Brazilian Mobilities

Brazilian Mobilities presents an overview of the diversity of mobility studies developed in Brazil. It builds a picture of a strong Latin-American perspective emerging in the field of mobilities research, which provides unique insight into the complex dynamics of mobilities in the emerging countries from the Global South.

Addressing such different areas as tourism, urbanization, media studies, social inequalities, marketing and mega-events, transport and technology, among others, the contributors use the new mobilities paradigm, or NMP (Sheller & Urry, 2006) as a starting point to reflect about the social changes experienced in the country and they also engage with newer literature on mobilities, including work done by Brazilian and Latin-American authors depending on the subject of each individual chapter.

Illustrating to scholars the uniqueness and complexity of the Brazilian social-political and economic context, the book was organized in order to be a representative sample of the studies carried out in Brazil, as well as to contribute to other academic investigations on (im)mobilities and different social realities in emerging countries.

Maria Alice de Faria Nogueira is a lecturer at Universidade Estácio de Sá (UNESA, Brazil). She is also National Coordinator of Social Communications Undergraduate Courses–Creative Economies Department at the same institution. Her research focuses on the interconnection of (im)mobility, communication, advertising and marketing.

Camila Maria dos Santos Moraes is a Tourism and Sociology Professor at Rio de Janeiro University (UNIRIO), where she coordinates the TurisData-RJ: Data base on Rio de Janeiro Tourism Reality and the Observatory of Favela Tourism.

Changing Mobilities

Series Editors: Monika Büscher, Peter Adey

This series explores the transformations of society, politics and everyday experiences wrought by changing mobilities, and the power of mobilities research to inform constructive responses to these transformations. As a new mobile century is taking shape, international scholars explore motivations, experiences, insecurities, implications and limitations of mobile living, and opportunities and challenges for design in the broadest sense, from policy to urban planning, new media and technology design. With world citizens expected to travel 105 billion kilometres per year in 2050, it is critical to make mobilities research and design inform each other.

Bicycle Utopias
Imagining Fast and Slow Cycling Futures
Cosmin Popan

Cycling
A Sociology of Vélomobility
Peter Cox

Sea Log
Indian Ocean to New York
May Joseph

Material Mobilities
Edited by Ole B. Jensen, Claus Lassen and Ida S. G. Lange

Brazilian Mobilities
Edited by Maria Alice de Faria Nogueira and Camila Maria dos Santos Moraes

For a full list of titles in this series, please visit www.routledge.com/Changing-Mobilities/book-series/CHGMOB.

Brazilian Mobilities

Edited by Maria Alice de Faria Nogueira and Camila Maria dos Santos Moraes

Routledge
Taylor & Francis Group
LONDON AND NEW YORK

First published 2020 by Routledge

2 Park Square, Milton Park, Abingdon, Oxon OX14 4RN
605 Third Avenue, New York, NY 10017

Routledge is an imprint of the Taylor & Francis Group, an informa business

First issued in paperback 2021

British Library Cataloguing-in-Publication Data
A catalogue record for this book is available from the British Library

Library of Congress Cataloging-in-Publication Data
Names: Nogueira, Maria Alice de Faria, editor. | Moraes, Camila, editor.
Title: Brazilian mobilities / edited by Maria Alice de Faria Nogueira and Camila Maria dos Santos Moraes.
Description: First Edition. | New York : Routledge, 2020. | Series: Changing mobilities | Includes bibliographical references and index.
Identifiers: LCCN 2019052956 (print) | LCCN 2019052957 (ebook) | ISBN 9780367172770 (hardback) | ISBN 9780429055966 (ebook)
Subjects: LCSH: Migration, Internal—Brazil. | Transportation—Brazil. | Culture and tourism—Brazil. | Social change—Brazil.
Classification: LCC HB2023 .B738 2020 (print) | LCC HB2023 (ebook) | DDC 304.80981—dc23
LC record available at https://lccn.loc.gov/2019052956
LC ebook record available at https://lccn.loc.gov/2019052957

ISBN: 978-0-367-17277-0 (hbk)
ISBN: 978-1-03-217424-2 (pbk)
DOI: 10.4324/9780429055966

Typeset in Times New Roman
by Apex CoVantage, LLC

Contents

Figures

Tables

Contributors

Thiago Allis holds a PhD in architecture and urban planning from the University of São Paulo (USP). He is Assistant Professor in Leisure and Tourism at the School of Arts, Sciences and Humanities (EACH) at the University of São Paulo. His scholar and research interests include urban tourism, regional and urban planning and tourism mobilities.

Luiz Adolfo Andrade is a journalist, game designer and researcher working on locative gaming. Visiting scholar at the Center for Computer Games Research, IT-University of Copenhagen, supported by CAPES Postdoctoral Scholarship, process number 88881.119487/2016–01. Adjunct Professor at the State University of Bahia (UNEB), Brazil. PhD in contemporary communication and culture (cyberculture) at the Federal University of Bahia, Brazil.

Rafael Castro has a DSc in transport engineering from the Federal University of Rio de Janeiro (PET/COPPE/UFRJ), Brazil. He is Lecturer at the Department of Tourism at Federal Center for Technological Education Celso Suckow da Fonseca (Cefet/RJ). His scholarly and research interests include tourism, air transport and tourism mobilities.

Bernardo Cheibub holds a PhD in history, politics and culture (CPDOC, Getulio Vargas Foundation) and a master's degree in leisure studies by Minas Gerais Federal University. Visiting scholar at the University of Surrey. He is currently a lecturer of the Master in Tourism of Fluminense Federal University (UFF) and Coordinates the research group Mobilities, Leisure and Social tourism (UFF).

Ariane Fernandes da Conceição holds a PhD in rural development, master's in rural extension from the Federal University of Santa Maria, 2012 and a degree in cooperative management (UFV), 2010 and administration (Faculdade Senac Porto Alegre), 2014. She was a visiting PhD student at Lancaster University, 2016. Currently she is a postdoctoral fellow in Rural Extension–Federal University of Viçosa.

Fernanda da Costa Portugal Duarte holds a PhD in communication, rhetoric and digital media from North Carolina State University. She is editor of

Mobility and Art for Transfers, an interdisciplinary journal for mobility studies, an associate professor in the Department of Communication and a Researcher at the Intermedia Connections Research Group (NucCon) at the Federal University of Minas Gerais, Brazil.

Jordania Eugenio has a master's in progress in Postgraduate Program in Tourism by Fluminense Federal University (UFF). Interdisciplinary bachelor's in human sciences by Juiz de Fora Federal University (UFJF). Bachelor's in tourism by Juiz de Fora Federal University (UFJF). Member of the research group Mobility, Leisure and Social Tourism (UFF).

Carla Fraga has a DSc in transport engineering from the Federal University of Rio de Janeiro (PET/COPPE/UFRJ), Brazil. She is adjunct professor in the Department of Tourism and Heritage of Federal University of the State of Rio de Janeiro (UNIRIO). Her scholarly and research interests include tourism and transport, tourism and cities, planning and management of tourism, tourism mobilities.

Bianca Freire-Medeiros is a sociology professor at Universidade de São Paulo. She has published extensively on urban issues and tourism mobilities. She was a visiting scholar at Princeton University, Colégio de Mexico, Lancaster University and was a Tinker Visiting Fellow at the University of Texas at Austin.

João Alcântara de Freitas is graduated in tourism (Fluminense Federal University–UFF, Brazil) and holds a PhD in history, politics and culture from Getúlio Vargas Foundation (FGV, Brazil). His research interests are in the mobilities paradigm, smart cities and tourism.

Camila Maciel Campolina Alves Mantovani is a professor at the Department of Social Communication of UFMG. Journalist (UFMG/2002) and PhD in information science (UFMG/2011) with research on "Narratives of mobility: communication, culture and production in informational spaces".

Filipe Marino is a Brazilian architect, urban designer and lecturer. He holds a PhD degree in urbanism (Federal University of Rio de Janeiro) and is adjunct professor of architectural project and urban design at Universidade do Grande Rio–UNIGRANRIO and Universidade Estácio de Sá–UNESA. He has a master's degree in urban planning (Federal University of Rio de Janeiro) and was a visiting researcher at the University of Montreal–UdM in 2012, at the Future Leaders of America Program.

Macello Medeiros holds a PhD in communication at the Federal University of Bahia (UFBA), Assistant Professor at the Federal University of Recôncavo of Bahia (UFRB) with emphasis in culture, languages and applied technologies. Coordinator of Environment of Research and Innovation in Media and Mobility (UFRB/CNPq), Harold Innis Award Winner (Media Ecology Association/2011).

Palloma Valle Menezes holds a degree in social sciences from the University of the State of Rio de Janeiro (UERJ) and a master's degree in sociology from the University of Rio de Janeiro Research Institute (IUPERJ). She holds a PhD in sociology from the Institute of Social and Political Studies of the University of the State of Rio de Janeiro (IESP/UERJ) and the Department of Social and Cultural Anthropology of Vrije Universiteit Amsterdam and postdoctoral fellow by the Center for Research and Documentation of Contemporary History of Brazil of the Getúlio Vargas Foundation (CPDOC/FGV). She is currently a lecturer at the Department of Social Sciences, Fluminense Federal University, researcher at the Collective of Studies on Violence and Sociability (CEVIS) and is an associate researcher on the FAPESP Thematic Project entitled Conflict management in the contemporary city.

Camila Maria dos Santos Moraes holds a PhD in history, politics and culture (CPDOC, Getulio Vargas Foundation) and a master's degree in social sciences. During her PhD, she was a visiting researcher at the Center For Mobilities Research/Lancaster University. She is a Professor in tourism, education and heritage in the Tourism and Heritage Department at Rio de Janeiro University (UNIRIO) and coordinates the TurisData-RJ: Data base on Rio de Janeiro Tourism Reality and the Observatory of Favela Tourism.

Leo Name has a degree in architecture and urbanism from Universidade Federal do Rio de Janeiro (2000), Specialization in urban sociology from Universidade do Estado do Rio de Janeiro (2002) and a master's degree and PhD in geography from Universidade Federal do Rio de Janeiro (2004 and 2008, respectively). Since 2014, he is a lecturer in architecture and urbanism and comparative literature at Universidade Federal da Integração Latino-Americana and its research and writings devoting attention, through a decolonial approach, to mobile Latin American bodies, landscapes, images, narratives and cartographies.

Maria Alice de Faria Nogueira holds a PhD in history, politics and culture (CPDOC, Getulio Vargas Foundation) and a master's degree in social communication (PUC-Rio). Current lecturer at Universidade Estácio de Sá (UNESA–Brazil), she is also National Coordinator of Social Communications Undergraduate Courses–Creative Economy Department at the same Institution. Her research focuses on the interconnection of (im)mobility, communication, advertising and marketing.

Sônia Caldas Pessoa is a Professor of the Social Communication Department and the Communication Postgraduate Program at the Federal University of Minas Gerais, Brazil. PhD and master's in linguistic studies (Poslin/UFMG) with an exchange program at Université Paris Est-Crèteil/Le Céditec (Centre d'Étude des Discours, Images, Textes, Écrits, Communication- Paris, France) about the research aesthetics of difference: contributions to the study of disabilities and social digital networks as mise en scéne devices.

Elton Santos Undergraduate in urbanism (UNEB), master's candidate in territorial studies (UNEB), experience as a trainee at Secretaria de Mobilidade of Prefeitura de Salvador and participation in different researches and projects during the undergraduate degree, discussing themes such as territorialities, mobility and accessibility. Former coordinator of academic directory of Course of Urbanism (2017–2018).

Sergio Schneider is a Professor at the Federal University of Rio Grande do Sul and member of the Graduate Program in Rural Development and Post-Graduate Program in Sociology. He holds a postdoctorate at City University of London with Prof. Tim Lang (2015–2016) and at the Institut of City and Regional Planning, Cardiff University/Wales/UK, with Terry Marsden (2007–2008) and is a co-postdoctoral fellow in rural extension at Federal University of Viçosa. Doctorate degree in Lancaster University, 2016. Master's in rural extension by the Federal University of Santa Maria, 2012. Has a degree in cooperative management (UFV), 2010, and administration (Faculty Senac Porto Alegre), 2014. Included the doctorate in sociology UFRGS/Université Paris X) in 1999, the master's in sociology (UNICAMP) in 1994 and the graduation in social sciences (UFRGS) in 1990.

Rita Vieira holds an MSc in statistics (UFRJ) and is an assistant professor at Universidade do Estado da Bahia (UNEB), working with statistics methods and probability, especially in courses of urbanism, engineering, information systems, social science and e-learning. Member of research groups that study urban and regional development, urban and regional planning, mobility, public engineering.

Acknowledgments

This book is about movements, encounters and exchanges of people and ideas. The present volume brought together 21 Brazilian scholars with different backgrounds. Thus, our first acknowledgment is to our contributors, who bought the idea and made this book happen. We would also like to thank all those who make this book possible. Monika Büscher from CeMoRe/Lancaster University and Gerhard Boomgaarden from Routledge, the first two persons to hear and discuss with us about this project. We would also like to thank Elena Chiu, Emily Briggs and Lakshita Joshi for their editorial assistance; Glauber Rosa for English proofreading and formatting of the manuscript; and Marcelo Baglione for his beautiful work with the images.

Preface

I was tasked with writing a preliminary text to introduce this book, which aims to discuss Brazilian mobilities as part of a series entitled Changing Mobilities. The first thing that came to mind was the idea that everything is always flowing everywhere.

Back in ancient times, there were discussions about the doctrine of flux and the cosmo-vision that fire is the source and nature of all things; pure energeia. When commenting on the Heraclitan thought, Plato provided an early reading, followed by Aristotle, that is still popular to the present moment. He claims that Heraclitus is a materialist monist who believed that all things are modifications of fire. Everything is in flux, in the sense that everything changes except the change itself; that is, some things can only remain the same by changing.

The world is in constant motion. We have witnessed the intensification of an accelerated modernity that privileges the global flows of people, information, objects and capital. At all times, the spatial boundaries are crossed as a result of the spatiotemporal compression that is characteristic of this not-so-new reality. Life "in motion" requires flexibility, adaptability and reflexivity to be able to live in a condition of dynamic stability.

This condition produces uncertainties in the way we relate and convey meaning to "place". Several places, mainly in the Global South, live a cultural and epistemological coloniality (e.g., cosmopolitanization of tastes) coming from the North, especially the United States and some European countries. This process produces a sense of displacement and loss of the "local". In contrast, several anti-globalizing movements have emerged as a form of resistance. Restoration and incentive policies for historical heritage aim to rescue or attempt to preserve a type of local identity in a process of romanticizing "place"; locality emerges as a sense of space of reaction.

The complex and diverse network of physical and digital mobility across territories resembles a constellation of mobilities. Local comes to be understood as a unique and particular meeting point or intersection of global flows or as articulated moments in the networks of human and machinic relations. Thus, the definition of local is criticized simply for its opposition to global in order to defend an understanding that comes from its complex relationship with the nonlocal. Then a dynamic and progressive sense of "local" is defended, one that includes awareness of connections with the global, positively integrating local and global.

Mobility became a key concept in the 21st century, representing both global and local flows (performed in smaller scale). All of these movements are important and central to both individuals and organizations, whether governmental or otherwise. A major contribution to the advancement and transformation of social sciences has been made by what has become known and has been regarded as the turning point of mobility. In addition to awakening to the investigation of new issues, this paradigmatic shift has crossed disciplinary boundaries and called into question sedentary and territorial precepts of modern science.

Mobility as a disciplinary field then assumes an important position in various research agendas. Recent advances in transport and communication infrastructures, along with new social and cultural mobility practices as well as political and economic challenges for representatives of various private or public institutions, have given rise to a range of new research initiatives that seek to understand mobility in the most varied forms. From then on, the different aspects of the study of mobility became fundamental to the understanding of various events (e.g., global warming, migratory crises, sustainable tourism, life at digital speed). This has contributed to the formation of a new mobilities paradigm composed of new theoretical and methodological approaches in the social sciences in particular and in the human sciences more broadly that seeks to deal with emerging and complex issues.

In this context of constant movement, we find a group of researchers with different views orbiting around the theme of mobility who are particularly interested in the Brazilian context. Addressing areas such as tourism, urbanization, media studies, social inequalities, marketing and mega-events, transport and technology, among others, *Brazilian Mobilities* captures the uniqueness and complexity of the Brazilian socio-political and economic context and shows how the mobilities paradigm provides a unique insight about the complex dynamics of mobility in emerging countries of the Global South based on the Brazilian experience.

The perspective of the epistemologies of the Global South is based on an epistemological reflection that aims to show how the modern scientific tradition is unable to deal with the rich diversity of experiences in the form of knowledge that exist in the world. This is a kind of rationality capable of provoking a true "epistemicide" of the original and distinct knowledge of the diverse locations of the Global South. This is because tradition disconsiders any forms of social knowledge or practices that do not fit the criteria of knowledge, culture and aesthetics of the Global North.

However, in order to respond to this waste and give voice and credibility to the silenced experiences and alternative movements, it is not enough to resort to the pioneering contribution brought by the new mobilities paradigm to social theory. At its roots, we find the same modern rational logic, which reduces social phenomena to entities endowed with attributes that are discrete and related through variance. Therefore, a transcendent rationality capable of dealing with sustainable and dynamic interactions between different ways of producing knowledge is necessary; a truly cosmopolitan rationality.

Brazilian Mobilities expands knowledge about mobility by rejecting the monoculture of modern scientific knowledge by exploring the plurality of alternative sciences and practices, as well as by enabling and cultivating interaction, interdependence and relational aspects between scientific and nonscientific knowledge. Therefore, existing conceptual tools can become credible according to the type of intervention they provide to the world while a growing need for new knowledge arises.

Bearing this in mind, Maria Alice de Faria Nogueira and Camila Maria dos Santos Moraes came together to bring to light an original and relevant undertaking. The set of texts that compose this book derive from the understanding that diversity in the study of mobility, inspired by research conducted in Brazil, is a key element for understanding modern life.

Recife
Sérgio Carvalho Benício de Mello[1]

Note

1 He has graduated in business studies and philosophy and has a PhD from the City, University of London, United Kingdom (1997). He is a full professor at the Federal University of Pernambuco (UFPE) and a research fellow (level 1D) at CNPq. He currently coordinates the Urban Studies and Politics of Mobility Laboratory (MOBIS) at UFPE.

Introduction

Maria Alice de Faria Nogueira and Camila Maria dos Santos Moraes

After two decades of military dictatorship (1964–1982), it took Brazil at least 20 years of political and economic effort to be considered one of the most important players in the global emergent market. This dramatic change did not occur without huge consequences for the local social scenario, particularly after the 2000s. Based on the increasing movement of people, objects, information, images, and ideas, a mobility culture (Urry 2003) imposed itself and involved everyone (individuals, government, and private sector) in new possibilities and experiences, as well as in new constraints, risks, and discourses, which should be studied.

Due to this historical scenario, the investigation of mobilities in Brazil is a new but dynamic field of research, with an increasing group of scholars interested in reflections about relevant aspects of today's society *and* all the uniqueness and complexity of the Brazilian social-political and economic background.

Since 2009, scholars in Brazil have been thinking about Brazilian issues through the lenses of the new mobilities paradigm (NMP). Through these years, we found more than 30 researchers, more than 40 papers published in journals, PhD dissertations, books, and book chapters, and 10 research groups addressing matters on tourism mobilities, student's motility, sociability on the move, potential mobilities and discourse, urban mobilities, immobilities and consumption, imaginative mobilities, international academic mobilities, mobilities and languages in contact, and mobilities in social movements.

The mega-events period was profitable for the mobilities studies in Brazil, especially in Rio de Janeiro. As highlighted by Zirin (2014), Brazil was the first country to host the 2014 FIFA Soccer World Cup and the Rio 2016 Olympic Games in such a short period of time, which made this organization challenging. In order to prepare for such mission, Rio hosted the Rio+20 conference in 2012. Between 2007 and 2016, the eyes of the world turned to Brazil and Rio de Janeiro a few times. The flows of people and investments intensified and generated an increase in the studies on mobilities, motilities, and immobilities. In addition, Brazilian media studies have showed how mega-events are an important marketing opportunity to release products on global scale.

During the early 2000s, most of the mobilities research done in Brazil had to do with tourism mobilities (the Brazilian edition of John Urry's book *The Tourist Gaze* was published in 2001), and it is still a preeminent field of research, as we can see in this edition. However, throughout these years, scholars from diverse academic backgrounds began to mobilize the new mobilities paradigm, or NMP (Sheller & Urry 2006, 2016) to think about all the changes Brazil was experiencing in areas such as economy and consumption, social mobilities, communication and technology, urban planning and transport, art and culture, education and health, among others, all of which were impacted by movement, mobility, and displacement of people, ideas, objects, and information like never before.

In this context, the University of São Paulo hosted in 2017 the first Advanced School of Mobilities: Theory and Methods – SPMobilities 2017. This conference gathered more than 100 participants interested to discuss and approach the NMP in their research. Among participants and the scientific committee, more than 20 lecturers from Brazilian universities followed the school's activities and are going to take the new approaches to the NPM in Brazil to their students. The school was also attended by around ten participants and professors from Latin America, which shows an attempt to maintain a dialogue between Brazilian and Latin American researchers.

It is important to notice that Brazil is a country with continental dimensions and more than 220 million people spread over five regions and 27 states. Marked by great social inequality, the mobilities, motilities, and immobilities reveal themselves as creative concepts to address Brazilian issues with innovative methods and questions.

Thus, the book was organized so as to be a representative sample of the studies carried out in different universities, groups of research, and areas of interest in Brazil. Although the authors use the NMP as a starting point to reflect about the social changes experienced in the country, they also engage with newer literature on mobilities, including work done by Brazilian and Latin American authors, depending on the subject of each individual chapter.

In this sense, the purpose of the book is not just to present an overview of the diversity of mobilities and mobilities studies developed in Brazil but also to build a Latin American perspective about this field of research. Furthermore, its aim is to "mobilize" this new perspective by causing the emerging countries from the Global South to go deeper in the subject and by providing new insights to Latin American contexts, as well as by putting new mobilities concepts and theories in dialogue with scholars on the mobilities paradigm from the Global North.

The book was organized to be a representative sample of the diversity of studies conducted in different universities and research groups and areas of interest in Brazil. The main idea of the book is to build a Brazilian (albeit limited) view of mobilities studies by creating a (small) cartography of what has been developed in the country in terms of research in the area. We put together 13 chapters, 21 authors, and 14 institutions from five states from three out of the five regions of the country.

We begin with the researches on tourism. In the first chapter, Thiago Allis, Rafael Castro, and Carla Fraga explore how mobile the tourism researches on transport in Brazil are. They look for researchable entities, types of mobilities, and mobile methods in Brazilian papers published between 1990 and 2015. They observe that the research on transport in tourism focuses on tourists despite the roles of other social groups, such as workers, and make use mainly of history and social sciences tools, such as oral history, participant observations, and travel diaries. In spite of a few papers that took the NPM into account, Allis, Castro, and Fraga defend that they open room for more scholars to experiment and employ new approaches and methods in research on tourism and transport in Brazil. Working in that direction are research groups in Brazil that are a creative environment for theoretical and methodological advances on tourism and transport mobilities research.

Still from the tourism perspective, Chapters 2 and 3 refer to studies related to the favelas, one of the strongest, most interesting, and well-known tourism research niches in Brazil. In Chapter 2 Bianca Freire-Medeiros and Palloma Valle Menezes explore how, since in its origin, the touristic favela benefited from the transcontinental mobility of people and ideas, images, and information. However, to be able to consolidate it in the market of poverty tourism, promoters of favela tourism also needed to ensure the circulation of very specific objects: souvenirs. Freire-Medeiros and Menezes discuss such "objects" that work as tangible markers of a particular cultural experience involving the conversion of the experience of poverty into a touristic product. The context of favela tourism offers a privileged point of view from which we can understand the paradoxes of the transnational flows directed towards certain favelas and projected in various directions. One of these directions is explored by Camila Maria dos Santos Moraes.

In the third chapter, Moraes presents how the favelas of Rio de Janeiro are places of contested meanings. If in the past these areas were signified as deforested, risky, poor, and violent areas, problems that affect "the wonderful city", in the context of the mega-events favelas, were under the spotlight. Recognized as official tourist attraction of Rio, public policies were conducted to expand favela tourism and re-signified these areas as green, safe, and cool. Based on multisited ethnography, Moraes moves through the expansion of tourism in the favelas and presents how tourism and the networks it mobilizes have provoked dispute regarding new meanings for the favelas and, in the specific case of this chapter, the contestation of a dogma – the anti-ecological favela.

We leave favelas and move to the "formal city". In the fourth chapter, João Alcântara de Freitas deals with one of the most important actions of the local government to prepare the city of Rio de Janeiro for the 2016 Olympics: the creation of the Rio Operations Center – COR. The creation of COR had a major impact on the management of the city and positioned it in the smart cities' scenario. Its centrality in the operation of the city demonstrates not only its functional but especially its symbolic importance. The COR presents itself not only as an instrument of so-called smart governance, but also as the technological materialization of the governmental control over the city and the urban experience of its population. COR's technical and symbolic power demonstrates its role in the narrative construction of Rio de Janeiro as a smart city, as well as highlights its own logic of action that constitutes the new forms of mobilities in Rio de Janeiro. Freitas explores how COR's impacts on the mobilities in and of Rio de Janeiro became a central tool in municipal management to showcase an administration that sought to be modern while having complete control over the city.

However, there is no way to talk about mobility without talking about immobility. The next chapters address the issue from different perspectives, but they shed light on the issue prior to displacement itself: the real and symbolic difficulties imposed by mobility, which translate into access and the right to come and go in cities.

Bernardo Cheibub and Jordania Eugenio bring to us in Chapter 5 the debate about tourism mobilities and immobilities in Brazilian cities. To do so, they conducted research about the street-living population and social and structural urban mobility policies. They present to us how in several situations, these individuals are excluded from exercising the universal right to come and go, the right to freely access the city's public spaces. Cheibub and Eugenio report the result of an agreement between a public social assistance unit called Centro Pop and a social project of the Fluminense Federal University (UFF), which offers tourist experiences to its poor students and workers. In this initiative, a group of homeless – users of Centro Pop – had the opportunity between November 2017 and April 2018 to visit some of the tourist attractions of the cities of Niteroi and Rio de Janeiro. During the planning of this experience, in meetings with the social workers, difficulties and limits in constructing a tour itinerary were noticed, taking into consideration the feelings and the previous experiences of this group. Through ethnographic research, this chapter reflects on the social relations identified through the social tourism project and the visible and invisible limits present in the way of life of homeless people.

Chapters 6 and 7 move us through the debate on mobilities and immobilities of people with disabilities. Camila Maciel Campolina Alves Mantovani and Sônia Caldas Pessoa share in Chapter 6 reflections on the ongoing research experiences in the Afetos: Research Group on Communication, Accessibility and Vulnerabilities. The centrality of the research is related to the presence of people with disabilities not only as subjects to be researched but also as an active part of encounters that awaken us as researchers to the potential of the new mobilities paradigm to reflect upon the correlations between mobility and immobility. In a world full of movement, what does it mean to not be able to move or to move with restrictions? The project I Exist and Move: Experiences and Mobility of People with Disabilities, an example of collaborative research methodology under construction with vulnerable subjects, points us to possible paths and relationships between mobility, immobility, and disability studies, since the interfaces between these fields not only can shed light upon central issues that arise from mobility research, but they can also contribute to broadening our understanding of disability.

On the same direction, Macello Medeiros, Rita Vieira, and Elton Andrade present an approach to people's right to the city, particularly the right of those with some physical limitation, who deserve to have their right to universal access to urban spaces and information guaranteed by the installation of adequate signs that allow their autonomy, without restrictions to public spaces. Medeiros, Vieira, and Andrade focus on problems related to the issue of mobility, in particular the obstacles faced regarding the movement of people with disabilities or reduced mobility in the urban space. The proposition presented in chapter seven derives from the execution of the *Ponto Certo* project ("The right point"), whose main purpose is to give visibility to these problems by analyzing the accessibility conditions at bus stops in the city of Salvador – Bahia, using geotechnologies through digital cartography (GIS).

Still on the mobility right, Chapter 8 brings to light how urban mobility has been a major challenge for Brazilian society, and its legal framework has been changing over the past 30 years. Filipe Marino analyzes the urban mobility in Brazil from its legal perspective and how the law can engender mobility itself by relating urban mobility with citizenship and urban rights. Marino shows us the evolution of the Brazilian legislation on this issue between 1988 and 2015, since the promulgation of the 1988 Brazilian Federal Constitution to the year when urban mobility became a social right. The observation of legal advances shows the maturity of Brazil after becoming a well-equipped country in terms of urban mobility laws, which evidences the importance of this discussion in contemporary Brazil.

Other important aspect of mobilities in Brazilian studies are virtual and imaginative mobilities, as we can see in the next chapters. We start with Luiz Adolfo Andrade's research on locative games, especially with Po*kémon GO*. In Chapter 9, Andrade discusses the application of the new mobilities paradigm as an attempt to understand locative games, particularly *Pokémon GO* (NianticLabs 2016). This locative game uses locative media as a resource for game design. It has become a blockbuster in the mobile game industry since it was released in mid 2016. Andrade's research supports that *Pokémon GO* can reflect the new mobilities paradigm by stimulating three levels of mobility in the gameplay: physical, informational, and imaginary. Different from previous locative games, such as *Code Runner* (Rocket Chicken 2011), *Ingress* (Niantic 2012), and so forth, *Pokémon GO* provides a special kind of imaginary mobility, which could connect its gameplay to the universe provided by Nintendo and Pokémon Co. in 1996. Thus, the main fascinating feature of *Pokémon GO* could be the connection provided by the imaginary mobility to the classic game, not the informational or physical mobility inherent to locative gaming.

Based upon the notion that communication is also mobility, in Chapter 10, Maria Alice de Faria Nogueira deals specifically with the link between mobility and brand strategies from the perspective of the new mobilities paradigm, or NMP (Sheller & Urry 2006, 2016). With special focus on the advertising discourse of brands, this chapter aims to demonstrate how advertising has been appropriating the contemporary compulsion for mobility in order to promote new products and services by selling mobilities – social, symbolic, potential, and imaginative – as one of the most important features offered by goods. The theory of "consumption of (im)mobilities" (Nogueira 2015) was used as a contribution to rethink the advertising discourse in a mobile risk society, within which objects can be seen as motility tools through which, depending on ready-to-handedness and on new affordances, they can (or cannot) support individuals' everyday compulsion for (im)mobility with some stability and less risk.

From advertising and consumption to journalism, in Chapter 11, Fernanda da Costa Portugal Duarte presents the experience of the journalism collective *BH nas Ruas* during the June Journeys, a wave of political protests that took over Brazil in 2013, and discusses how journalism practices, formats, genres, and ethos are reconfigured by the appropriation of mobile medialities (Sheller 2013). The protests initially stood against an increase in public transportation fares and were later expanded to include a range of issues. These issues include responsible governmental expenditures, triggered by the budget deficit caused by the sponsorship of mega-events (the 2014 FIFA World Cup and the Rio 2016 Summer Olympics), a stand against government corruption, and the defense of social justice and minority rights. During the June Journeys, streets and communication networks were occupied by dissatisfied citizens who used smartphones to both record and disseminate images of the protests. The independent reporting that occurred during these events prompted the deployment of media activism and mobile journalism tactics by groups such as *Mídia NINJA* and *BH nas Ruas*. This chapter demonstrates the contributions of a mobilities perspective to media studies as it decenters the agency of mobile devices in practices of mobile journalism to address how politics of information mobility forge journalism formats and genres.

So far, all the chapters have dealt with mobilities from the perspective of the big cities. However, following what seems to be a trend, even if incomplete, of the research on mobilities in Brazil, mainly due to the country's dimensions, Chapter 12 moves us to the rural mobilities, which could not be disregarded. The rural environment has undergone several transformations, mostly connected to the concepts of new ruralities, and became a space of services as well as a site for leisure and new economic sources through pluriactivity. In this sense, Ariane Fernandes da Conceição and Sergio Schneider promote the debate on family farming and the Internet in Chapter 12. The authors show us how the information and communication technologies (ICT), especially the Internet, have been adopted by family farmers in rural areas and what the direct impacts on the daily life of those who live there are. Not only a cultural change is observed but also a change in daily activities, through the search for new practices, new markets, and new experiences made available by the advent of communication. Fernandes and Schneider analyze the influence of the increasing use of the Internet on mobility in rural areas. To this end, they look into the growth of the Internet in rural areas and data on an empirical research carried out with family farmers from the municipality of

Santa Rosa de Lima, state of Santa Catarina. This new scenario seems to present new possibilities, such as access to information, insertion into new markets, differentiated forms of production, and, in a way, greater contact between producer and consumer.

Finally, Leo Name questions the centrality of research in the area from the point of view of the geography of knowledge and its asymmetries, largely due, but not only, to the language most commonly used in academia: English. In Chapter 13, Name states that the increase in the number of Latin American intellectuals affiliated with the new mobilities paradigm is concomitant with an internationalization of scientific production that broadens the global circuits of researchers and academic literature. In spite of that, on the one hand, studies on the new mobilities are still dominated by concepts, models, theories, researchers, and writings originating in the Anglo-Saxon world, and on the other hand, they have not had their fundamental books and articles translated into Spanish or Portuguese. The new mobilities paradigm, therefore, is permeated by asymmetries of power that are characteristic of the modern-colonial matrix of scientific production, which create unequal circuits of production and diffusion of knowledge and restrict its application by those whose native language is not English. Based on the decolonial theory, Name points out the effort of Brazilian scholars to make the NPM known and applied in Brazilian studies.

From this brief introduction, we can see that our contributing authors are among the leaders of the mobilities studies in Brazil, and this edited book is an attempt to connect and disseminate the knowledge produced in Brazil about Brazilian studies on mobilities to the non-Portuguese-speaking academia. In this sense, we would like to think of this book as one more step towards understanding mobilities in the global South and specially in Latin America.

References

Code Runner [Locative Game.] 2011. Vancouver, Canada: Rocket Chicken.

de Faria Nogueira, M. A. 2015. *Mobilidade em potência e discurso publicitário na sociedade contemporânea globalizada: Brasil, 1982–2014*. PhD dissertation – Centro de Pesquisa e Documentação de História Contemporânea do Brasil, Programa de Pós-Graduação em História, Política e Bens Culturais. Rio de Janeiro. Available at: http://hdl.handle.net/10438/13704.

Ingress [Locative Game.] 2012. San Francisco, CA: NianticLabs, Inc.

Pokémon GO! [Locative Game.] 2016. San Francisco, CA: NianticLabs, Inc.

Sheller, M. 2013. Mobile mediality: Location, dislocation, augmentation. 309–326. In Witzgall, S. & Vogl, G. eds. *New mobilities regimes in art and social sciences*. London: Routledge.

Sheller, M. & Urry, J. 2006. The new mobilities paradigm. *Environment and Planning A*, 8(2), pp. 207–226.

Sheller, M. & Urry, J. 2016. Mobilizing the new mobilities paradigm. *Applied Mobilities*, 1(1), pp. 10–25.

Urry, J. 2003. *Mobile cultures*. Published by the Department of Sociology, Lancaster University, Lancaster LA1 4YN, UK. Available at: www.comp.lancs.ac.uk/sociology/papers/Urry-Mobile-Cultures.pdf.

Zirin, D. 2014. *Brazil's dance with the devil: The world cup, the Olympics, and the fight for democracy*. Chicago, IL: Haymarket Books.

Chapter 1

Moving on

How mobile is tourism research on transport in Brazil?

Thiago Allis, Rafael Castro and Carla Fraga

Introduction

The relationship between transport and tourism is intrinsic, with transport being an essential element for the distribution of tourist flows and, in some cases, becoming the very attraction for tourism. Thus, considering different approaches, it is undeniable that this interface is rooted in the vast universe of mobilities studies. The aim of this chapter is to approach transport and tourism from a theoretical and conceptual discussion under the umbrella of mobilities studies considering the new mobilities paradigm, particularly the application of mobile methods. This chapter will be divided into three main sections: the first introductory part aims to situate theoretically and conceptually the relationship between transport and tourism; the second part presents the methodological scheme; the third part holds a discussion on the new mobilities paradigm and mobile methods, presenting and analyzing a selected list of publications in Brazilian tourism journals. To conclude, we make our final remarks and point out some perspectives for future developments on tourism mobilities as a specific research field.

Approaching transport and tourism through mobilities studies

To start responding to the question "How mobile is tourism research on transport in Brazil?", this first part of the chapter aims to theoretically and conceptually present the interface between transport and tourism. It is undeniable that the tourism phenomenon implies movement, so it is necessary to use a mode of transport to reach tourist destinations, as well as to circulate within them and return to the place of origin (Palhares 2002).

In this sense, there are efforts to create tourism schemes, models, and whole systems that represent these dynamics, such as the one developed by Palhares (2005), titled "Whole Model of Tourist Transport Systems", by presenting the various patterns of movement imbricated in the tourist phenomenon. Movement is considered here in its more explicit sense – that is, "corporeal travel" (Urry 2000), as an elementary component of travel and, therefore, characteristic of tourism.

From the idea that "mobility is movement imbued with meaning" (Adey 2017, p. 63), one can consider, in alternative perspectives, the idea of mobility as a defining element of tourism beyond the implications of physical travel (raw materials, money, garbage, etc.), images and virtualities (Urry 2000) as well as models and cultures of being and doing tourism.

Fraga et al. (2013), based on the postulates of Kaul (1985) on the interface of transport and tourism and the multiplicity of representations of transport in tourism systems and models, spatial models – tourist trip, origin-destination, structural, and evolutionary (Pearce 2003) – provide an important framework for understanding the theoretical and conceptual aspects that mark the advance of knowledge about this topic. The Leiper (1990) model, for example, presents, among other elements, three geographic (regions of origin, transit, and destination), in which transport is represented, even indirectly, as necessary for the movement between and within these regions.

Castro et al. (2013) also address the theoretical and conceptual issue, but from the point of view of planning, approaching tourism, and transport planning. The authors, on the one hand, consider the role of transport in the planning stages of tourism (analysis of the environment, diagnosis, prognosis, development of strategies, implementation, and evaluation) and, on the other hand, they discuss the reasons for using sequential models as a tool for the integrated planning of transport and tourism. Based on Campos's [n.d.] work, they explain the following concepts: trip generation, trip distribution, modal choice, and route assignment. In addition, also based on Campos's (n.d.) ideas, these authors discuss the transport cycle from the perspective that goes hand in hand with tourist mobilities: "Changes in Land Use and Occupation"; "Generation of Movements"; "Demand for Transport"; "Transportation Offer"; "Increased Accessibility"; and starting the cycle again with new "Changes in Land Use and Occupation".

Before addressing the new mobilities paradigm, two observations are relevant: (1) the systemic view seems to be the paradigm in the treatment of tourism, and this influences the view on transport and tourist mobility, and (2) there are groups of researchers who have different views toward tourism, notably on tourism being a science. For example, there is a group that does not consider tourism to be a science but a field of study. They believe there are no research methods and/or research objects already developed by the tourism academia. In Tribe's (1997) model about the creation of tourism knowledge, it is evident that knowledge is produced in what was called the "Band K", where K stands for knowledge, from the interface of the "N" disciplines with the tourism fields (Tourism Field I – study of commercial aspects of tourism/Tourism Field 2 – study of non-commercial aspects of tourism) (Lohmann & Panosso Netto 2010). Thus, the production of a new knowledge about transportation problems that are caused in the Field of Tourism I and/or II could be treated from varied disciplinary perspectives. That is Fraga's (2011) proposition when addressing the interface of rail transport and tourism to generate methodological contributions for the deployment of tourist trains in Brazil.

Thus, it can be observed that, although the new mobilities paradigm may dialogue with these theoretical and conceptual perspectives, it can also highlight the discussion about the interface of transport and tourism from other perspectives – including the large range of mobile methods reclaimed on its framework from several disciplines.

The exercise of studying tourism through the lens of mobilities is relatively recent. Sheller and Urry (2004), Burns and Novelli (2008), and Hall (2009) represent organized efforts in this sense, in which tourism – besides being studied as an economic and commercial activity – is studied as a practice and a particular manifestation of the universe of mobilities. Allis (2018) briefly informs that the studies dealing with tourism through the aspect of mobilities – or tourism mobilities – are distributed in some large research fields, namely: (a) environmental impacts; (b) tourist destinations planning; (c) approaches to social, cultural, and political elements; (d) technologies, materialities, and meanings of the transport systems, and (e) migration studies.

In any case, there are few references to research and publications on tourist mobilities in Latin America (for recent contributions, see Zunino Singh et al. 2018), so understanding their representativeness, specifically in Brazil and when it comes to transportation and tourism, is still a challenge.

Methodological procedures

As mentioned in the previous section, tourism research objects and issues are generally addressed in a varied number of disciplines, often leading to multidisciplinary and interdisciplinary studies. In this sense, one can foresee that the relationship between transport and tourism is also addressed in this way, and thus scientific data on tourism were considered for the data collection.

Therefore, the objective of this section of the chapter is to present and analyze publications on transport published in Brazilian tourism journals. The website Publications on Tourism (http://publicacoesdeturismo.com.br), which includes 31 indexed Brazilian scientific journals, has been used as a search engine.

In a first search with the descriptor "transport" in any field (title, keyword, or abstract), 67 papers published in 21 journals from 1990 to the present were found. From this list, we excluded papers in which transport was treated in a collateral manner – for example, when the theme was only a part of an analysis of tourist destinations; or when it dealt with indirect issues (as the use of geographic information systems – GIS – for tourism). In addition, studies dealing broadly with mobility (rather than transport) issues – such as studies on trails and tourist routes – or which, although published in tourism journals, did not address tourism issues (in the case of papers on logistics and transport multimodality in general, for example). Thus, for the analysis presented, we considered 29 papers published between 1990 and 2015.

As regards the scope of this study, the selected papers were analyzed in terms of the research units in the field of mobilities (people, objects, information, and

Table 1.1 The new mobilities paradigm and the mobile methods

Criteria	*Description*
Researchable entities (Büscher et al. 2011)	1. People 2. Objects 3. Information 4. Ideas
Types of mobilities (Urry 2000, 2007; Büscher et al. 2011)	1. Corporeal travel of people (work, leisure, family life, pleasure, migration) 2. Physical movement of objects 3. Imaginative travel (images of places and people moving across multiple media) 4. Virtual travel (enables presence and action at a distance) 5. Communicative travel (person-to-person contact via different supports: texts, messages, mobile, etc.)
Mobile methods (Büshcer et al. 2011)	1. Observing people's (also objects') movement, 2. "Walking with" 3. Mobile video ethnography (anticipating the movement) 4. Time-space diaries (textual, pictorial, digital) 5. Virtual mobility (texting, websites, blogs, listservs, etc.) 6. Art and design interventions 7. Mobile positioning methods (combining with ICT) 8. Capturing atmosphere 9. Memories (postcards, letters, souvenirs, photographs) 10. Moving places (on the go or that are no longer on the go) 11. Examinations of conversations 12. Analysis of "transfer points" or "interspaces"

Source: Urry (2000, 2007), Sheller and Urry (2006), Büscher et al. (2011).

ideas), the types of mobilities (corporeal, physical, virtual, imaginative, and communicative), and the use of mobile methods – with reference to the principle of Büscher et al. (2011), Urry (2000, 2007) and Sheller and Urry (2006) (Table 1.1).

To support the discussion, the following section summarizes the concepts that guide this field of research, starting from the "mobility turn" that is observed in sociology, which will provide the basis for proposing a "new mobilities paradigm" and then the construction of a range of mobile methods that have been gathered and applied in research in this field.

Transport and tourism and the use of mobile methods

This section is subdivided into two parts: the first one deals with theoretical aspects related to the new mobilities paradigm (NMP) and mobile methods, and in the second one, we discuss the scientific production on transport in Brazilian tourism journals.

New mobilities paradigm (NMP) and tourism

Over almost 100 years, multiple approaches have been adopted aiming to understand tourism practices and to frame it theoretically. Nevertheless, greater focus has been given since World War II, given the expansion of tourism, with the increase of flows and consequently its economic importance. Economics, management, geography, psychology, anthropology, and ecology are some of the many fields of knowledge that contribute to the interpretation of the many variables that structure the phenomenon in its determinants, practices, impacts, and possibilities (for an overview on the early days of tourism studies, see Panosso & Jäger 2015). Something that can hardly be questioned from any perspective is that it is an essentially mobile phenomenon. However, of course, immobilities should not be disregarded, since, for the sake of ever-growing tourist flows, there is a set of fixed elements to support them, from buildings (hotels, terminals, roads, theme parks, etc.) to social groups (namely, operational labor force that, at least momentarily, is rooted in given places to provide services in specific locations).

In this context, from the perspective of social sciences, a look at tourism as a form of mobility still seems to be recent, with initiatives starting in this century. Urry (2000) generically proposes a question that may seem so obvious – but perhaps little explored – in the study of tourism: "Why do people physically travel, what are its uses, pleasures and pains and what social and physical ramifications does such a movement possess?" As elementary as it may seem, this questioning starts from a very poignant observation, in a political, economic, social, and cultural framework in which tourism is inserted: "being physically mobile has become for both rich and even for some poor a 'way of life' across the globe" (Urry 2000, p. 4). A lifelong lifestyle (for millions of new or habitual tourists), desired (in spite of the dreams and imagery associated with tourism) and, in many cases, to be avoided – both for those who travel compulsively for work and for those who move as a migrant or refugee as their last choice for survival.

Theories and methods on mobilities in this perspective bring together what is being called the "mobility turn" on social sciences, "mobilizing analyses that have been historically static, fixed, and concerned with predominantly a-spatial 'social structures'" (Urry 2000, p. 6). For him, the broad idea of mobilities "includes various kinds and temporalities of physical movement" from walking to flying and comprises a large array of technologies – such as boats and crutches. On the temporal scale, "[m]ovements range from the daily, weekly, yearly, and over people's lifetimes", and it is not reduced to people or objects but also "the movement of images and information on multiple media, as well as virtual and one-to-many and many-to-many through networked and embedded computers" and many other devices, such as mobiles and tablets (Urry 2000, pp. 8–9).

Echoing G. Simmel, Urry (2000) urges expanded, complex, and revisionist ways of addressing and acting on multiple aspects and dimensions of mobilities in the contemporary world. That is, a *mobility paradigm*, "which involves a post-disciplinary, productive way of doing social science, especially in the new century where mobility issues would seem to be evidently centre-stage" (Urry 2000, p. 18). Without being contradictory, to pursue a NMP means to question both the *static* tradition of the social sciences and the "grand narrative" of *deterritorialization* (Sheller & Urry 2006) – as if, in the wake the globalization, borders and controls were collapsing equally for all social groups.

In fact, concerning tourism studies, Coles et al. (2005, p. 38) claim that "a post-disciplinary approach has clear potential by mobilizing tourism research towards considerations of other forms of human movement. . . . [Thus] studies of tourism must be able to formulate a coherent approach to understanding the meaning behind the range of mobilities (including tourism) undertaken by individuals, not just tourists". Broadly speaking, "tourism implies forms of travel that lead to the movement (or immobilization) of ideas and models of society, capital, workers, waste (including environmental pollution), almost always without a clear division between one or the other" (Allis 2016, p. 103).

Following this rationale, a specific critique emerges on traditional approaches in transport studies based on "technological determinism", which represents a cornerstone for this chapter: "It little examines the complex social processes that underlie and orchestrate the uses of such transports. There is we might say too much transport in the study of travel and not enough society and certainly not enough thinking through their complex intersecting process" (Urry 2000, pp. 19–20) – including travel and other movements associated with tourism.

Based on this framework, we ask: how mobile is tourism research on transport in Brazil? In order to answer this research question, the studies selected were analyzed in their general structure, especially with regard to the theoretical and methodological component – although, objectively, most of them did not use the specific literature on mobilities.

How mobile is the tourism research on transport in Brazil?

Overall, the scientific production on tourism and transport in Brazil is quite limited: considering a spectrum of about 25 years (1990–2015), there is an average of just over one paper per year published in national research journals. Amongst the 29 papers published in this period, the majority ($n = 16$) was published in *Revista Turismo em Análise* ($n = 7$), followed by *Revista Visão e Ação* ($n = 4$) and *Revista Brasileira de Pesquisa em Turismo* ($n = 4$).

Santos and Allis (2013) identified that the year of 2008 was the peak of publications for the period 1990–2011, with an emphasis on air and rail transport modes.[1] In the selection for this chapter, most articles (*n* = 25) were published after 2002 and had a clear focus on air transport (13 out of a total of 29), with a focus on airport studies (Kunz et al. 2015; Favorito 2013; Ferreira et al. 2012; Mattozo et al. 2012; Maia & Borges 2006), followed by others focusing on airlines – particularly operational and commercial aspects (Corrêa 2010; Ferraz & Oliveira 2008; Brasil 2006; Valente & Cury 2004; Feitosa 2002; Pelizzer & Scrivano 1990) but also historical ones (Godoy & Guimarães 2014; Gastal 2010). The second-most-expressive group refers to studies on urban mobility, with studies on tourist services (Bandeira et al. 2008) or on tourist uses of urban public transport systems – particularly road transport (Simon et al. 2014; Fernandes et al. 2013) and also underground systems (Graciose 1999). As for Zanirato (2008), he proposes a broader discussion on the impacts of automotive transport to historic city environments.

The rail mode is the next one (*n* = 4), with an emphasis on tourist trains (Mamede et al. 2008; Lohmann & Oliveira 2008) and other studies on current and potential uses of regular rail transport for tourism (Siqueira & Delage 2010; Ribeiro 2009). With the same amount of papers (*n* = 4), water transport is represented by studies on maritime cruises (Fujita & Andrade Júnior 2014; Trigo 1999; Zancudo & Alvarez 1997) and on river transport (Rodrigues & Castro 2011).

Finally, three other studies deal with multiple aspects of the relationship between tourism and transport: planning (Almeida 1992), cycling, and environmental education (Gonçalves Junior et al. 2011), and the relevance of road transport to tourism (Lacerda 2005).

The expression "mobility" itself appears very timidly among the selected papers, only as of 2008. Zanirato (2008) addresses mobility and accessibility in a similar way, emphasizing physical-spatial aspects of historical centers and their connection with tourism. Similarly, Fernandes et al. (2013) study the urban mobility of Curitiba, Brazil, and its implications and uses for tourism with attention to the public transport system. It should be noted that, in both cases, the emphasis is on infrastructure, bringing an analysis of the services and structures that allow the movement of tourists in during their visits. Simon et al. (2014), on the other hand, incorporate more subtle aspects of mobility in its interface with tourism, also in relation to the uses of urban public transportation – although, in the theoretical and methodological field, the framework that supports the new mobilities paradigm was not used.

In the case of research on transportation and tourism, most of the papers were expected to have *people* as researchable entities. On the other hand, despite the fact that they do not address a reflection about *objects*, some researches focus on particular structural components of transportation systems, in which people (passengers, tourists, travelers) represent an indirect approach. For example, Kunz et al. (2015) discuss the management of waste produced at airports, and Fernandes et al. (2013), when studying an interface between public transportation and tourism in Curitiba, focused on the analysis of folders, sites, and design and information available at bus stops.

Research has been undertaken on transport terminals (airports and bus terminals) (Bandeira et al. 2008; Ferreira et al. 2012; Ribeiro 2009). However, one cannot say that mobile methods – for instance, analysis of transfer points, observation of people's movement – is employed. This is because they do not seek to analyze the spaces themselves; instead, those terminals are solely taken as a spot to conduct an applied research (in general, interviews and surveys). In a way, Mattozo et al. (2012) aim to capture how passengers react to the *ambience* of the airport, since their research proposes to analyze satisfaction. That would suggest the employment of the method *capturing the atmosphere*. However, by employing quantitative techniques, it distances itself from more subtle analyses concerning the complex interaction between people (passengers, visitors, workers) and spaces (airports).

Among all the selected papers (n = 29), only seven have employed mobile methods, even when their authors were not aware of that. From the identification of the research tools employed, we can look for a correspondence with the list of mobile methods, although the methodological framework of these works does not clearly denote such intention. Therefore, by doing this, it is our intention to depict mobile tourism research on transportation in Brazil (Table 1.2).

With the exception of the interviews, in most cases, the techniques used reveal that the subjects under observation are in coadjuvant conditions – that is, the agency on the use of mobile methods relies on the researcher, with little or no protagonism of the studied subjects. For example, diaries have been used as a tool for researchers (as a field report, similarly to ethnographic approaches) – not as a way to collect people's perceptions, including audio and digital (and not only written) versions.

Interestingly, most of the works that use mobile methods – although not expressly – are concentrated from 2010 (Simon et al. 2014; Godoy & Guimarães 2014; Mattozo et al. 2012; Corrêa 2010; Siqueira & Delage 2010). In these cases, for the purpose of research on transportation and tourism, they employed methodological resources well consolidated in other areas, especially in social sciences – such as participant observation and travel diaries – and history (oral history).

More complex resources regarding the use of digital technologies are also practically absent in the selected papers – except for content published electronically in social networks (Corrêa 2010; Mattozo et al. 2012). In the same sense, the use of GIS technologies is also absent – which, in a certain sense, is not so different from the international context, since the researches with this methodological approach have only increased over the last 10 to 15 years (Allis 2018).

Final remarks and further developments

If tourism is only one (although complex) piece of the contemporary mobilities puzzle and if its existence depends on the means of transport that represent the

Table 1.2 Employment of mobile methods on tourism and transport research in Brazil

Paper Title [our translation]	*Authors*	*Research tools*	*Types of mobilities*	*Mobile methods*
Mobilidade e Turismo: hospitalidade no transporte coletivo em Caxias do Sul/RS. [Mobilities and Tourism: hospitality on public transport in Caxias do Sul/RS.]	Simon et al. (2014)	Observation Field notes (diary) Photograph Interviews	Corporeal travel	Time-space diaries Walking with Observing people's movement
Turismo, história, memórias e imaginários dos Tempos da PANAIR. [Tourism, history, memories and imagery of PANAIR's time.]	Godoy and Guimarães (2014)	Oral history	Corporeal travel	Memories
Aplicação adaptativa do modelo Fodness e Murray na avaliação da satisfação de passageiros no Aer. Intern. Augusto Severo utilizando regressão multivariada [Adaptative application of the Fodness and Murray model in the evaluation of passenger satisfaction at Augusto Severo International Airport using multivariate regression.]	Mattozo et al. (2012)	Literature review Interviews Statistics Webography	Corporeal travel	Examinations of conversations Analysis of transfer points
TAM Linhas Aéreas no Twitter: canal de comunicação ou rede social? [TAM Airlines on Twitter: communication channel or social network?]	Corrêa (2010)	Webography Content analysis	Communicative travel	Examinations of conversations
Imaginário e representações sociais a bordo do trem de passageiros Vitória Minas. [Imagery and social representations aboard the Vitória Minas passenger train.]	Siqueira and Delage (2010)	Interviews Observation Photograph Field notes (diary)	Corporeal travel	Walking with Time-space diaries
O continente da solidão. [The solitude continent.]	Trigo (1999)	Experience report Interviews Observation Documentary survey	Corporeal travel	Walking with Observing people's movement
Turismo e metrô: parceria viável. [Tourism and metro: viable partnership.]	Graciose (1999)	Documentary survey Observation	Corporeal travel	Walking with

mechanisms that provide flows and accessibility, one can no longer understand both areas (tourism and transport) as remote dimensions. A very stimulating and auspicious way to frame the issues, methods, and concepts of both areas seems to be under mobilities – despite the contributions from the social sciences.

As we have seen, on the one hand, the constitution of a new mobilities paradigm (NMP) is a recent but vigorous and growing process, within which an emerging tourism scholarship is/to be developed; on the other hand, with specific regard to the scientific knowledge in tourism that deals with transportation in Brazil, the gaps are still relevant – despite consistent (and perhaps not conscious) efforts to fill them. Hence, understanding how transport is being treated under the umbrella of mobilities could be a way of questioning and deepening some taken-for-granted elements in the tourism theories themselves. It is but an interdisciplinary effort, which might help mobilize tourism and transport.

The Transport and Tourism Research Group-GPTT (based at the Federal University of the State of Rio de Janeiro, Unirio), the Research Group on Transport, Tourism, and Economic Development-GPTTDE (University of Brasilia, UnB), and the Research Center on Transport and Tourism-PlaneTT (Federal University of Rio de Janeiro, UFRJ) pioneered the discussion of the interface between transportation and tourism in Brazil. Therefore, in the near future in Brazil, those seem to be the thriving environments for theoretical and methodological advances, using mobilities as a source of inspiration.

Note

1 Methodological note: the cited work incorporated more articles because the search has been based in several descriptors; we decided here to focus the searches exclusively on the descriptor "transport", expecting to identify specific adherence of the works to this field of study. For an extended list of papers on transport and tourism published in Brazil, see Santos and Allis (2013).

References

Adey, P. 2017. *Mobility*. London, New York: Routledge.

Allis, T. 2016. Em busca da mobilidades turísticas. *Plural*, 23(2), pp. 94–117.

Allis, T. 2018. Movilidad y turismo. In Zunino Singh, D., Giucci, G. & Jirón, P. eds. *Términos clave para los estudios de movilidad en América Latina*. Buenos Aires: Biblos, pp. 131–138.

Almeida, E. M. 1992. Transportes e planificação do turismo. *Turismo em Análise*, 3(2), pp. 83–91.

Bandeira, R. A. M., Ariotti, P. & Marins, L. M. 2008. Análise da qualidade de um serviço de transporte turístico: estudo empírico da linha turismo de Porto Alegre. *Turismo Visão e Ação*, 10(2), pp. 164–184.

Brasil, V. S. 2006. O impacto dos canais de distribuição no comportamento de compra no turismo: uma análise das relações entre satisfação, valor e lealdade na aquisição de passagens aéreas através de canais interpessoais e canais baseados em tecnologia. *Turismo Visão e Ação*, 8(3), pp. 361–378.

Burns, P. & Novelli, M. eds. 2008. *Tourism and mobilities: Local-global connections*. Oxfordshire: CABI International.

Büscher, M. et al. eds. 2011. *Mobile methods*. New York: Routledge.

Campos, V. B. G. 2013. Planejamento de Transportes: conceitos e modelos. Rio de Janeiro: Interciência, 2013.

Castro, R., Fraga, C. & Lohmann, G. 2013. Planejamento e Gestão dos Transportes e Destinos Turísticos. In Lohmann, G., Fraga, C. & Castro, R. eds. *Transportes e Destinos Turísticos: Planejamento e Gestão*. Rio de Janeiro: Elsevier, pp. 63–95.

Coles, T., Hall, C. M. & Duval, D. 2005. Mobilising tourism: A post-disciplinary critique. *Tourism Recreation Research*, 30(2), pp. 31–41.

Corrêa, C. H. W. 2010. TAM Linhas Aéreas no Twitter: Canal de Comunicação ou Rede Social. *Revista Brasileira de Pesquisa em Turismo*, (4)3, pp. 85–108.

Favorito, F. 2013. Aeroporto: suas relações e identidade. *Revista Brasileira de Ecoturismo*, 6(2), pp. 414–423.

Feitosa, W. R. 2002. Estratégias e políticas de preços no mercado de aviação: caso da Gol Transportes Aéreos. *Turismo em Análise*, 13(1), pp. 48–65.

Fernandes, D. L. et al. 2013. A utilização do transporte coletivo pelo turista em Curitiba. *Anais Brasileiros de Estudos Turísticos*, 3(2), pp. 55–64.

Ferraz, R. B. & Oliveira, A. V. 2008. A estratégia de overbooking e sua aplicação no mercado de transporte aéreo brasileiro. *Turismo em Análise*, 19(1), pp. 103–124.

Ferreira, J. B. et al. 2012. Motivadores de compra nos aeroportos brasileiros: uma tipologia para o consumidor em aeroportos. *Revista Brasileira de Pesquisa em Turismo*, 6(1), pp. 32–47.

Fraga, C. C. L. 2011. *Contribuição Metodológica para a implantação de trens turísticos no Brasil*. DSc Thesis. Transport Engineering Program. Federal University of Rio de Janeiro. Rio de Janeiro, Brazil.

Fraga, C. C. L. et al. 2013. Destinos Turísticos e Transportes: aspectos teóricos e estado da arte. In Lohmann, G., Fraga, C. & Castro, R. eds. *Transportes e Destinos Turísticos: Planejamento e Gestão*. Rio de Janeiro: Elsevier, pp. 31–64.

Fujita, D. M. & Andrade Júnior, H. F. A. 2014. Cruzeiros marítimos: histórico, evolução e tipologia voltados à hospitalidade comercial. *Revista Acadêmica Observatório de Inovação do Turismo*, 8(2), pp. 1–30.

Gastal, S, A. 2010. Correio aéreo e aviação civil: os primeiros passos da Varig. *Turismo e Sociedade*, 2(2), pp. 185–211.

Godoy, K. E. & Guimarães, V. L. 2014. Turismo, História, Memórias e Imaginários dos Tempos da PANAIR. *Revista Rosa dos Ventos*, 6(2), pp. 124–138.

Gonçalves Junior, L., Carmo, L. S., Colloca, E. D. & Corrêa, D. A. 2011. Projeto de Educação Ambiental e Lazer (pedal): Dialogando a partir do Cicloturismo na Escola. *Licere*, 14(4), pp. 1–16.

Graciose, V. F. 1999. Turismo e metrô: parceria viável. *Turismo em Análise*, 10(1), pp. 58–74.

Hall, C. M. 2009. *El turismo como ciencia social de la movilidad*. Madrid: Síntesis.

Kaul, R. N. 1985. *Dynamics of tourism: A trilogy* (vol. 111). Transportation and marketing. Nova Delhi: Sterling Publishers.

Kunz, J. G., Conto, S. M. & Demori, M. K. 2015. A geração de resíduos sólidos aeroportuários e suas interfaces com o turismo: o caso do Aeroporto Hugo Cantergiani, Caxias do Sul-RS, Brasil. *Revista Brasileira de Pesquisa em Turismo*, 9(1), pp. 59–75.

Lacerda, W. J. C. 2005. Turismo e transporte: importância do transporte rodoviário. *Revista Turismo & Desenvolvimento*, 4(1), pp. 9–21.

Leiper, N. 1990. *Tourism systems: An interdisciplinary perspective*. Palmerston North, Nova Zelândia: Department of Management Systems, Massey University.

Lohmann, G. & Oliveira, M. V. O. 2008. Transporte ferroviário de passageiros turísticos: o estado da arte. *Turismo em Análise*, 19(1), pp. 137–154.

Lohmann, G. & Panosso Netto, A. 2010. *Teorias de turismo: conceitos, modelos e sistemas*. São Paulo: Aleph.

Maia, A. I. W. & Borges, M. P. 2006. Turismo em Cabo Verde: perspectivas de crescimento com o aeroporto internacional da praia, Ilha de Santiago. *Caderno Virtual de Turismo*, 6(2), pp. 25–32.

Mamede, D. M. J. A., Vieira, G. L. & Santos, A. P. G. 2008. Trens turísticos e patrimônio cultural: como o turismo ferroviário tem resgatado, preservado e valorizado o patrimônio cultural. *Caderno Virtual de Turismo*, 8(2), pp. 81–94.

Mattozo, T. C., Silva, G. S., Costa, J. A. F. & Fernandes Neto, A. P. 2012. Aplicação adaptativa do modelo Fodness e Murray na avaliação da satisfação de passageiros no Aeroporto Internacional Augusto Severo. *Revista Iberoamericana de Turismo – RITUR*, 1(2), pp. 58–74.

Palhares, G. L. 2002. *Transportes Turísticos*. São Paulo: Aleph.

Palhares, G. L. 2005. Transportes para Turistas: Conceitos, Estado da Arte e Tópicos Atuais. In Trigo, L. G. G. ed. *Análises Globais e Regionais do Turismo Brasileiro*. São Paulo: Roca, pp. 641–669.

Panosso Netto, A. & Jäger, M. 2015. Robert Glücksmann (1877–1942): Founder of Berlin school of tourism research. *Anatolia*, 27, pp. 1–10.

Pearce, D. G. 2003. *Geografia do Turismo: Fluxos e regiões no mercado de viagem*. São Paulo: Aleph.

Pelizzer, H. A. & Scrivano, N. B. 1990. Relacionamento entre agência de turismo e fornecedores de serviços turísticos: agência de turismo e transportador aéreo. *Turismo em Análise*, 1(2), pp. 24–43. Publicação de Turismo. Available at: http://publicacoesdeturismo.com.br [Accessed on June 1, 2018].

Ribeiro, D. A. 2009. Demanda para trens de passageiros no eixo Rio de Janeiro – São Paulo. *Itinerarium*, 2, pp. 1–19.

Rodrigues, S. M. & Castro, F. M. M. 2011. Transporte fluvial e turismo: uma análise das potencialidades dos cânions do rio São Francisco e do atracadouro da Terra Caída em Sergipe (Brasil). *Turismo e Sociedade*, 4(2), pp. 323–342.

Santos, G. E. O. & Allis, T. 2013. Produção científica sobre transportes em periódicos de turismo. In Lohmann, G., Fraga, C. & Castro, R. eds. *Transportes e Destinos Turísticos: Planejamento e Gestão*. Rio de Janeiro: Elsevier, pp. 46–55.

Sheller, M. & Urry, J. eds. 2004. *Tourism mobilities: Places to play, places in play*. London: Routledge.

Sheller, M. & Urry, J. 2006. The new mobilities paradigm. *Environment and Planning A*, 38, pp. 207–226.

Simon, S., Gastal, S. A. & Santos, M. M. C. 2014. Mobilidade e Turismo: Hospitalidade no Transporte Coletivo em Caxias do Sul/RS. *Revista Brasileira de Pesquisa em Turismo*, 8(3), pp. 552–567.

Siqueira, E. D. & Delage, R. G. A. 2010. Imaginário e representações sociais a bordo do trem de passageiros Vitória Minas. *Revista Rosa dos Ventos*, 2(2), pp. 103–115.

Tribe, J. 1997. The indiscipline of tourism. *Annals of Tourism Research*, 24(4), pp. 638–657.
Trigo, L. G. G. 1999. O continente da solidão. *Turismo Visão e Ação*, 2(3), pp. 9–26.
Urry, J. 2000. *Sociology beyond societies: Mobilities for the twenty-first century*. London and New York: Routledge.
Urry, J. 2007. *Mobilities*. Cambridge: Polity Press.
Valente, F. J. & Cury, R. M. 2004. Transporte aéreo e a integração logística com as atividades turísticas. *Turismo Visão e Ação*, 6(1), pp. 27–43.
Zancudo, G., M. T. & Alvarez, G. 1997. El negocio de líneas de cruceros y el modelo de estrategias competitivas. *Turismo em Análise*, 8(2), pp. 59–66.
Zanirato, S. H. 2008. A Mobilidade nas Cidades Históricas e a Proteção do Patrimônio Cultural. *Revista Eletrônica de Turismo Cultural*, 4, pp. 1–16.
Zunino Singh, D., Giucci, G. & Jirón, P. eds. 2018. *Términos clave para los estudios de movilidad en América Latina*. Buenos Aires: Biblos.

Chapter 2

The mobilities of the favela and the social life of souvenirs

Bianca Freire-Medeiros and Palloma Valle Menezes

The "things" of favela tourism

Institutional spaces and editorial initiatives in various disciplines have long since addressed the study of material culture, objects and their materiality, and the conditions of production and consumption. However, these themes have gained greater relevance and have come to be seen through another theoretical approach as of the publication of the collection *The Social Life of Things*, edited by Arjun Appadurai, in 1986. In opposition to the idea that things have intrinsic and measurable value, Georg Simmel argues that value is always contingent and relative in space and time. Appadurai follows this line of thought, extending it to the study of the movements of objects in history, social contingencies, and policies that form their cultural biography. Although the focus had previously been on the forms and functions of the exchange, in the context of material culture studies post-1980, the "exchanged" element becomes central.

In general, the study of souvenirs reveals the relationship between material culture, social representations, market strategies, and consumer practices present in the context of a social experience – tourism, the existence of which is based on transcontinental transits (Urry 1990, 2001, 2007). Historians, anthropologists, and sociologists (among others) have explored the role that souvenirs play as objects of memory (Swanson 2004) and as condensing signs of the travel experience (Gordon 1986) as well as the crucial importance they have in the relationship of reciprocity so dear to contemporary travelers (Kim & Littrell 2001; Ward & Tran 2007).

In the specific case of favela tourism, the examination of these "things" allows us, on the one hand, to trace the very trajectory of the "traveling favela" (as proposed by Freire-Medeiros 2013) and, on the other hand, to examine the relationship between the mirroring of the favela as the territory of imagination and changes in the empirical materiality of the different touristic favelas. The notion of the "traveling favela", by favoring the mobility of and within the favela, seeks to explain how its transformation into a tourist destination and brand is far from being unambiguous. On the contrary, this is a complex and contradictory process in which poverty acquires an exchange value in the globalized market in an unpredictable and enigmatic manner (for poverty as a tourist attraction, see Frenzel

2016; Frenzel et al. 2012). It is not surprising that souvenirs, as one of the material media that guarantee the continuous circulation of the favela as a trademark, while benefiting from its perpetuation as a tourist destination, are absorbed in contradictory logics that elude interpretative predictability.

Where do souvenirs, which transform the experience of favela tourism into something tangible and collectible, come from? What is their trajectory, and what are the motivations for putting them into circulation? What do these "things" mean, to whom, and why? How, in the production of these souvenirs, does the dialectic relationship between massification and singularization, between the local and the global, so typical of the contemporary tourist experience, occur?

We seek to offer an answer to this set of issues by turning to reflections made over the last decade. We conducted participant observation at the points of sale of souvenirs in the Rocinha and Santa Marta favelas, in addition to interviews with tour guides and tour operators, souvenir producers and vendors, residents, tourists, and local leaders. At the end of 2015, when Santa Marta was already fully consolidated as a tourist destination, we returned to the field to interview producers and souvenir shop owners as well as to map out the products they marketed. Despite the extent of our previous research, the intention here is rather limited: to trace the social life of the "favela souvenirs" by revisiting the spirals of representation and meaning that move from empirical territory to objects and vice versa. With this objective in mind, we develop our argument by drawing together two main lines of thought: on the one hand, we chose paintings over the multitude of other objects that are sold as souvenirs in Rocinha (Nunes 2010) and Santa Marta; on the other hand, we concentrated on the point of view of craftspeople and shop owners as opposed to that of tourists – but this does not mean that the demands of this public are forgotten. Consumers, as we shall see, are a constant presence in the speech of craftspeople and those who trade souvenirs while functioning as a source of creative inspiration and practical constraint.[1]

In the following section, we will discuss exchanges, transfers, and appropriations produced within the context of touristic favelas and made apparent by a cross-examination of its souvenirs in relation to its topography. We will begin with the colors that are brought to life in paintings by the artists of Rocinha and which are reproduced on the colored walls of houses not only in that area but also in the "other" touristic favela: Santa Marta.[2] We will shed a light on the specificities of the life of the souvenirs produced here, in the first "pacified" favela in the city of Rio de Janeiro,[3] with the intention of tracing its continuous paths between imagination and materiality. In this reclaiming of the biography of the touristic favela from its material culture, our conclusion seeks to reflect on the death of (anti-)souvenirs or, in other words, what seems to be the exhaustion of possibilities of representing the favela as a trademark.

"Paint a watercolor with the colors of misery"

Rocinha, summer 2007. On one of the main streets of the favela, where most tour operators stop, craftspeople exhibit and market a variety of products: bags and belts made of aluminum rings; magnets and figurines made of medicine boxes, matches, and telephone wires; handbags and hats made of plastic bags. While groups of tourists listen to the explanations of the tour guide and photograph the stunning view of Christ the Redeemer and Rodrigo de Freitas Lagoon, Maicon sets up to work on one of his many paintings (Figure 2.1). Bigger than the others exhibited here – the artists know that tourists usually prefer small paintings that are easier to carry, such as those to the right of the photograph – the canvas draws the attention of "gringos" and researchers.[4] It is not that its subject is remarkable – after all, paintings that depict the houses of the favela, a theme also largely privileged by tourists' cameras, abound (see Menezes 2007; Freire-Medeiros et al. 2008). However, the combination of the mass of colored houses, the starry sky, and the spectacle of the circle of residents on the purple-tinted ground is enough to catch the eye.

"I started painting little colored shacks, which I think reminded me of the Rocinha of my childhood," Maicon recalls. "But then I looked around and realized that there are almost no shacks left in Rocinha; what was left were tall buildings, two and three floors high. I stopped painting little shacks and ended up painting

Figure 2.1 A resident of Rocinha sets up to paint and attract the attention of the tourists who pass by along the street.

Source: The authors.

the buildings." In fact, that view, which is sold to the tourist market as "the biggest favela in Brazil," leaps out at the eye and impresses due to the quantity of buildings with or without plastering whose half-constructed concrete slabs show the intention to keep going further up. How does one therefore explain the modest multicolored wooden houses that inhabit the souvenirs on display? "I tried to paint the buildings, but it didn't work. I didn't sell anything. What tourists really want is the colored shacks," Maicon concludes.

Seven years later, another picture takes us from Rocinha to Santa Marta (Figure 2.2). The shades of purple, pink, yellow, blue, and green seem to have leapt off Maicon's canvas and onto the walls of the first "pacified" favela. The typology of its constructions, the proximity of the houses, the lack of streets, and even the way the houses are painted, with white frames delimiting the shades of color, greatly resemble each other in the two images. The difference between the landscape and the painting is less quality than quantity: the existence of a large number of unpainted houses in Santa Marta gives the impression that the landscape of the favela is still an unfinished replica or a sketch of the work of the painter from Rocinha.

Let us carefully examine what the photograph reveals and the recent history of Santa Marta. On the left, we see a large concrete wall, which the state government erected in 2009 with the justification, challenged by the residents, that it was necessary to restrain the growth of the favela into the forest. To the right, the funicular opened at the beginning of 2008, which has five stops and ensures the increase of mobility in the area, the steepest favela in Rio. Between these two points, there are many-floored buildings that evidence the process of verticalization that has been occurring in Santa Marta since the beginning of the year 2000. Finally, our eyes land on the fourth element – the presence of buildings painted with different colors that move away from the typical monochromatic pattern of buildings in the favelas – which, in this narrative of the touristic favela, requires further reflection.

First, we must remember that the deliberate use of colors in the construction of the favela is much older than first thought. In 1959, Mario Saladini, then director of tourism and exhibitions of the city, suggested that painting the shacks in different colors would improve "the aesthetic and hygiene aspect" of the favelas and "attract visitors". According to an article published in *Diário Carioca* on October 3, 1959, with the title "Favela will show 'colored misery'",[5] favela residents would be responsible for cleaning up the shacks that would then be photographed and, from these images, artists hired by the city hall would determine the appropriate colors. If "the problem of miserable housing" was, as Saladini argued, "universal" and unobstructed in its entirety, it was the responsibility of the public authorities "to improve their appearance and even to turn them into a tourist attraction."

The project earned countless reactions, both supportive and critical, from the public. The bluntest and most forceful opposition was led by the then-Archbishop of Rio and creator of Cruzada São Sebastião,[6] Dom Hélder Câmara. However, it was in the magazine *O Cruzeiro*, on October 31, that we found the deliberation

Figure 2.2 Panoramic photograph of Santa Marta in 2014.

Source: The authors.

that best reveals the difficulty of accommodating the favela in the narrative of a city whose *status* as capital of the Republic had been withdrawn but that was struggling to maintain itself as the country's main showcase:

> Everyone knows and deplores them – the favelas are a social sore, a shame, a tragedy. However, the Director of Tourism is not guilty of that, nor does he

> have the authority to interfere with the problem. He is only a kind of makeup artist for the city.
>
> (*O Cruzeiro*, Oct. 31, 1959)

The following lines make clear the anxiety caused by the semantic approach between tourism and poverty:

> It may be claimed then that caring for tourism at a time when everyone is hungry is futile. But that is another kettle of fish. Tourism is now a serious business, it is an industry, and it is worth millions of dollars. It is not profitable here because it doesn't exist yet. If tourism were bringing in money, who knows if it would not be able to urbanize the favelas? Even though I doubt that, after bringing in the cash, people would remember favelados.[7] They would say it was picturesque, that the favelas are a tradition of the city.
>
> (*O Cruzeiro*, Oct. 31, 1959)

The proposition also inspired Jota Júnior and Oldemar Magalhães to write the song "Favela Amarela" ("Yellow Favela"). In their verses, the difficulty at that time of finding a way to classify a colorful and potentially touristic favela, except ironically, is once again made evident: "The irony of life. Paint the favela. Paint a watercolor with the colors of misery". Saladini's plan did not prosper, but the song guaranteed the singer Araci de Almeida the title of Queen of the Carnival in 1960 and the posterity of the poetic history of that episode.

Secondly, although the focus on the tourist potential of a colorful favela is nothing new, one must recognize that the recent coincidence of various economic circumstances – what literature came to call "the context of the megaevents" – offered the conditions for legitimating that idea and materializing what had previously been only the extravagant delirium of a public figure or the fruit of an artistic imagination. The "colored versions" of Rocinha and Santa Marta are, therefore, part of a larger set of spectacular interventions that have targeted their physical landscape and the conduct of their inhabitants.

The colorful chapter in the biography of the two touristic favelas began to be written in 2010. In Rocinha (Figure 2.3), according to the Ministry of Planning, BRL 278.8 million were spent on the work for the Growth Acceleration Plan (PAC in Portuguese), which included, among other things, a sports complex, a footbridge designed by Oscar Niemeyer, a community library, the urbanization and the enlargement of the streets, and the creation of a set of nine apartment buildings with 144 apartments. These new buildings as well as a series of houses located at the entrance of Rocinha were painted in vibrant colors, forming a colorful corridor that conducts the flow of tourists within the favela.[8]

In the case of Santa Marta (Figure 2.4), about 450 buildings were painted by 2014 – a comparatively smaller number than in Rocinha – thanks to a partnership between the state government and the company Tintas Coral.

Figure 2.3 The colorful buildings, which came from the painted canvases for consumption by gringos and which invaded the physical landscape of Rocinha, keep catching the eye of the tourist.

Source: The authors.

A closer examination of this alignment between public and private interests, between the state government and a Dutch paint factory, shows not only the new order that aims to depoliticize the city and govern it according to market demands (Leite 2015; Telles 2015) but also the mobilities of various orders that interfere with the vocation of the touristic favela. Its inaugural milestone – the so-called Michael Jackson's laje[9] – celebrates a long globalized Santa Marta: there is the statue of the pop star, created by the trendy sculptor and cartoonist Ique, and the reproduction of his face on a colored wall signed by the "international" artist Romero Britto, both evoking the controversial memory of Jackson visiting the area in the 1990s.[10]

The process of the aesthetic conversion of the Cantão square into a tourist attraction repeats the same strategies for the implementation of the physical landscape of the favela in the broader narrative of "poor-chic" (Halnon 2002). It is not surprising, therefore, that two Dutch visual artists, Jeroen Koolhaas and Dre Urhahn, were invited so that the initiative could hit international headlines. In the midst of their prestigious "Favela Painting" project,[11] the young artists, known as

Figure 2.4 The geometric coloring of the Cantão square in Santa Marta is intended to single out the location but at the same time limits it to the cliché of the touristic and globalized favela.

Source: The authors.

Haas & Hahn, redefined the Cantão square with the instrumentation of colors and geometric patterns.

This crossing over of the touristic favela through idealization and transnational flows is consistent with the dynamics of a mobile and unsubstantiated entity such as the "traveling favela" (Freire-Medeiros 2010). That does not mean, however, that these negotiations between the global and the local, the general and the specific, which the colors of Santa Marta express so well, are free of tension, as we shall see in what follows.

Souvenirs in the spirals of representation and color

In recent years, Santa Marta has seen an increase in the number of tourists circulating around the favela. The growth in the number of residents who have become active in the local tourist trade is also evident, either as guides, craftspeople, or souvenir vendors. Different products – keychains with Michael Jackson's face, blouses, hats, bags, mugs, pillows, notebooks, postcards, and boards, among others[12] – are sold in the gift shops spread across the area.

The iconography of the favela in the souvenirs, while evoking the representation of their physical landscape, is composed of a very similar set of residences: there is hardly any variation in the type of construction material employed in the architectural style or in the size of the houses. The only element that escapes this reductive routine is the color of the facades: on the surface of many items, the favela resembles a rainbow.

Andrea Miranda, the owner of one of the most successful gift shops in the neighborhood, offers an explanation for the presence of such a colorful favela in the touristic Santa Marta's material culture, inserting it into the spirals of representation that range from the artist's aesthetic intention to the physical landscape of the favela and back to the imagination materialized in the souvenir:

> Before, it was black and white, but due to the fact that Santa Marta is today one of the most colorful favelas in Rio de Janeiro, because of the Tintas Coral project, now everything is colorful to us, you know? Today we, the residents of Santa Marta, are all colorful. Because everything takes on color. And one thing that draws the attention of the tourists are the colors.

A resident of Santa Marta, craftsperson, and tourist guide, Barbosa, has been questioned over the last few years about the strategies of representation he uses in his drawings, illustrations, and paintings. He said that initially, he thought of depicting not only Santa Marta but other neighborhoods in his work. From a reflection full of ambiguities, however, it ended up becoming a representation of:

> A characterless favela. It's a favela. You don't need to identify which favela it is. My first project was to portray identifiable favelas. This is a product of Santa Marta, the first pacified favela. Rocinha has Niemeyer's work right at the entrance. Alemão has something different, the tram [cable car]. So, I wanted to work with this. But at the same time, there are artists in these areas, right? My mark is a more indefinite favela, you cannot tell if it is in Rio or in São Paulo. It's just a favela. You recognize that these features are a favela but cannot recognize which one it is.

To treat his own place of residence in a general way without the specificities of other neighborhoods would be more advantageous to Barbosa for two main reasons. On the one hand, it pleases the tourists, as gringos only seem to care about what is typical of the favelas in general. On the other hand, the appeal to typical and generic traits allows these products to circulate more and to be sold in other areas of the city. Through a partnership with an NGO, Barbosa managed to launch a line of notebooks with his drawings of the generic favela (in black and white or in color), which can be found in the gift shops of Santa Marta, in the stationery shops of large malls, and in museum gift shops in Rio.

The success of the sale, however, was not enough to appease Barbosa, who continues to question whether he, as someone born and raised in the favela, should produce different souvenirs for tourists who specifically visit Santa Marta:

> This is a question I ask myself: will I create two types of products? Am I going to make a type of product for the tourists in Santa Marta? So, my idea is to create one, two, or three products with the face of Santa Marta, with the funicular, with the colorful houses that people see and recognize as Santa Marta.

If, as Sheller and Urry argue (2004, p. 6), "places are neither fixed nor are given, but are in play with multiple mobilities", Barbosa's considerations help us remember how ingrained Santa Marta is in the global flows of tourism – for better and for worse. On the one hand, such insertion allows the favela to burst with a positive visibility; on the other, it requires that it be domesticated and that it not let go of its empirical diversity.

Crispim, an artist from Santa Marta, who paints the favela on wooden panels and canvases, points out that he seeks inspiration for his work in past memories and in desires projected into the future. His paintings, more than portraying reality, would express his desire for a transformation in progress:

> I aim to move forward and go beyond the reality that we are living in, painting a wholly colorful favela. When you look up from down here, you see some colorful houses, but it is not fully and completely colored. . . . On my canvases, [I seek] a dreamlike favela that you can look at and identify as beautiful. . ., a harmonious, cheerful, exciting, and pleasant thing to be seen.

In the picture represented in Figure 2.5, Crispim reveals a less dense favela, with wooden shacks surrounded by trees and bushes and not superimposed on top of each other like in previous illustrations. One cannot say that this image is a faithful portrayal of Santa Marta, because on Crispim's canvas, the houses, despite being made of wood, seem to be painted in diverse and intense colors. According to the artist, his decision to portray the favela of the past in color is justified for two reasons: on the one hand, he has lived in a shack and has always dreamed that his house could be as colorful as the ones on the canvas; on the other, he thinks that the colors do not serve only as an element to draw the tourists' attention, but they also make it possible to portray a positive image of the favela to the foreign eye:

> I lived in a shack. I can say that I still live in a shack. . . . And I always dreamed of living in a colorful shack. And so, I ended up bringing that to the canvas. Actually, they [colored shacks] even existed, but there weren't many. Today, if I were able to not live in the modern world, I would build a wooden

Figure 2.5 Crispim idealizes an old and colorful favela.

Source: The authors.

Figure 2.6 The human element portrayed in the paintings exhibited in one of the souvenir shops in Santa Marta corresponds, as a rule, to the narrative of typicality.

Source: The authors.

> house on the hill, totally painted. If I could, I would still do that, like I do on the canvas. But, on the other hand, I make them colorful because for tourists that does not transmit an idea of sadness and poverty, but one of joy.

On Crispim's canvas, as well as on most of the canvases, shirts, mugs, and magnets sold as souvenirs in Santa Marta, the favela is almost always represented as a set of houses without the residents present. When there is a human element, it rarely portrays a common resident going about everyday life. The characters that inhabit the canvases are baianas, capoeira dancers, Samba musicians, etc., as seen in Figure 2.6.

Once again, the souvenir makers justify that they represent these typical characters because they anticipate that is what tourists desire to see and consume. They also evoke the desire for a cheerful favela in the paintings, with residents playing instruments or doing capoeira. Favela residents who dance samba and who know, despite all adversity, how to live a happy life. In Andrea's words, some paintings have:

> Capoeira dancers, there's the guy with the accordion, because everyone in the neighborhood is a musician, everything here is a reason to dance samba. This is what the guys (tourists) look for in the favela!"

Final considerations: the death of the "anti-souvenirs"

The option of painting a cheerful and harmonious favela means that many of the everyday problems faced by the residents – power and water shortage, bad sanitation and infrastructure, arbitrary police behavior – are not portrayed in the souvenirs. As we have seen here, artists justify the absence of negative aspects of life in the neighborhoods because, on the one hand, this would not interest tourists and, on the other, that would not represent the image of the favela that they wish to sell to the world.

And what if an artist dared to create souvenirs that showed not only the beauty but also the ills of life in the favela? This is what the Rio artist Rafucko[13] did on the eve of the Rio 2016 Olympic Games, in what he called the "Monstruário 2016: Rio de Janeiro's anti-gift shop for the Olympics". In a video of the shop's opening, the "artivist" exhibited and contextualized the products that were part of the exhibition:

> These are the postcards. . . . One of them portrays the *apartheid*, with young black teenagers being searched in front of the Olympic rings. And there's this one, which is a photo of the Vila Autódromo, a community forcibly evicted. . . . We also have custom-made Havaianas flip-flops with the image of young black teenagers being searched in front of the bus on the way to the beach. It costs 30 reais. Here we have a toy car shot by the Military Police of Rio de Janeiro. 111 shots, and it costs 111 reais. . . . This one is the most popular item: the mug with Beltrame's face [former Secretary of Security of Rio de Janeiro]. It costs 40 reais. . . . Here every drink is undrinkable. And here are stuffed toys for the children. . . . The big tractor, used for demolition and illegal evictions. And "caveirinho", the stuffed keychain shaped as the "caveirão", BOPE's[14] armored vehicle that kills. Finally, we also have decorative plates. They come in three prints. One is the uniform of the Special Police Operations Force (BOPE) who restrain the demonstrations. The other is the official logo of BOPE. And one is in commemoration of the Army's occupation of the Maré favela complex. . . . The Monstruário 2016 exhibit is open to the public until May 21 here at the Hélio Oiticica Cultural Center, and we await you to come and take a look at our anti-souvenirs that reflect the reality of Rio de Janeiro.

Rafucko's creation was criticized by the people of the favelas and the advocates of the black movement[15] who questioned the artist's "standpoint" – a middle-class white male, speaking in the name of the black people – and the fact that the souvenirs do not only play a part in a performance, but they are also being sold. Faced with commercialization that seemed immoral to them, these residents of the favelas and advocates organized an act against the Monstruário exhibition. Defending himself against accusations that he would be profiting from other people's pain, Rafucko released an open letter in which he stated that:

> Selling is an important part of the work, because it reproduces/reveals this commercialized and monstrous logic that transforms the city into a theme park for the few while the black youth are being slaughtered. It is important to state that despite the products being sold, there was no profit. . . . The sales, which were made in a space belonging to the city hall, are also a criticism of how the state insists on selling the city of Rio de Janeiro as wonderful, even in the midst of so much blood and pain. I used the official logo of the Olympic Games to make clear that the memory that should be taken from this event is also that of those who were excluded from the celebrations because their homes or their lives and those of their loved ones were destroyed.

Apart from any moral or aesthetic assessment that may be made on Rafucko's products, the fact is that the controversy around the initiative is the explicit and summarizing argument that runs through this article: it is essential to maintain a historical perspective in the approach to the theme of the "touristic favela". Only by going back in time can one understand the controversy around Rafucko's pieces without appealing to the polarization between representations "from within" and "from outside". The fact that the favela is appropriated as an element of artistic representation by a subject who is alien to it is nothing new. On the contrary, there is a long list of painters, writers, poets, and musicians who, being residents of other parts of the city or even as foreigners, have used it as a main theme. The "colorful" favela, bucolic and atavistically rural, long before inhabiting the paintings of the artists residing in Rocinha and Santa Marta, was present, for example, in the revered paintings by Tarsila do Amaral (*Morro da favela*, 1924) and Di Cavalcante (*Favela*, 1958).

This temporal perspective enables us, moreover, to problematize "native art" as the carrier of an immaculate authenticity, apart from the other consecrated works whose principles of representation are based on a shared imagination of the favelas. In this way, the anxieties explained by the local artists, which we reproduce here, may be understood as arising from their commitment to the interest of the market, but also from the pressures imposed upon them by certain artistic conventions, enshrined in the official history of Brazilian art.

Faced with the controversy generated by the anti-souvenirs, we must ask: is it possible for these objects, which have the function of turning the experience of the touristic favela into something tangible, to reveal the violent dynamics and the pain that are part of everyday life for those who inhabit the margins of the city? Will the objects produced for tourist consumption be destined to travel the world, taking with them only positive memories of their destinations? Or can they also carry representations that are not dislocated from reality and the everyday problems that are often invisible to tourists but that are experienced by the residents? Can souvenirs serve as devices of political fight by helping to internationally disseminate what the official propaganda of the tourist destinations tends to erase? By placing Rio's production of souvenirs at the center of the debate about favelas and city representations, we seek not only to map out how and by whom the souvenirs are produced but also to analyze some of the dilemmas involved in the materialization and transformation of inequality, social exclusion, racism, and state violence into products.

Notes

1 For a detailed examination of the consumer practices of the tourists in Rocinha and Santa Marta, see Freire-Medeiros et al. (2008) and Freire-Medeiros and Vilarouca (2015).

2 In the context of the mega-events that took Rio as a stage, other favelas – Babilônia, Vidigal, Complexo do Alemão, to name a few – were incorporated into the tourist maps of the city by the initiative of private and/or public actors. It was in Santa Marta, however, that the volume of paid tours became comparable to that of Rocinha: at the time of research, they received an average of 4,000 tourists per month.

3 In November 2008, Santa Marta was occupied by the military police, and a new "proximity policing" project, named the Pacifying Police Unit (UPP), was tested. Over the last decade, while Rio de Janeiro was preparing to receive mega-events such as the 2014 World Cup and the 2016 Olympic Games, 38 UPPs were inaugurated (Menezes 2015). Especially in Santa Marta, soon after the beginning of the "pacification" process, investments were made – through a project called the Rio Top Tour – to promote the neighborhood as an official tourist destination of the city, to train local guides, and to promote commercial activities aimed at foreign and Brazilian visitors who came to visit the "model favela" (Freire-Medeiros et al. 2013).

4 In the summer of 2006, the authors, accompanied by research assistants Fernanda Nunes and Livia Campello, conducted intense fieldwork to observe the relationships between tourist guides, tourists, vendors, and souvenir producers, which were concentrated mainly on "Rua 1". We thank both for their dedication and partnership.

5 This and the other reports mentioned in this section are available on http://favelatemmemoria.com.br/bonita-por-fora/. Accessed on April 2016.

6 Dom Hélder Câmara, while an archbishop of the Archdiocese of Rio de Janeiro, seeking a "rational, human, and Christian solution to the problem of the favelas" (Valladares 2005, p. 77), created Cruzada São Sebastião. The idea was to favor the residents of the favelas while keeping them close to their place of work and leisure. The only favela that was in fact entirely urbanized by the Cruzada was Praia do Pinto, located in Leblon, a neighborhood that, as Don Helder had anticipated, ended up becoming a most valued place in the city (Simões 2008, p. 2).

7 *Favelado* is a term used to refer to those who live in favelas. For decades, the term has been associated with the stigma linked to the favela, as *locus* of poverty and criminal behavior. As well as being used to refer to those people that live in these criminalized areas of the city, the term is also used generally to refer to people that behave in ways that are considered rough or unrefined. In recent years, various social movements and

leaders of favelas have been defending the use of the term and redefining it as a synonym of struggle and resistance, a source of pride and not embarrassment.

8 In May 2018, Mayor Marcelo Crivella caused outrage by giving the order to paint in gray and beige the facades of the 150 apartment buildings and houses of Rocinha facing Autoestrada Lagoa Barra, multicolored until then. As highlighted in an article in the newspaper *O Estado de São Paulo*, titled "Rio de Janeiro's City Hall Paints Rocinha Gray", the initiative did not sit well with the residents of the favela, who claimed that "in addition to deleting the unique colors of the community, the intervention is literally a facade, because it does not solve real problems such as open sewers, the accumulation of waste, and power shortages in many side streets. Not to mention the war between criminals and police troops which, for nine months, have caused shootings in the community."

9 The turning of Santa Marta into a tourist destination was the result of an agreement signed with the Ministry of Tourism that allowed the installation of bilingual tourist signs in the favela and the creation of promotional materials for the favela. As well as the signage, a bronze statue of Michael Jackson was constructed on the same *laje* (rooftop) where the pop star filmed part of his "They Don't Care about Us" video in 1996. The creation of the space that has become known as "*Laje do Michael Jackson*", despite having been welcomed by a large portion of the residents, was criticized by some leaders who believe the space should continue to be called "*Laje do Ambulatório do Dedé*", the name it had been given in tribute to a previous resident who contributed significantly toward the improvement of service provision in Santa Marta.

10 In 1996, Michael Jackson filmed several scenes for his music video "They Don't Care about Us" in the Santa Marta favela. At the time, the newspaper *O Globo* published on its front page that director Spike Lee had hired a Brazilian producer to negotiate prices and locations with Marcinho VP who, at the time, was a "Lord of the Favela". A public prosecutor reacted and asked for a judge to decide to suspend the shooting. Filming crews did not follow the order, and the images of the favela circulated globally along with Jackson's music (see Freire-Medeiros 2009).

11 See www.favelapainting.com.

12 When we started our fieldwork in Rocinha, industrialized products almost didn't gain space in the market of Rua 1, where more rustic souvenirs made from recycled materials were sold in stalls. In Santa Marta, there are other shops where many articles produced en masse are marketed and that arrive in the favela from different parts of Brazil. One interviewee revealed to us that several of these "are more generic products but some are from the favela. A company in Santa Catarina [in the south of the country], for example, created mugs and pillows with the image of colorful houses and, as we already have this matter of the colorful favela, we acquire those to sell here".

13 Rafucko is an artist and advocate from Rio who identifies as a "modern fool and a multimedia artivist. A freelance VJ, a video editor, a model, and a VIP presence in protests". He currently has 84,800 followers on his Facebook page. Source: https://rafucko.com/bio/. Accessed on April 2016.

14 A Special Police Operations Force in Rio de Janeiro.

15 Robin Batista, a student of Afro-Diasporic Visual Arts, for example, published a blog post on the blog page of the Guerilla Collective's site, an independent media collective, criticizing Rafucko's initiative harshly. See: www.guerrilhagrr.com.br/sobre-a-dor-negra-e-periferica-como-souvenir-da-esquerda-branca/. Accessed on April 2016.

References

Appadurai, A. 1986. *The social life of things: Commodities in cultural perspective*. Cambridge: Cambridge University Press.

Freire-Medeiros, B. 2009. *Gringo na laje: produção, circulação e consumo da favela turística*. Rio de Janeiro: FGV Editora.

Freire-Medeiros, B. 2010. Felicidade é . . . uma favela violenta com vista para o mar. In Freire Filho, J. ed. *Ser feliz hoje: reflexões sobre o imperativo da felicidade*. Rio de Janeiro: FGV, pp. 257–273.

Freire-Medeiros, B. 2013. *Touring poverty*. London and New York: Routledge.

Freire-Medeiros, B., Menezes, P. V. & Nunes, F. 2008. Ética, estética e consumos possíveis: Notas etnográficas sobre turismo em uma favela carioca. *Os Urbanitas*, 5, p. 3. São Paulo.

Freire-Medeiros, B. & Vilarouca, M. G. 2015. Would you be a favela tourist? Confronting expectations and moral concerns among Brazilian and foreign potential tourists. In Diekmann, A. & Smith, M. K. eds. *Ethnic and minority cultures as tourist attractions*. Bristol: Channel View Publications, pp. 151–168.

Freire-Medeiros, B., Vilarouca, M. G. & Menezes, P. V. 2013. International tourists in a "pacified" favela: Profiles and attitudes. The case of SantaMarta, Rio de Janeiro. *Die Erde*, 144, pp. 147–159.

Freire-Medeiros, B., Vilarouca, M. G. & Menezes, P. V. 2016. *A pobreza turística no mercado de pacificação: reflexões a partir da experiência da Favela Santa Marta*. Salvador: CRH.

Frenzel, F. 2016. *Slumming it*. London: Zed Books.

Frenzel, F., Koens, K. & Steinbricnk, M. 2012. Introduction. In Frenzel, F., Koens, K. & Steinbricnk, M. eds. *Slum tourism poverty, power and ethics*. London: Routledge.

Gordon, B. 1986. The souvenir: Messenger of the extraordinary. *Journal of Popular Culture*, 20(3), p. 135146.

Halnon, K. 2002. Poor chic: The rational consumption of poverty. *Current Sociology*, 50(4), pp. 501–516.

Kim, S. & Littrell, M. A. 2001. Souvenir buying intentions for self versus others. *Annals of Tourism Research*, 28(3), pp. 638–657.

Leite, M. P. 2015. De territórios da pobreza a territórios de negócios: Dispositivos de gestão das favelas cariocas em contexto de "pacificação". In Birman, P., Leite, M. P., Machado, C. & Carneiro, S. S. ed. *Dispositivos urbanos e trama dos viventes: ordens e resistências*, 1, pp. 377–401. Rio de Janeiro: FGV Editora.

Menezes, P. V. 2007. Objeto e sujeito da fotografia: gringos e câmeras na favela da Rocinha. *Cadernos de Antropologia e Imagem*, 25, pp. 65–78.

Menezes, P. V. 2015. *Entre o "fogo cruzado" e o "campo minado": uma etnografia do processo de "pacificação" de favelas cariocas*. Tese de doutorado em sociologia, Instituto de Estudos Sociais e Políticos da Universidade do Estado do Rio de Janeiro, Rio de Janeiro.

Moraes, C. 2016. Turismo em favelas: notas etnográficas sobre um debate em curso. *Revista Plural*, 23, pp. 65–93.

Nunes, F. 2010. As representações da favela e seus significados: o caso dos souvenires "by Rocinha". In Panosso Netto, A. & Gaeta, C. eds. *Turismo de experiência*. São Paulo: Editora Senac.

Sheller, M. & Urry, J. eds. 2004. *Tourism mobilities: Places to play, places in play*. London: Routledge.

Simões, S. 2008. *Cruzada São Sebastião do Leblon: Uma etnografia da moradia e do cotidiano dos habitantes de um conjunto habitacional na Zona Sul do Rio de Janeiro*.

Tese de Doutoramento, Programa de Pós-Graduação em Antropologia da Universidade Federal Fluminense da Universidade Federal Fluminense.
Swanson, K. 2004. Tourists' and retailers' perceptions of souvenirs. *Journal of Vacation Marketing*, 10, pp. 363–377. London: Sage.
Telles, V. S. 2015. Cidade: produção de espaços, formas de controle e conflitos. *Revista de Ciências Sociais (UFC)*, 46, pp. 15–42.
Urry, J. 1990. *The tourist gaze*. London: Sage.
Urry, J. 2001. *Globalising the tourist gaze*. Lancaster: Lancaster University.
Urry, J. 2007. *Mobilities*. Cambridge: Polity Press.
Valladares, L. 2005. *A invenção da favela: do mito de origem ao favela.com*. Rio de Janeiro: Editora FGV.
Ward, C. B. & Tran, T. 2007. Consumer gifting behaviors: One for you, one for me? *Services Marketing Quarterly*, 29(2), pp. 1–17.

Chapter 3

Green favelas

Past, present, and futures of favela tourism in Rio de Janeiro

Camila Maria dos Santos Moraes

Introduction

On a sunny morning in January 2011, on a tour to Babilônia and Chapéu Mangueira, I was introduced to the "green favela". A title that was conferred by an international organization due to the reforestation carried out in the area since the late 1980s by the residents to contain the fires that occurred at the top of the hill during the period of drought. The project was presented at Rio +20, the Conference for Sustainable Development of the United Nations held in 2012 in the city, 20 years after Eco 92.

This green face of the favela was the one mostly unknown until then, since favelas were built on the hills where formerly we could find the Atlantic Forest, as we can observe in the article published on OGlobo.com in June 2010. The article claims that favelas occupy partially or totally preservation areas demarcated by the federal government, the state government, or the municipality, and indicates a growth of 282.3% in the previous five years. There were 17 favelas in this situation in 2003, according to a study by the Municipal Court of Auditors, and in 2010, there were at least 65 (*O Globo* 2010).

In March 2011, an article of the same newspaper entitled "A Greener Rio" (*Um Rio Mais Verde*) presented a new project announced by the State Department of the Environment – the Green Pacifying Police Unit (UPP Verde), whose pilot was going to be deployed in Babilônia. The article explains that the favela was chosen for several reasons, among which is the fact that it is a pioneer "in a successful reforestation program of Atlantic Forest seedlings" that counts on the participation and engagement of residents in the Cooperative of Reforesters (Cooperativa de Reflorestadores da Babilônia – CoopBabilônia; *O Globo* 2011).

As we can see, Babilônia, formerly considered an anti-green favela, was elected in 2011 by the state to be a laboratory of green public policies that would be presented at Rio+20. Since then, new green initiatives have been launched there, such as the Living Green Program (*Morar Carioca Verde*) by the City Hall, which aimed at the eco-friendly urbanization of this favela; *Favela Orgânica* (Organic Favela), a local project founded to promote knowledge about the total food cycle, from its production to its preparation using barks and stalks, avoiding waste, until the seeds' return to the land for a new production; and, later on, *Revolusolar*, a project that aimed to install solar energy panels in houses in Babilônia. According to the president of the Residents Association, all these projects and his work as the head of the Association aimed to make Babilônia a "sustainable favela that offers quality of life for its residents".

The abovementioned initiatives emerged and were highlighted in the context of mega-events in the city of Rio, such as the 2014 FIFA World Cup and the 2016 Olympic Games. To prepare the city, Rio also hosted Rio+20 in 2012, and public policies were launched to groom the city. In this context, selected favelas got new security and urbanization public policies, and the state saw tourism in the favelas as an important ally to these policies. Consequently, favelas experienced a new flow of people and investments that enabled a presentation/visibility of a green favela that contested the widespread image of the antigreen favela.

To better understand the favelas of Rio de Janeiro and its contested meanings, the new mobilities paradigm (NPM) offers a new lens of analysis. Proposed by Sheller and Urry, the NPM brings the new mobilities to the center of social studies. Sociologists considered that time and space compression was a result of the innovations and expansion of access to transport and new information and communication technologies, which brought people around the world closer and increased the flows of data, travelers, migrants, tourists, images, capitals, and objects (Sheller & Urry 2004, 2006, 2016). These new flows produced, among other things, new tourist destinations, such as the favelas of Rio de Janeiro.

According to Freire-Medeiros (2013), the combination of the favela both as a tourism destination and as a brand occurs through the "circulation of images, meanings, objects, and bodies responsible for creating and mobilizing the tourist favela", which became a worldwide phenomenon at the turn of the millennium (Freire-Medeiros 2013, p. 24). As a consequence of that, Frenzel (2016) sees tourism in poverty areas as a discursive field where social issues are negotiated and where political spaces are created to respond to social problems. In this sense, tourism would be a way of accessing poverty issues, to know or learn about inequality, and while the tourists learn, they revalue these places (Frenzel 2016, p. 4).

Thus, if we think about the case of Rio de Janeiro's favelas, to Frenzel (2016), tourists would not be familiar, for example, with the so-called dogmas about the favelas, identified and elaborated by sociologist Lícia Valladares, who found in her research a series of statements made about the favelas in the media at the governmental level and in the academic world itself, which were named by the researcher as "dogmas" (Valladares 2005, pp. 148–152). The first dogma refers to the specificity of the favelas. According to the researcher, the favelas have always been considered "different". Geographers draw attention to the differential of irregular occupation of the territory, architects emphasize buildings and urbanization that escape the rationality of architecture, and official agencies highlight irregularities and illegalities. The second dogma refers to the categorization of the favelas as the "locus of poverty and violence", that is, the territory par excellence where the poor reside. As a territory of poverty, it becomes a symbol in the territory of social problems and precarious physical space and social fabric. Such symbolization comes from the idea of the favela as an enclave, a "ghetto". Therefore, it is elected by the academy for studies, and by governmental and non-governmental social projects for investments. The third dogma that Valladares works on refers to "uniqueness", the unique analytical and political treatment given to the favelas, that is, the term *favela* is little relativized and is generalized; politically and analytically, we "fall into the error" of dealing with the favelas in the singular rather than in the plural.

In Frenzel's interpretation, these values or these dogmas are not known by tourists in some of the cases observed by the researcher. However, I believe that the dogmas identified by Valladares (2005), although unknown to international tourists, are still present and reproduced in the tourist favelas. They are marketed by major operators as something specific and particular to the city of Rio de Janeiro, as poor and violent, and as if they were all the same, especially in the trade in this type of tourism by large companies. Consequently, for many tourists, knowing one favela would be the same as knowing all of them.

Having said that, in this chapter, I offer an overview on favela tourism and its mobilities that allowed the "discovery" of the green face of the favelas and contested the widespread image of the antigreen favela. That is because the favelas are places of contested meanings, that produce ruptures and disjunctions due to the complex combinations of movements provided by the favela tourism. The frequent visits to green initiatives in favelas put into circulation the image of the green favelas, which challenges the historical antigreen meanings imposed on favelas.

To better understand how these meanings are elaborated and challenged through history, I turn to Reinhart Koselleck, who proposes a relativization of past, present, and future according to the social group and the time, which modifies the way in which such concepts of time are perceived and projected, as well as the relations between them (Koselleck 2006).

Therefore, this chapter is organized in three historical times – past, present, and future – that symbolize different meanings imposed and disputed for the favelas. The first one, the past, before the city hosted mega-events, when favelas were seen as antigreen; the second one, the present time, when it became a host city from 2009 to 2016, a period when Rio de Janeiro hosted the 2014 FIFA World Cup and the 2016 Olympic Games; and the future, after hosting mega-events, when new meanings will be disputed in the favelas. It is important to mention that the distinction between meanings and historical times is not exact but rather illustrative of the thoughts and disputes presented. However, discourses on antigreen, tourism, and green favelas coexist in past, present, and future perspectives.

It is also important to explain the selection of the mega-events period as a reference of present time. The central analysis on the mega-events period is justified, as highlighted by Zirin (2014), because Brazil was the first country to host the 2014 FIFA Soccer World Cup and the Rio 2016 Olympic Games in such a short space of time, which rendered the organization rather challenging. In order to prepare for this mission, Rio hosted the Rio+20 conference in 2012. Between 2009 and 2016, the eyes of the world turned to Brazil and Rio de Janeiro a few times. There was an intensification of flows of people and investment, which generated an increase in the number of tourists and a potential increase in the number of tourist places to meet this new demand.

According to Sheller and Urry (2004), a mega-event city moves out of the commonplace and becomes a "host city", a city that looks into the future and prepares for those events that produce and intensify flows of people and investments. Because they are considered unique, they involve moments of "global condensation", that is, intense localization of people and investments (Roche 2000, p. 224, cited in Sheller & Urry 2004, p. 9). That is exactly what happened in Rio between 2002 and 2016. Rio de Janeiro ceased to be an ordinary city and began to prepare itself to be a host city. Flows of people and capital were intensified and arrived in selected favelas of Rio in the shape of public policies that moved new favelas into the international tourist system.

Therefore, I conducted a multisited ethnography in the new tourist favelas of Rio de Janeiro, following the expansion of tourism to these areas. During fieldwork, I noticed that the metaphor of the green favelas also spread throughout the city and gained visibility in the context of mega-events, especially after Rio+20. Green initiatives were found in eight other groups of favelas besides Babilônia, namely: Rocinha; Vidigal; Tabajaras and Cabritos; Pavão, Pavãozinho and Cantagalo; Santa Marta; the Alemão complex; and the favelas of Tijuca and Vale Encantado. Together, these favelas represent nearly 500,000 out of the 6.5 million residents of Rio. In this multisited research I was in contact with residents engaged in tourism and green initiatives, as well as state agents that operate in these areas.

The antigreen favela past

In the city of Rio de Janeiro, favelas were originally formed on hillsides, encroaching on remnant areas of Atlantic Forest. In the 1970s, some of the main hills of Rio were designated as environmental conservation units (UC). Therefore, favelas were considered antigreen areas that occupied environmentally fragile zones. Former meanings imposed on the favelas were added to these characteristics, such as precariousness of the buildings and illegal occupation, causing them to be classified as areas of environmental, social, and political risk (Soares Gonçalves 2012).

Brazilian research about favelas and the environment is still relatively sparse. Most papers are concerned with landslides and illegal spread of housing into forested areas, focusing on reforms in housing and civil defense policies. These studies indicate favelas are the most affected areas of the city, especially because of their location on hillsides and precarious structures (Allen 1989; Amaral & Amaral 1989).

An analysis of public policies in favelas located close to or within the Atlantic Forest was made, and a few projects and technical reports can be found in the former State Foundation for Environmental Engineering (*Fundação Estadual de Engenharia e Meio Ambiente* – FEEMA), now called the State Institute of Environment (*Instituto Estadual do Ambiente* – INEA). These reports presented a diagnosis of deforestation in the city of Rio de Janeiro and proposed a series of eco-development projects in the favelas. The aim was to create a method to address environmental problems in poverty areas (FEEMA 1982). These reports identified the need for a study to examine the relation between favelas and deforestation, as these are often considered the cause of all the city's problems.

Throughout history, therefore, a series of public policies sought to contain, define, and control the expansion of favelas, if not eliminate them with the designation of "occupation of environmentally protected areas" or "risk areas". Therefore, the state, the media, and academia considered favelas an "environmental problem" and a risk to the city.

In this sense, during the 2000s, the idea of an antigreen favela was intensified by public policies, such as the ecolimits. Created to contain the spread of favelas in 2001, when the Municipal Environmental Office created a project that included the "construction of delimiters to protect green areas subject to invasions" and presented three types of delimiters to be applied in accordance with local conditions: chain-link fences, steel wire fences, and solid walls. These ecolimits would have the "function of preserving the Atlantic Forest remnants in several communities in Rio de Janeiro and stop the process of irregular occupation of forests, which has marked the history of the city" (Tito 2003, p. 13).

In 2004, former mayor Luis Paulo Conde (1997–2001) and the former Secretary of Environment and Urban Development during the administration of former governor Rosinha Garotinho proposed the construction of walls around certain favelas (Camargo 2012; Machado 2013; Compans 2007). In 2009, after a study commissioned by the Federation of Industries of Rio de Janeiro (FIRJAN) compared the dimensions of 219 favelas in the city of Rio de Janeiro between 2002 and 2007, governor Sergio Cabral Filho declared he had a "special concern with the growth of favelas" (Nunes 2012, p. 8). This led him to enact Municipal Act 245 in 2009. The main objective of such act was to ensure the integrity of the fauna and flora of the city of Rio de Janeiro and prevent the uncontrolled growth of 11 favelas located in the south zone of the city: Santa Marta, Rocinha, Chapéu Mangueira, Benjamin Constant, Chácara do Céu, Parque da Cidade, Morro dos Cabritos, Tabajaras, Pavão-Pavãozinho, Cantagalo, and Vidigal. The walls, about three feet high, were to be constructed along the boundaries between the favelas and the areas to be preserved, replacing the old fences installed in 33 favelas since 2001 (Camargo 2012; Machado 2013; Compans 2007).

This stirred up heated controversy, and the idea was rejected by most academics and most people living in the favelas. In a series of articles on the ecolimits, most authors agreed that the environmental discourse supporting the project hid the real interests behind the project, which were to reinforce sociospatial segregation (Camargo 2012; Machado 2013; Compans 2007).

Against this ongoing backdrop of controversy justified by the growth of favelas, an environmental protection action was taken in favor of the middle and upper classes' private interests. However, the idea of the antigreen favela has been challenged, and several favelas have become not only tourist attractions but ecotourism destinations, famous for their green initiatives.

The favela tourism present

Favela tourism is the local expression of a global phenomenon: tourism in poverty areas. According to Frenzel et al. (2015), the so-called slum tourism presents itself as a mass tourism phenomenon that occurs in some areas of the Global South. In the last 20 years, the offer of these tours has increased, as well as the number of tourists interested in knowing these areas. It is estimated that more than 1 million tourists are distributed annually in South Africa and Brazil (Rio de Janeiro), which accounts for 80% of this flow, and the other 20% are distributed in India, Kenya, and Mexico, among other countries (Frenzel et al. 2015).

In Brazil, favela tourism started in the 1990s, more precisely in Rio de Janeiro – Rocinha in the 1992 Earth Summit in Rio (Eco 92), when leaders of various social movements and Greenpeace organized a visit to Rocinha, which became the model for favela tourism (Freire-Medeiros 2013; Frenzel & Koens 2012).

In the 2000s, Rocinha has become one of the main tourist attractions of Rio de Janeiro, and favela tourism appears in other favelas as a response to internal and external initiatives. A key role in this expansion of favela tourism is played by public policy. In the most frequently visited favelas, public policies such as the Growth Acceleration Program (*Programa de Aceleração do Crescimento* – PAC) and the Pacifying Police Units (*Unidades de Polícia Pacificadora* – UPP). PAC and UPP have promoted and supported the expansion for social and developmental ends and to aid the improvement of security (Frenzel et al. 2015).

The PAC for favelas

In a partnership between the federal government and the government of the state of Rio de Janeiro, the PAC for favelas was launched, an urbanization program in selected favelas of Rio: Rocinha; Pavão, Pavãozinho, and Cantagalo; the Alemão and Manguinhos complexes. In all of these favelas, the urbanization project involved improvements in the access to this areas and new buildings to solve housing issues in these areas. In two groups of favelas, we also find an urban mobility project. In Pavão, Pavãozinho, and Cantagalo, a panoramic lift was build, which connects a metro station in one of the main areas of the Ipanema neighborhood to the top of these favelas. In the Alemão complex, a cable car with seven stations was built to connect the Bonsucesso neighborhood to the favelas and to connect the favelas of the complex to one another.

According to Cavalcanti (2013), the PAC for Favelas was designed following the requirements of strategic planning and urban marketing that are giving it the political, discursive, and imaginary tone of a suitable city to host mega-events, such as the 2014 FIFA World Cup and the 2016 Olympic Games. From the standpoint of strategic planning, the biggest obstacle to this process was the so-called public security crisis, which for three decades has been converging with the idea of the "problem of favelas" (Burgos et al. 2011). In this sense, the PAC for Favelas was only one aspect of a broader arrangement of the city and favelas under construction for mega-events. The next step was to solve the security issues.

UPP

Launched by the government of the state of Rio de Janeiro in the end of 2008 in selected favelas of Rio de Janeiro, the Pacifying Police Unit (UPP) is a public security police based on the permanent occupation of the favelas by the military police, under the premise of "recovering territories" and "integrating these spaces with the city" (Carvalho 2013). Since its implementation, the UPP has been interpreted, investigated, and questioned by locals, NGOs, and social movements (Menezes 2015). The UPP was presented by the state government as a public security solution and an inaugural step toward a new and safer life in the favelas, which would also bring other social programs.

The "pacified" favelas, the ones with UPPs, became prime locations for public and private investment in social programs, for the expansion of public services, and for the regularization of existing services and businesses. According to Cavalcanti (2013), the space distribution of UPPs in Rio de Janeiro leaves no doubt that the tourist sites are favored, in particular the south region of the city and areas near sport arenas of the FIFA World Cup and the Olympic Games.

Favelas tourism and public policy

In Rio de Janeiro, favela tourism has been part of urban tourism planning for almost a decade, appearing for the first time in Providência in 2006, with plans for an open museum (Menezes 2008), and then in Pavão, Pavãozinho, and Cantagalo in 2008, with its Favela Museum, created with the support of the Growth Acceleration Program to value the local culture and to attract tourists to these favelas (Moraes 2010). The third time we can see favela tourism as a subject of public policies is after the launch of the Pacifying Police Unit (UPP), which was first installed in Santa Marta in 2008. After that, in 2010, there was the Rio Top Tour Program, inaugurated as a part of the pacification of the Santa Marta favela (Freire-Medeiros 2013). It was originally going to be developed in three other groups of favelas – Chapéu Mangueira and Babilônia; Pavão, Pavãozinho, and Cantagalo; and Providência, which received their UPP in between 2009 and 2010. The program aimed to develop tourism in these favelas, to train local guides, and to create promotional material. However, the project could only be completed in Santa Marta due to political issues inside the other favelas and also some changes in the government (Moraes 2011). The fourth time, also as part of the Growth Acceleration Program (PAC), was when the Alemão complex cable car was launched in 2011, which has "increased tourist numbers from zero to several thousand in just a couple of years. The cable car was never meant to be only a tourism attraction, but tourism was part of the strategy to make the investment viable" (Frenzel et al. 2015). Finally, the Providencia cable car was launched in 2015, but this one did not have the same effect as the Alemão cable car in increasing tourist visitors, something I could observe from my fieldwork.

In other favelas, we also saw the expansion of favela tourism. This is mainly due to the effort of residents that want to be part of this new market niche and because of the UPP and projects that follow this public policy.

This expansion of favela tourism, allied with public policies in urbanization and security areas, gave visibility to former ecological projects in favelas and encouraged new projects, as we can see in the selected case of Babilônia and Chapéu Mangueira.

"The Green Favelas" – Babilônia and Chapéu Mangueira

Named Green Favelas by an international NGO because of the Reforestation Project carried out by the community since the end of the 1980s, Babilônia and Chapéu Mangueira were chosen by the City Hall to receive the *Morar Carioca Verde* program (Green Carioca Living). This program promotes the construction of "green buildings", which reuse rainwater and use LED lighting, among other actions, and during Rio+20, it attracted high-profile visitors like New York Mayor Michael Bloomberg.

The *Morar Carioca Verde* program focuses on sustainability and on a new type of land occupation, changing the opinion about these areas, which are usually known for their risks, so that they are seen as safe places for the population. In Babilônia and Chapéu Mangueira, this program is considered to be in an advanced stage. Among the sustainability actions of the project are the use of alternative building materials in these favelas, a rainwater reuse system, and selective waste collection.

In addition to this program, Babilônia is also acknowledged for the Organic Favela project, led by a local woman who organized workshops about the total use of food and food cycle. In her workshops, she teaches recipes with vegetable peels and stems that normally would go to waste. She also talks about the total cycle of food, especially vegetables. She explains in every lecture that we must know how and where the vegetables that we buy were produced and all their cooking possibilities, and after that, she explains that whatever we cannot use, we should give back to the earth. So, she teaches how to build urban farms on the *lajes* of favelas (favela houses' rooftops), how to compost the food that is not edible anymore, and how to use the composted material in the urban farm.

After Rio+20, these favelas became more and more visited by tourists looking for a quiet place to stay in Rio de Janeiro near the beach and he nature. They come to Babilônia to visit trails and to take part in some workshops by Organic Favela.

According to the community association president, they "aim to transform Babilônia in a sustainable favela". He is working with Organic Favela and CoopBabilônia to bring more green initiatives to the favela. The most recent project is Revolusolar, an NGO that is installing solar panels in selected houses of the community.

Favelas' contested futures

Thinking about favela tourism and green favelas stimulates a reflection on the future of favelas and tourism in these areas. Inspired by the future of the cities designed by John Urry in the book *What Is the Future?* (2016, pp. 151–189), I imagined four contested futures for favelas, namely: fast-mobility favela, fortress favela, digital favela, and green favelas.

In the first future scenario, I described the fast-mobility favela. It would involve large investments for the occupation of airspace, which could be used for tourist visits on the move. The verticalization of these areas would also be a feature, considering that, throughout history, favelas were verticalized by individual urbanization or public policies for the expansion of local houses and businesses. However, the high investments required for this scenario render it unlikely, considering the political and economic situation of the state, as well as the great rejection that the mobility equipment or verticalizations proposed by the state have suffered in Rio de Janeiro after the mega-events (see Moraes 2017, pp. 213–216).

The fortress favela or the fortress city scenario with favelas outside this urban perimeter presents itself with greater possibility. The resumption of the removal process or recovery of the ecolimits can be reedited at law or in urbanization projects to create new boundaries between favelas and green areas, or between the favelas and the city, since the deforestation and polluting image of the favela remains. The biggest example in this sense is the Horto community, where the removal justified by an environmental discourse was revived immediately after the Olympic Games.

In this perspective of a fortress favela or favelas outside the city, the possibility of a virtual visit in favelas would be tempting for some curious people and already exists on the platform Beyond the Map, which is part of the On the Map project (*Tá no Mapa*). The idea of this project is not directly related to tourism, but its discourse is similar to the favela's local guides. The platform and the project seek to give visibility and promote the inclusion of favelas, residents, and their businesses in the digital life, using the format of script or tour. Launched on the eve of the Rio 2016 Olympic Games, the platform was possibly intended to move tourists and visitors to these favelas by putting them on the map.

Finally, we come to the future that may have a better dialogue with this chapter: the future of the green favelas. For many, this idea is still far from being possible, because favelas would represent the opposite of the "green idea". However, if the favelas are a part of the city, green favelas would be possible only in the livable city. However, as pointed by Urry (2016), the livable-cities future is very unlikely, since this future would require a significant inversion in the economic, energy, and transport systems. Urry's livable city is much like a green favela and very similar to the aims of the green initiatives in Babilônia and Chapéu Mangueira. In the livable city, favelas would be green, but it would be necessary to reverse the current logic of the favela and city relationship for that. It would be necessary to revalue the favelas as green but to also revalue Rio de Janeiro itself as a livable city. So the final question is: green favelas? Is this a possible future or a utopia to be pursued?

Developed by Levitas (2013), the idea of utopia as a method is a useful exercise, since it is based on a hermeneutic methodology related to "transforming initiatives for a better world", which can be observed in the cases presented in this article. In Babilônia, the residents' association group seeks to transform this favela into a "sustainable favela". In other favelas such as Laboriaux–Rocinha, the NGO Green Favela seeks "the urban sustainability of favelas adjacent to protected natural areas, aiming at the coexistence between natural and urban systems". Therefore, utopia ceases to be just an idealization, but it can be a method to think of a better future for the favelas with alternative social practices and opposed to the status quo.

It is important to mention that the futures illustrated here could coexist and be deemed utopia for some or dystopia for others. What is important here is to reflect on these possibilities, to prepare ourselves, to challenge ourselves, and to opt for our utopia, which some favela dwellers are already doing. Engaged in green initiatives, these actors chose their utopia and made a method out of it to create a better favela.

Final thoughts

Between 2016 and 2017, Brazil went through some important changes. The impeachment of the president and the local elections for the city mayor and city council members caused some significant modifications. In Rio, the state went broke after the Olympic Games, and an unprecedented crisis has taken place, which is reflected in the main public security policies in the favelas. Individually or in local groups, tourism guides and entrepreneurs maintain their interrelation to continue their work. However, favela tourism is now in retraction in the face of the news about unsafety in favelas and changes to public policies.

As we saw in this chapter, favela tourism and tourism mobilities in the favelas of Rio contrast different images of these areas. These mobilities gave some visibility for a green face of the favelas and contested the generalized idea of an anti-green favela. In this sense, with the tourism retraction and the increased unsafety in favelas, old meanings can be re-valued or new meanings can be attributed to these areas in order to contain the "favela problem". Such scenarios have been encouraging analysts, residents, and social movements to reflect on the future of favelas, and this chapter sought to contribute in this sense.

References

Allen, E. 1989. *The flood which became a disaster: Housing and the poor in Rio de Janeiro*, Discussion Paper, 25. Glasgow: Centre for Housing Research University of Glasgow.

Amaral, C. P. & Amaral, F. P. 1989. Impactos ambientais derivados do processo de favelização nas encostas do Rio de Janeiro. *Simpósio de geografia física aplicada*, 3, Friburgo.

Burgos, M. B., Cavalcanti, M., Brum, M., Amoroso, M. & Pereira, L. F. A. 2011. O efeito UPP na percepção dos moradores das favelas. *Desigualdade & Diversidade*, 11, pp. 49–98. Rio de Janeiro.

Camargo, J. C. G. January 25, 2012. Ecolimites ou Sócio-Limites? Da preservação ambiental à segregação sócio-espacial. In *Portal do Observatório das Metrópoles*. Rio de Janeiro: IPPUR/UFRJ.

Carvalho, M. B. 2013. A política de pacificação de favelas e as contradições para a produção de uma cidade segura. *O Social em Questão*, 29, pp. 285–308. Rio de Janeiro.

Cavalcanti, M. 2013. À espera, em ruínas: urbanismo, estética e política no Rio de Janeiro da PACificação. *Dilemas: Revista de Estudos de Conflito e Controle Social*, 6, pp. 191–228. Rio de Janeiro.

Compans, R. A. May 2007. Cidade contra a favela: a nova ameaça ambiental. *Revista Brasileira Estudos Urbanos e Regionais*, 9(1), pp. 83–99. São Paulo.

FEEMA. 1982. *Projeto Ecodesenvolvimento. Favelas, desmatamento e reflorestamento no município do*. Rio de Janeiro: FEEMA.

Freire-Medeiros, B. 2013. *Touring poverty*. New York: Routledge.

Frenzel, F. 2016. *Slumming it*. London: Zed Books.

Frenzel, F. & Koens, K. 2012. Slum tourism: Developments in a young field of interdisciplinary tourism research. *Tourism Geographies*, 14(2), pp. 1–18. London.

Frenzel, F., Koens, K., Steinbrink, M. & Rogerson, C. 2015. Slum tourism: State of the art. *Tourism Review International*, 18(2), pp. 237–252.

Koselleck, R. 2006. *Futuro Passado*. Rio de Janeiro: Editora PUC Rio/Contratempo.

Levitas, R. 2013. *Utopia as method: The imaginary reconstitution of society*. New York: Palgrave Macmillan.

Machado, A. B. 2013. Ecolimites e gestão das descontinuidades internas da cidade do Rio de Janeiro IN: *Anais dos Encontros Nacionais da ANPUR*. Available at: www.anpur.org.br/revista/rbeur/index.php/anais/article/view/4314.

Menezes, P. 2008. *Interseções entre novos sentidos de patrimônio, turismo e políticas públicas: um estudo de caso sobre o museu a céu aberto do Morro da Providência*. Master's thesis, Instituto Universitário de Pesquisas do Rio de Janeiro – IUPERJ, Rio de Janeiro.

Menezes, P. 2015. *Entre o "fogo cruzado" e o "campo minado": uma etnografia do processo de "pacificação" de favelas cariocas*. PhD dissertation, Instituto de Estudos Sociais e Políticos, Universidade do Estado do Rio de Janeiro, Rio de Janeiro.

Moraes, C. M. S. 2010. Caminhos do Pavão, Pavãozinho e Cantagalo. *Revista Intratextos*, 1, pp. 32–46. Rio de Janeiro.

Moraes, C. M. S. 2011. *Museu de Favela: pensando turismo e patrimônio no Pavão, Pavãozinho e Cantagalo*. Master's thesis, Programa de Pós-Graduação em Ciências Sociais, Universidade do Estado do Rio de Janeiro, Rio de Janeiro.

Moraes, C. M. S. 2017. *Favela Ecológicas: passado, presente e futuro da favela turística*. PhD dissertation, Centro de Pesquisa e Documentação de História Contemporânea do Brasil (CPDOC), Fundação Getúlio Vargas, Rio de Janeiro.

Newspaper Archives O avanço sobre o verde no Rio. *O Globo*. June 27, 2010, p. 19.

Nunes, J. S. 2012. "Remoções em Foco: Políticas Públicas para as Favelas Cariocas em Tempo de Megaeventos". *Anais VI Enapegs Eixo Temático Gestão Social*. São Paulo: PUC.

Sheller, M. & Urry, J. 2004. *Tourism mobilities: Places to play, places in play*. New York: Routledge.

Sheller, M. & Urry, J. 2006. The new mobilities paradigm. *Environment and Planning A*, 8(2), pp. 207–226.

Sheller, M. & Urry, J. 2016. Mobilizing the new mobilities paradigm. *Applied Mobilities*, 1(1), pp. 10–25.

Soares Gonçalves, R. 2012. A construção social do risco e as remoções das favelas cariocas. 36 ANPOCS, 2012. *Anais do 36 ANPOCS*. Aguas de Lindoya: ANPOCS.

Tito, M. F. 2003. *A Importância Do Ecoturismo Para A Preservação Do Parque Nacional Da Tijuca*. Final paper presented in the *Lato Sensu* graduate program Projeto a Vez Do Mestre, Universidade Cândido Mendes.

Um Rio mais verde. *O Globo*. March 20, 2011, p. 42.

Urry, J. 2016. *What is the future?* Cambridge: Polity Press.

Valladares, L. P. 2005. *A invenção da favela: do mito de origem à favela*. Rio de Janeiro: FGV.

Zirin, D. 2014. *Brazil's dance with the devil: The world cup, the Olympics, and the fight for democracy*. Chicago, IL: Haymarket Books.

Chapter 4

After COR

Social impacts of a smart city initiative on Rio de Janeiro's mobilities

João Alcântara de Freitas

Introduction

Over a decade (2007–2016), Rio de Janeiro has experienced a unique moment in its history, hosting several mega-events such as the Pan American Games, Rio+20, World Youth Day, the World Cup, and the Olympic Games, among others. To be ready to host such events, the city needed to meet a number of prerequisites, some related to basic infrastructure. In April 2010, the city suffered one of the biggest tragedies of its recent history: heavy rains and flooding caused hundreds of deaths and brought chaos to the city, showing the total unpreparedness of the government to handle emergencies (Boghossian et al. 2011).

In this context, the government of Rio, in partnership with IBM, developed the Rio Operations Center (COR): a control room that integrates the data and monitoring functions of approximately 30 municipal and state agencies and utilities under the same roof. With the promise of increasing the efficiency of services and improving responses to outages and service failures, the Operations Center was created with the intention to make Rio de Janeiro a more sustainable, safer, and integrated city.

By applying ICT in urban management, COR was supposedly the main body responsible for making Rio de Janeiro a smart city, being pointed out as a kind of role model (Sennett 2012). Although it has won international awards in the area of smart urbanism, as in the case of the World Smart City 2013, the city rarely uses the title of "smart city" locally. However, on the international scene, Rio occupies a relatively important place when it comes to smart cities. Because of its repercussion, COR has systematically received politicians from other cities, researchers, lobbyists, policymakers, and entrepreneurs who wish to know a little about its operation. This remarkable flow would characterize Rio as a destination for "urban policy tourism" (González 2011).

The heterogeneity of cities claiming the smart city title makes it very difficult to make a precise critical assessment of what the so-called smart urbanism actually represents. At the same time, it is the mobilization of the "smart city" label, as a distinctive mark, that better positions these cities in the global financial flows, clearly configuring a strategy of urban entrepreneurship (Harvey 1989).

The purpose of this chapter is to discuss how the implementation and use of COR affected the urban mobilities in Rio de Janeiro. It is important to clarify that the objective is not to assess whether urban mobility has improved or worsened but to debate the transformations generated by COR in relation to mobilities and how this affects the way people live in Rio de Janeiro.

The analysis presented here is composed in the interval between 2010 – year in which COR is projected – and 2016 – last year of former mayor Eduardo Paes's administration. After Mayor Marcelo Crivella took office in 2017, COR underwent some significant changes, and that demands relative chronological distance for them to be evaluated.

This chapter is the result of a research developed for a dissertation on a process that I called "the invention of Rio Smart City". In addition to the visits I made to COR, the research included interviews with people who worked at COR between 2011 and 2016 and with an IBM representative. I guaranteed their anonymity. I also interviewed Eduardo Paes, whom it would be impossible not to identify during the dissertation. It will be structured as follows: after these opening words, brief remarks will be made about the new mobilities paradigm, underscoring its importance to the approach intended here. In the next section, I will contextualize the emergence of smart cities to then be able to explore the case of Rio. Finally, I will make some comments about the transformations that the COR generated in the way that urban mobilities are performed in Rio de Janeiro.

The new mobilities paradigm

According to Kuhn (1991), a paradigm refers to a shared network of conceptual, theoretical, methodological, and instrumental commitments and adhesions. The new mobilities paradigm (NMP) has in its center the movement – real, virtual, and potential – of people, capitals, images, objects, and ideas. Sheller and Urry (2006) point out that the NMP enables a much more comprehensive analysis of complex relational systems of infrastructure and social interaction at multiple scales. I also emphasize the importance of addressing "mobilities" in the plural form, as Urry underlines (2007), so as to comprehend that it is a complex set of movements.

The NMP permeated, in different ways, the research that gives rise to this chapter. It is important to emphasize that "to speak of mobility is in fact to speak always of mobilities. Mobility is never singular but always plural. It is never one, but necessarily many" (Adey 2009, p. 18). First, the very discourse of smart cities emerges as a sustainable alternative to a model of city – society, in fact – in which cars are the protagonist (Sheller & Urry 2000). Second, the concept of policy mobility has helped us understand how these smart-cities policies have spread in less than two decades on five continents and deciphered their circulation channels and the actions of the various actors involved (Wiig 2015). Third, mega-events involve a set of mobilities not only of people but also cultures, objects, capital, businesses, services, diseases, media, images, information, and ideas (Salazar 2017). The inauguration of COR took place during one of the visits of the then-International Olympic Committee (IOC) president, Jacques Rogges, and was announced as the first work completed for the Olympic Games (Freitas 2018).

Besides these questions, I emphasize that COR plays a key role in managing the daily spatial mobilities. Kellerman (2012) defines as daily spatial mobilities those comprised in: public transport, walks, private cars, and bicycles. I opt for such a distinction because I understand that there is a striking difference between "daily spatial mobilities" and "urban mobilities", the latter being more extensive and complex.

From the theoretical perspective of the NMP, urban mobilities would comprise all the mobilities that manifest themselves in urban space, be they corporeal, physical, communicative, virtual, and/or imaginative – following the categories proposed by Urry (2007). The ways in which people perform their daily mobilities tell a lot about the society of which they are a part, clearly revealing social inequalities. So to approach the mobilities does not mean to be attentive only to the physical movement but to a certain extent to its opposite: the potential movement, the impeded movement, the immobility, and residence (Büscher & Urry 2009). As announced in the introduction, it is precisely Rio's urban mobilities that I will address in this chapter.

The progress of smart cities: a brief contextualization

For the first time in history, the number of people concentrated in the cities has surpassed the number of people living in the countryside. According to a United Nations report, in 2018, 55% of the world's population live in urban areas, and such proportion is expected to increase to 68% by 2050 (United Nations 2018). This increase implies the need to build new cities, especially in countries of recognized high population density, such as India and China (Greenfield 2013). Greater concentration of people in cities also tends to multiply urban problems, such as natural resource scarcity, increased pollution, land speculation, traffic intensification, and increased crime, among others.

While the city is a perfect representation of the 21st century's urban problems, it also emerges as a key place for social experimentation and the search for solutions. Demographic pressure, coupled with global warming crises and economic instability, has propelled a range of new city concepts and policy prescriptions that place the city at the center of solutions to these problems (Shelton et al. 2014).

Characterized mainly by the extensive use of information and communication technologies (ICTs), smart cities appear as a celebrated solution for urban problems. There is great imprecision in determining their true origin, but several authors (Hollands 2008; MacLeod 2013; Harrison & Donnelly 2011) point to two likely influences: (1) the early-1980s New Urbanism movement in the United States, which questioned the urban model of high car dependency and the structuring of the city based on that, seeking to improve the quality of life and the environment by reducing land occupation, traffic congestion, and disturbances; and

(2) the idea of Smart Growth, which proposed compact cities, rational use of land, valuation of pedestrian spaces, reduced car use, and multiple-use communities.

Although the references are clear, the various fields that study smart cities have yet to agree on a unified approach (Nam & Pardo 2011). The concept remains fuzzy: some cities define themselves as a smart city when they identify some of their own features as "smart" but without referring to a standard meaning (Cocchia 2014). Generally, the smart-city vision is related to the application of a set of technologies to urban management, but it cannot be just about technologies.

The transformations prescribed in a smart-city project depend on the involvement and commitment of the population. To encourage this, the debate needs to match people's cultural preferences and practices, compliance with legal standards, and local planning requirements. The deployment of new information technology (IT) solutions in cities should not be limited to developing and pushing technologies to users. The transformations proposed by a smart city initiative have a clear and challenging sociological nature (Carvalho 2015). Urban life is multifaceted and extremely complex. Problems such as poverty, discrimination, social inequality, crime, and even environmental issues have important social, political, and cultural dimensions and will not be solved merely by IT solutions (Hollands 2015).

Gaffney and Robertson (2016) reiterate this perspective by arguing that the smart city paradigm is unable to meet the most pressing needs of cities with chronic deficits in urban infrastructure and the absence of robust civil society institutions. As such, smart urban systems can actually contribute to the securitization and fragmentation of urban space, exacerbating socioeconomic and political divisions. It should thus be considered that the so-called smart urbanism involves not only the implementation of new technologies but also a new geometry of power relations, which demands the production and circulation of knowledge, rationalities, subjectivities, and directed morals for the management of the smart-city projects (Vanolo 2014).

By analyzing the projects that carry the title of smart city, one notices how heterogeneous they are, since they prescribe actions for different spheres of the city. Smart cities could be divided into at least six dimensions: smart economy, smart people, smart governance, smart mobility, smart environment, and smart living (Giffinger et al. 2007). Even if these categories contribute to a better understanding of this universe, they are not always sufficient, since these dimensions sometimes overlap and reinforce the polysemy of the concept.

COR at the core of Rio's smart-city policy

Between 2007 and 2016, Rio de Janeiro hosted several mega-events, with the World Cup and the Olympic Games being the two most relevant. Immersed in several security and economic problems, the city needed to invest vigorously to be able to host these mega-events. In this context, the city of Rio de Janeiro, during the first administration of Mayor Eduardo Paes (2009–2013), signed a partnership with IBM. The mayor's intent was to use the expertise of the North American company to improve Rio's management. IBM, in turn, could showcase the use of its services in a city with great visibility, where they would be even more in evidence due to the mega-events.

In an interview with one of the leaders of the IBM Smarter Cities and Government team in Brazil, it was possible to understand the company's participation in the development of COR. The relationship between the City of Rio de Janeiro and IBM in regard to smart cities began in 2009, when Rio became one of the first cities to participate in the IBM Smarter Cities Challenge. The reward was consulting services provided by IBM to help cities become *smarter*, valued at around USD 500,000. To participate, managers and city leaders must apply on behalf of their cities by reporting on critical issues that could be resolved with the help of the IT company. The initiative began in 2010. By 2016, IBM had selected more than 132 cities whom they plan to help cope with chronic problems through the use of consulting, sophisticated software, and data management expertise. Analyzing the results of the projects, it is possible to notice a pattern in the actions of the company: it seems that, instead of seeking solutions to the problems of the city, IBM is looking for problems for its "smart solutions".

Participation in the challenge generated very specific actions in Rio de Janeiro, such as: (1) the institutionalization of digital practices, evidenced by the creation and fulfillment of the position of chief digital officer; and (2) the creation of *Rio Negócios*, an investment promotion agency based in the governance model defined by the IBM team (IBM 2010). Rio's participation in the challenge led to a strengthening of the city's relationship with IBM and the decision to continue the partnership. In order to find the best way to contribute to Rio de Janeiro, a two-day workshop with key city figures and IBM experts was scheduled for May 2010. Then, in April 2010, Rio de Janeiro recorded the highest volume of rainfall in a day in 50 years. The strong storm – and the city's lack of preparedness to deal with the emergency – left more than 250 dead in the metropolitan region of Rio de Janeiro, where entire neighborhoods were flooded and lost electricity (Barrionuevo 2010).

In the wake of the floods, the workshop was redesigned with the goal of making the city more resilient, improving the city's response in emergency situations. Based on this need and on demands made by IOC, COR was inaugurated on December 31, 2010, with the announcement that Rio was on its way to becoming a smart city. The announcement states that COR's mission is "to consolidate data from various urban systems for real-time visualization, monitoring, and analysis. The system was initially created for predicting floods and other related emergencies, but it is extensible for any event occurring in the city" (IBM 2010). The discourse of an urban control system is central to IBM's vision of a smart city, where the complexity of the urban condition and its governance can be reduced to manageable data variables through computerized control systems (Wiig 2015). In a short time, COR assumed important functions and became an indispensable tool for the day-to-day management of Rio de Janeiro. In a spacious hall located in a modern three-story building in the Cidade Nova neighborhood, a wall inside the COR headquarters is covered with 104 screens that allow staff to monitor images provided by more than 1,500 cameras and to manage actions in real time.

The room with "a screen larger than that of NASA", as former mayor Eduardo Paes boasted (Urbanized 2011), centralizes city control. COR is a significant example of computational scrutiny, which makes all city processes visible to those responsible for their management and makes the previously opaque or indeterminate not merely knowable but actionable (Greenfield 2013).

When asked why COR was successful, one of the former employees I interviewed said the project was "well publicized". Through COR, Rio succeeded before any other city in creating a control room that centralized the management of all the infrastructure of the city and disseminating it. Former mayor Paes used a TED Talk presentation in 2012 to show how COR technology facilitates governance. During the talk, Paes made a video call to Carlos Osório, COR's chief executive at the time, and, within two minutes, managed to display live images of weather satellite radar, cameras in the city center, and the location of garbage trucks that rolled around the streets (Paes 2012).

The operations center is deemed a landmark of so-called smart governance (Kitchin 2014) and is the main thing responsible for Rio's 2013 World Smart City Award (Bernardes et al. 2017). Competing against 200 other cities from 35 different countries, Rio de Janeiro submitted a package titled "Management of High Performance", which basically encompasses three projects: (1) COR; (2) *Central 1746*, a telephone center that concentrates a large part of the services of Rio de Janeiro City Hall; and (3) *Porto Maravilha*, which includes the revitalization works of Rio's Port area. Rio de Janeiro edged out the finalists cities of Buenos Aires, Berlin, Dayuan, Copenhagen, and Sabadell and was unanimously voted World Smart City 2013. Pedro Paulo Carvalho, the mayor's chief of staff at the time, spoke shortly after the event: "The jury evaluated mainly Rio's capacity to integrate several public agencies through service platforms that rely on state-of-the-art technology, which allows more interactivity for the citizen" (Magni 2013). In addition, the city was a finalist of the Guangzhou International Award for Urban Innovation (2014), won two consecutive Latin America Geospatial (2014 and 2015), and was prominently featured in Waze W10 as the first city to have a formal partnership with the most-used navigation app.

Not only COR but Rio de Janeiro was well publicized as a smart city internationally; however, the "smart city" title is used sparingly in Rio de Janeiro. The actions that boast the title of smart city locally are very punctual, and there is little relation to COR. On the occasion of its 450th anniversary, the city government incorporated "Rio Smart City" branding in information provided to tourists and locals on bus itineraries, bus stops, and tips on touristic spots. The systematization of the information about public transport in Rio de Janeiro is very important, but by using the branding just for that, the city downplays other initiatives and contradicts the title itself. Even after the mega-events, the domain riosmartcity.com remains active, but consists of an interactive map of bus stops and some tourist information. The fact is that there is a difference in the way that the title of smart city is mobilized locally and internationally, and it reiterates, to a certain extent, how "smart city" is more related to a narrative than actually to technologically oriented social transformations.

A proof of the positive repercussions of COR is that it attracts many visitors, both Brazilian and foreigners (politicians, policy makers, researchers, university groups, businesspeople, lobbyists, etc.), who are interested in learning about the functioning of the center. Due to its relatively large volume of visits, it is possible to characterize COR as an urban policy tourism destination. According to González (2011, p. 1398), urban policy tourism would be "short fact-finding trips by urban and planning professionals to other cities to learn about their transformation". A former employee said that at the beginning of the operation, the center was not expecting to receive requests for visits, because Rio's public agencies receive visitors only in very specific cases. As requests arrived, the agency gradually organized itself and developed a protocol to receive visitors. Internal statistics indicates that COR received 10,000 national and international visitors between 2011 and 2016 – a very expressive milestone. Among the visits, one was highlighted more than once by the interviewed employees: the governor of Tokyo, Yuriko Koike, and her entourage. Tokyo will succeed Rio de Janeiro as the next venue for the Olympic Games to be held in 2020. Governor Koike visited the facilities of COR to understand how Rio's control room was designed and operated for the Games. Considering that the International Olympic Committee requires host cities to have a command center during Games, there is some chance that something remotely similar to COR will be replicated in the Japanese capital.

Smart-city policies – as an object of discourse and actions – arise from a very specific set of conditions produced by late capitalism, in which cities compete with each other to be attractive destinations in search of both economic and social capital. Smart cities are the embodiment of what Harvey (1989) characterized as urban entrepreneurialism. In this sense, the success of Rio de Janeiro as a smart city is strongly related to the construction and dissemination of COR's image (Freitas 2018). This image was not only built by Rio's managers. Söderström et al. (2014) argue that the repercussions of COR are due in part to IBM's rhetorical appropriation of this installation as one of its success stories. The intention of the company was to be able to use the expertise acquired in Rio de Janeiro to eventually sell its solution package to other cities. The characterization of any city as smart is not limited to the implementation of ICTs in city management but involves the efforts of social actors (politicians, lobbyists, corporations, and others) to label a given city as smart to meet economic and political demands (Freitas 2018).

Rio de Janeiro's mobilities after COR

COR made it possible for managers in the city of Rio de Janeiro to make quicker and more informed decisions. The fact of having cameras scattered throughout the city as well as satellite information, application integration, near ubiquity in social networks, and media support imparts an idea of total control, which is ambiguous. While demonstrating to the population that the city is being monitored and managed 24/7, this vigilance ensures to the government a kind of power that can be dangerous. The technocratic discourse of ICT-oriented management carries an isonomic and neutral veneer; however, technology is a tool (Latour 2002) that can be appropriated and mobilized in different ways.

Rekow (2015) reports that Rio de Janeiro's security forces also benefited from the use of this technological apparatus, claiming they used it, for example, during the protests that took place in the year 2013. With the promise of a more orderly society, the technology was used to support a series of demonstrations of power as well as violence, including extensive surveillance, intimidation tactics, and so-called predictive policing, in which suspects are arrested before committing any crime. To the extent that these actions prevent legitimate protest, they ensure a more mechanized and inorganic society – where surveillance is used to capture and reproduce a set of power relations (Sadowski & Pasquale 2015).

The speed and intensity of the actions of COR led Sadowski and Pasquale to classify the process as a smart shock: "a shock therapy method, wherein a city undergoes a quick, large-scale integration of 'smart' ideals, technologies, and policies into an existing landscape" (2015, p. 3). This integration can be detailed in two aspects: (1) between agencies and departments of the city; and (2) COR with the population.

The COR integrates representatives of practically all agencies and city departments under the same roof. Even while it is based on experiences of control rooms in other cities, such as New York and Madrid, this interagency integration is very particular to the case of Rio. Some of the interviewees stated that COR only developed because it was a pet project of the former mayor. The management of the city of Rio de Janeiro is complex, and the long-standing rivalries among some agencies and city departments could jeopardize COR's entire operation. According to Paes, he negotiated directly with the heads of the agencies and departments so that the city hall could count on their support and have at least one representative of each agency and department present. Perhaps that is what Sandulli et al. (2017, p. 9) summed up as the "combination of strong political and organizational commitment", to which IBM attributes the success of the project. Paes failed to help elect the mayoral candidate he supported: Pedro Paulo Carvalho even advanced to the second round of the elections. The elected mayor, Marcelo Crivella (whose term of office began in January 2017), needed to demonstrate great bargaining power to maintain the support of agencies achieved during the previous administration. During the first year of Crivella's administration, COR had four different chief executives, double the number it had in the first six years.

COR's integration with the population is due to the way the information obtained by the center reverberates and tends to impact Rio's daily life. The management of a network's infrastructure is often invisible to the population; it is accompanied only by the city managers. One aspect that draws a lot of attention and that differentiates it from other control rooms is how COR conveys the idea of transparent management. Its press room is located in a mezzanine, within full sight and hearing for everyone. It is a room with computers, televisions, and a camera set up for daily live links to the local and national television news. The city's main news media monitor and report the entire operation. This type of relationship between government and the press is fairly uncommon in Brazil. Despite all of the problems in the structure and operations of the city, officials do not hide them from the press and civil society.

However this "integration" should not be interpreted as democratic inclusion. The city of Rio de Janeiro experiences historical socioeconomic problems; its reconfiguration due to mega-events, including COR's creation, has not only failed to solve these problems but has widened the socioeconomic divide (Sánchez & Broudehoux 2013). An example is the uneven distribution of cameras through the city: the number of cameras is higher in the more affluent areas than in other areas of the city. According to COR's operating model, the places with the most cameras are the places that get most attention. Gaffney and Robertson (2016) categorize these gaps in Rio's "smart" geographic coverage as "peripheralization of dumbness".

Although the main motivation for its creation was to make the city more resilient in emergencies, COR stands out for the way it enhanced the conduct of daily operation, especially with regard to urban mobility. Despite all of the infrastructure investments made for the World Cup and the Olympic Games, the mobility situation remains critical. In 2016, the population of Rio spent an average of 164 hours in traffic jams (TomTom 2017). Assuming that the working day in

Figure 4.1 Situation room, as seen from the mezzanine of the press room.

Source: Author's personal collection.

Figure 4.2 Avenida Venceslau Braz, information about the traffic situation.

Source: Taken and provided by Maria Alice Nogueira.

Brazil is usually eight hours long, this number of hours spent in traffic would amount to 20.5 working days in the year. In 2013, the "(im)mobility cost" reached BRL 29 billion in the metropolitan areas of Rio and São Paulo. After completion of the works for the mega-events, this number was expected to fall to BRL 25 billion in 2014 and 2015, but if there were no new investments in the coming years, these figures would rise proportionally with the increase in traffic congestion (FIRJAN 2014). The consequences of this astonishing number of days that the *carioca* population wastes in traffic jams not only reflects in the economy, but it also impacts quality of life.

Luque-Ayala and Martin (2016) state that in this way, COR not only tries to inform the population, but it is also a key component of its operation in the city. In order for the information obtained by Rio's control room to have impact, it is essential, first, that it reach the population quickly and reliably, and secondly, that people's actions be in response to this information. In addition to the partnership with the press, traffic and navigation applications, such as Waze and Google Maps, are also integrated with the COR system, and they include alerts sent directly by the center (to the users) through the applications themselves. Digital clocks scattered along the main thoroughfares of the city tell drivers how long they will spend on certain routes and allow them to avoid more congested roads. COR is a keen user of social networks like Facebook, Twitter, Instagram, and Periscope and estimates that it reaches about 0.8 million in normal conditions and 2.1 million people in emergency situations, when publications have more shares.

Adey and Bevan (2006) work with the concept of cybermobilities to explain how, with the overt use of technology, physical and virtual mobility are increasingly intertwined. The physical mobility of the car and its driver is facilitated by virtual information mobility. This virtual component of cybermobility, in this same example, is generated from physical movement (or inertia) of other cars. The concept reinforces how these two dimensions of mobility are mutually dependent and necessary: "Cybermobilities are the combination of virtual and physical movements, which are produced symbiotically and mediated by each other" (Adey & Bevan 2006, p. 48). "Space-time choreography" is no longer limited to physical urban spaces, but also encompasses the use of a multiplicity of electronic networks and spaces, as mobile devices are used as mediators of everyday life, and due to the media itself they begin to take the form of global electronic networks (Graham & Marvin 2002).

By acting strongly on the frontiers between physical, virtual, and communicational mobilities, the Rio de Janeiro Operations Center is an example of how these mobilities overlap and create new ways of perceiving the city. The COR system has an integration interface with Waze, Moovit, and Google Maps. These applications get information from satellites and GPS to assess the traffic situation in real time.

Its overexposure and its centrality in the operation of the city demonstrate not only the functional importance of COR but especially its symbolic importance: COR presents itself not only as an instrument of so-called smart governance but also as the technological materialization of government control over the city and the urban experience of its population. COR's technical and symbolic power demonstrates its role in the narrative construction of Rio de Janeiro as a smart city, as well as highlights its own logic of action that constitutes the new forms of mobilities in Rio de Janeiro (Freitas 2018).

Mobility is a kind of capital – which, by definition, is distributed unevenly – in which not only speed matters but also the practicality and flexibility of individuals in choosing routes and managing their mobilities according to their agendas (Kaufmann et al. 2004). In the case of cybermobilities, the analogy with capital is reinforced, since the physical, virtual, and communicative dimensions of mobility are not fairly distributed either. The very configuration of the urban mobility system of Rio de Janeiro tends to cause the information passed by COR to privilege individuals who use cars, since they can use alternative routes to reach their destination, unlike users of the public transportation system, which does not often have many options and is generally more vulnerable to traffic congestion.

Final words

With the blatant increase in the concentration of people in urban areas, the smart-city policies have been treated as the solution for the urban problems of the 21st century. In practical terms, it is still very difficult to assess whether so-called smart urbanism has the capacity to deliver on its promises. For now, smart cities have been presented as a kind of rhetorical strategy of urban entrepreneurship. COR has been treated as a success story internationally because Rio de Janeiro was the first city to put all its agencies and departments under one roof. The fact that they are working in the same space is not necessarily synonymous with an integrated operation, but it is a virtual potentiality.

In addition to facilitating the daily management of the city's infrastructure and emergency protocols, the use of this management tool in the planning and operation of the city during mega-events proved the importance of this equipment to the city. All the repercussions that COR's case had in the studies on smart cities are maybe an indication that Rio can prefigure the types of systems that will be constructed and implanted in other cities in the near future. The fact that the center has become an urban policy tourism destination will contribute to the dissemination of this model of smart initiative.

The success and effectiveness of policies, however, should not be based solely on their media repercussions or on their branding and marketing. Such policies need to consider and have a positive impact on the daily lives of the population. The implementation of ICT in city management is of great value, but it is not what will solve, almost by decree, the problems of Rio's mobilities. Most of the problems that the city faces are not related to lack of technology, but they are mostly results of secular social inequalities. Even in these conditions, COR does not hide its operation; the press practically lives there and incessantly observes the operation of the city. This transparency of operations – which does not mean total management transparency – demonstrates, in a calculated manner, a certain organizational maturity. In transmitting to the population an image of ubiquitous management, the smart-city operations center allows people to see that the urban machine is constantly at work.

References

Adey, P. 2009. *Mobility*. New York: Routledge.

Adey, P. & Bevan, P. 2006. Between the physical and the virtual: Connected mobilities. In *Mobile technologies of the city*. London: Routledge, pp. 44–60.

Barrionuevo, A. 2010. Rain multiplies woes of Rio de Janeiro's squatters. *The New York Times*, 14 April. Available at: www.nytimes.com/2010/04/15/world/americas/15brazil.html.

Bernardes, M. B., de Souza, R. M. S., de Andrade, F. P. & Novais, P. 2017. The Rio de Janeiro, Brazil, experience using digital initiatives for the co-production of the public good: The case of the operations centre. In Rocha, Á., Correia, A., Adeli, H., Reis, L. & Costanzo S. eds. *Recent advances in information systems and technologies*. WorldCIST 2017. Advances in Intelligent Systems and Computing, vol 569. Cham: Springer, pp. 18–27.

Boghossian, B. et al. 2011. Catástrofe no Rio: 271 mortos. *Estadão*, 13 January, p. 7.

Büscher, M. & Urry, J. 2009. Mobile methods and the empirical. *European Journal of Social Theory*, 12(1), pp. 99–116.

Carvalho, L. 2015. Smart cities from scratch? A socio-technical perspective. *Cambridge Journal of Regions, Economy and Society*, 8(1), pp. 43–60.

Cocchia, A. 2014. Smart and digital city: A systematic literature review. In *Smart city, progress in is*. Berlin: Springer, pp. 13–43.

FIRJAN. 2014. *Os Custos Da (I)Mobilidade nas Regiões Metropolitanas do Rio de Janeiro e São Paulo*. Brasil: Nova Técnica, no. 3.

Freitas, J. 2018. *A invenção da Cidade Inteligente Rio: uma análise do Centro de Operações Rio pela lente das mobilidades (2010–2016)*. Tese de Doutorado. Rio de Janeiro: CPDOC/FGV.

Gaffney, C. & Robertson, C. 2016. Smarter than smart: Rio de Janeiro's flawed emergence as a smart city. *Journal of Urban Technology*, pp. 1–18.

Giffinger, R. et al. 2007. *Smart cities: Ranking of European medium-sized cities*. Vienna, Austria: Centre of Regional Science (SRF), Vienna University of Technology.

González, S. 2011. Bilbao and Barcelona 'in motion'. How urban regeneration 'models' travel and mutate in the global flows of policy tourism. *Urban Studies*, 48(7), pp. 1397–1418.

Graham, S. & Marvin, S. 2002. *Telecommunications and the city: Electronic spaces, urban places*. London and New York: Routledge.

Greenfield, A. 2013. *Against the smart city (The city is here for you to use)*. New York: Do Projects.

Harrison, C. & Donnelly, I. A. 2011. *A theory of smart cities*. Proceedings of the 55th Annual Meeting of the ISSS-2011, Hull, UK, Vol. 55, No. 1.

Harvey, D. 1989. From managerialism to entrepreneurialism: The transformation in urban governance in late capitalism. *Geografiska Annaler. Series B, Human Geography*, The Roots of Geographical Change: 1973 to the Present, 71(1), pp. 3–17.

Hollands, R. 2008. Will the real smart city please stand up? *City*, 12, pp. 303–320.

Hollands, R. 2015. Critical interventions into the corporate smart city. *Cambridge Journal of Regions, Economy and Society*, 8(1), pp. 61–77.

IBM. 2010. *IBM's Smarter Cities Challenge Rio de Janeiro Summary report*, l. Available at: http://bit.ly/2xva0r0.

Kaufmann, V., Bergman, M. & Joye, D. 2004. Motility: Mobility as capital. *International Journal of Urban and Regional Research*, 28, p. 745–756.

Kellerman, A. 2012. Potential mobilities. *Mobilities*, 7(1), pp. 171–183.

Kitchin, R. 2014. The real-time city: Big data and smart urbanism. *GeoJournal*, 79(1), pp. 1–13.

Kuhn, T. 1991. *A estrutura das revoluções científicas*. São Paulo: Perspectiva.

Latour, B. 2002. Morality and technology: The end of the means. *Theory, Culture & Society*, 19(5/6), pp. 247–260.

Luque-Ayala, A. & Marvin, S. 2016. The maintenance of urban circulation: An operational logic of infrastructural control. *Environment and Planning D: Society and Space*, 34(2), pp. 191–208.

MacLeod, G. 2013. New urbanism/smart growth in the Scottish Highlands: Mobile policies and post-politics in local development planning. *Urban Studies*, 50(11), pp. 2196–2221.

Magni, É. 2013. Rio de Janeiro ganha prêmio de cidade inteligente do ano. *O Globo*, 21 November. Available at: https://oglobo.globo.com/rio/rio-de-janeiro-ganha-premio-de-cidade-inteligente-do-ano-10843951.

Nam, T. & Pardo, T. A. 2011. *Conceptualizing smart city with dimensions of technology, people, and institutions*. Proceedings of the 12th Annual International Conference on Digital Government Research, ACM, s. l, pp. 282–291.

Paes, E. 2012. *Eduardo Paes: The 4 commandments of cities [Video file]*. Available at: http://bit.ly/1KSLvqH: s.n.

Rekow, L. 2015. Police, protests, and policy in Rio de Janeiro: Mega-events, networked culture, and the right to the city. In *Citizen's right to the digital city*. Singapore: Springer, pp. 119–135.

Sadowski, J. & Pasquale, F. 2015. The spectrum of control: A social theory of the smart city. *First Monday*, 20(7).

Salazar, N. B. 2017. Exposing sports mega-events through a mobilities lens. In *Mega-event mobilities: A critical analysis*. Abingdon: Routledge, pp. 1–32.

Sánchez, F. & Broudehoux, A.-M. 2013. Mega-events and urban regeneration in Rio de Janeiro: Planning in a state of emergency. *International Journal of Urban Sustainable Development*, 5(2), pp. 132–153.

Sandulli, F. D., Ferraris, A. & Bresciani, S. 2017. How to select the right public partner in smart city projects. *R&D Management*, 47(4), pp. 607–619.

Sennett, R. 2012. No one likes a city that's too smart. *The Guardian*, 4 dezembro.

Sheller, M. & Urry, J. 2000. The city and the car'. *International Journal of Urban and Regional Research*, 24, pp. 737–757.

Sheller, M. & Urry, J. 2006. The new mobilities paradigm. *Environment and Planning A*, 38(2), pp. 207–226.

Shelton, T., Zook, M. & Wiig, A. 2014. The 'actually existing smart city'. *Cambridge Journal of Regions, Economy and Society*, 8(1), pp. 13–25.

Söderström, O., Paasche, T. & Klauser, F. 2014. Smart cities as corporate storytelling. *City*, 18(3), pp. 307–320.

TomTom. 2017. *Rio de Janeiro traffic congestion statistics*. s.l. Available at: http://bit.ly/2v5roA5.

United Nations, Department of Economic and Social Affairs, Population Division. 2018. *World Urbanization prospects: The 2018 revision*. New York: United Nations.

Urbanized. 2011. [Movie] Director: Gary Hustwit. United States and United Kingdom: Plexifilm.

Urry, J. 2007. *Mobilities*. London: Polity Press.

Vanolo, A. 2014. Smartmentality: The smart city as disciplinary strategy. *Urban Studies*, 51(5), pp. 883–898.

Wiig, A. 2015. IBM's smart city as techno-utopian policy mobility. *City*, 19(2–3), pp. 258–273.

Chapter 5

I live here, but I've never been inside it

Narratives on social tourism of the homeless population in the metropolitan area of Rio de Janeiro, Brazil[1]

Bernardo Cheibub and Jordania Eugenio

Introduction

"I live here, but I've never been inside it". That was a black male street dweller's reaction to a printed image of Solar do Jambeiro[2] Cultural Center, located in a middle-class neighborhood in the city of Niterói, in the metropolitan region of Rio de Janeiro. After being asked why he had never entered that cultural center, he pointed out that he had already been treated aggressively when trying to enter it, despite its free admission. He said that in a "natural" manner and with a shy and at the same time embarrassed laugh – perhaps in an attempt to demonstrate that he had not suffered from the expulsion or that the attitude of the guard was justified. This situation allows us to reflect on how far from social justice society is, especially regarding homeless people: a social group composed of people who have their rights ignored, who become invisible to the eyes of the state and other citizens (Santana & Castelar 2014).

In this chapter, we intend to reflect on the tourist experience of homeless people in the metropolitan area of Rio de Janeiro, based on the partnership between UFF's Social Tourism project[3] and the Specialized Reference Center for the Street Population (Centro Pop)[4] of Niterói. This article is based on the qualitative research method with the use of ethnography, carried out in the Master's Program in Tourism of Fluminense Federal University (UFF).

The idea of integrating homeless people in the study of the Social Tourism project, which originally served the university students and staff only, came from some of UFF's undergraduate students, who first saw the possibility of a partnership between that extension project and Centro Pop. Thus, the partnership organized two outings to some of the tourist attractions and cultural and educational venues in the cities of Niterói and Rio de Janeiro by a group of approximately 30 homeless people who are users[5] of Centro Pop, respectively on November 17, 2017, and April 25, 2018.[6]

In this chapter, we present some observations, interpretations, and analyses carried out by the students and the coordinator of the UFF Social Tourism project as well as professionals who work at Centro Pop and its users, who participated in the "preparatory" meetings and in the tours offered. With the use of ethnography as a scientific approach, by observing and talking to the homeless and other people involved in the tours, we were able to reflect on a complex scenario: people who live on the streets getting to know places that are usually intended for upper- or middle-class visitors, places they have no access to in another context, which limits their ways through the city. We believe that an ethnographic approach brings interesting contributions to qualitative research, "in particular for studies interested in social inequalities, exclusion processes, and social interactional situations" (Mattos 2011, p. 3).

Social tourism: tourist experiences as possibilities for inclusion

Tourism is an important source of income in many countries. Even if they do not properly organize or work on it in a comprehensive way (considering its social, cultural, political, and spatial dimensions), some countries can generate large revenues from the development of the tourism sector. Therefore, we argue that tourism should be considered a social right, not only due to the economic benefits obtained from it, but to what this activity represents in a globalized world.

We understand leisure as a social right and social tourism as a phenomenon that historically collaborates with the enjoyment of this right. Considering that public policies on leisure are necessary, there must be an understanding from society and the state that leisure is a social right (present in the Brazilian Federal Constitution, dated 1988) as important as others – health, education, housing, security, transportation, etc. (Melo 2007).

To discuss leisure, it is necessary to briefly go through the history of resistance and struggles of the proletariat in the 20th century. While we are currently part of an economic and social system in which most of the working class has the chance to rest at home on Sundays and have 30 days of paid vacation at least once a year, this exists because in the past free time became something fundamental to citizens' quality of life. To consider leisure a right of minor importance means to disregard a history of conquests through labor demands – especially in the early decades of the 20th century in most of the Western world – that achieved the decrease in daily working hours. When these facts are related to the reality of homeless people, who are usually unemployed, some questions arise: What is their relation with leisure? What does free time mean to these individuals?

Considering tourism as an option of leisure, we can say that the implementation of public policies connected to this practice enables the poorest population to have access to tourism experiences, even in their own home city. When experiencing the city where they live, citizens move and consume several urban spaces, which are accepted as their right, reducing the sense of not belonging to certain locations, perceived mainly by people who are on the margins of society (Cheibub & Eugenio 2018).

One of the foundations of social tourism is the understanding of tourism as a public service to citizens. The International Social Tourism Organisation (ISTO)[7] defines it as:

> A set of relationships and phenomena resulting from participation in tourism of a very low social class is possible or is facilitated by well-defined social policies, in which the idea of service rather than profit is implied.
>
> (Bureau 1996)

The ISTO has two fundamental principles: (1) tourism is an integral part of contemporary social life; (2) access to tourism should be seen as an inalienable right of the individual (Carta de Viena 1980). Despite the fact that the Brazilian Ministry of Tourism conceptualizes social tourism in its documents, initiatives in this area were assumed by the Commercial Employee Social Service (Sesc in Portuguese),[8] which demonstrates the lack of public policies in all governmental sectors that organize, or at least regulate, the activity in the country. Besides Sesc, some trade unions and other class associations contribute to making the tourism experience more accessible to their members, through organized tours and summer camps. Some nonprofit organizations and universities – through their extension programs – also organize similar activities. It can be observed that almost all social tourism initiatives in the country are intended for working-class families. What about street dwellers? Could they broaden their personal horizons from tourist experiences?

The (in)visibility of homeless people

The right to the city is ignored when there is no recognition and acceptance of forms of sociability other than bureaucratic, consumerist, and planned actions, which mutilate the personality and authenticity of people as real citizens (Lefebvre 1967). The statement by the street dweller – a Centro Pop user – in the title of this article reflects the reality of these individuals. The fact that he takes shelter on the sidewalk in front of the mentioned cultural center characterizes him as an individual excluded from the daily "normality" and places him on the opposite side of the pre-established social and economic order in contemporary society, attracting dubious looks from those who live according to the existing social and economic system (Frangella 2004).

The image associated with homeless men and women is usually pejorative, and they are stigmatized as: beggars, bums, dangerous, mentally ill, pitiable, etc. According to Mattos and Ferreira, "the social representations of the homeless population reinforce the construction of identities based on negative values" (Mattos & Ferreira 2004, p. 48). After some time, street dwellers begin to ask themselves, "who am I?", "where do I come from?", which reaffirms that they belong to the streets. In the words of Helena Ferreira, "the belonging to a territory implies the construction of an identity related to it" (Ferreira 2010, p. 136); the street population throughout the years seems to build a relationship of familiarity and identity with the streets, and in some cases they refuse to return to traditional models of housing.

When some individuals refuse to leave the streets, which demonstrates familiarity with this way of living, there is no understanding from society. This, in turn, reinforces the discourse that those people are only in such a condition because they want it and deserve it (since they do not accept the help the state offers), a kind of celebration of fatalism.

The nonacceptance of the way of life of those people is partly determined by the idea that they have "failed in life", and it is the main reason for biased attitudes toward that population (Frangella 2004). In the capitalist economic and social order, the person who is not inserted in the working world is considered unproductive and is seen in society as a vagabond, one of the most common words used to refer to the street population. A usual element of the excluded groups is the condition of supposedly being superfluous and unnecessary individuals to work and production (Escorel 1999).

In the social sciences, there is not a single concept regarding the expression "social exclusion"; the binomial is present in several themes that deal with poverty and inequalities. According to Hannah Arendt (1989), exclusion is a process involving a path of vulnerability, fragility, precariousness, and even breaking the ties with socio-family relations, with work, cultural representations, citizenship, and life. It is possible to observe that the social exclusion imposed on the street population is not only linked to material deprivation but also related to the disqualification of the individual as a citizen, thus reinforcing their invisibility to the state.

When we have contact with the way of life of homeless people, such as the one we had during our research, the invisibility of these people in society and the reasons they often choose to remain on the streets are clear. For this analysis, Elliott and Urry (2010) stated that the paradigms of contemporary mobilities are essential, due to the network capital, which is a new cause of social inequality, since it is related to the ability individuals have to build and keep social relations that generate emotional, financial, and practical benefits in a kind of network in which they are supposed to have intermittent virtual and co-presence meetings. From that perspective, it is possible to point out that network capital is also a factor that contributes to the continuity of men and women living on the streets, since they have gradually "lost" the ability to have new social relations with different people and remain restricted to the same views of society and to the same forms of existence, in which they are judged as marginal and thus are not recognized as individuals who can benefit a certain social context. At the same time the (new) mobilities can challenge and even reverse the power relations around the world. Paradoxically, network capital intensifies and extends inequalities and distances between people. In the words of the coordinator of Centro Pop in Niterói, there is only one difference (which arouses every prejudice and discrimination) between those individuals and the rest of society: "the fact that those people are living on the streets". Moreover, in her opinion, all individuals have similar feelings, desires, and needs.

Could the partnership between Centro Pop and UFF's Social Tourism program help homeless people expand their networks and generate new associative and affective perspectives? Sociability is represented here as a behavioral foundation of the construction of the individual in interactions with others, and it seems to be re-established by them on occasion. In the tour to Sugar Loaf,[9] there were interactions between Centro Pop users and conventional tourists, either commenting on the beautiful view or reporting some previous experience. This encounter may cause strangeness, but at the same time, it demonstrates new possibilities of social interactions. That is why it clearly brought pleasure to some Centro Pop users who were there. Besides, they could see themselves as sociable people again. This feeling resulting from the activity could be observed in different moments and circumstances and will be discussed further in what follows.

The relationship between homeless people and the city

Lefebvre (1967) considers that citizens are more objects than subjects in the social environment, and because of that, the state and society do not allow all citizens to participate in the development of their own city. According to the author, the state is authoritarian and strict and solves possible urban problems just in an administrative, technical, and scientific way, thus keeping citizens alienated. The state builds an urban scenario in which everyone should adapt to the existing way of life, although it was built without them (Lefebvre 1970). This panorama for street dwellers can be even more exclusionary.

If the city is recognized as a multicultural entity that gives free access to its citizens, many people would meet in different environments and find a sense of belonging. Since certain places are public, they should not only belong to one group or another but should be recognized as "ours" by all the inhabitants of a city.

The members of the Social Tourism project and the professionals of Centro Pop considered it important for the homeless users to be included in deciding the places to be visited. In one of the first meetings at Centro Pop, the interns of the project brought photographs of some tourist attractions and cultural centers of Niterói so that users could choose the tour destination. The interaction was conducted by a social worker who led a group of nine users. The statement that introduces this article, "I live here, but I've never been inside it" was made during this meeting, when others also reported negative previous experiences at those tourist attractions, involving repression and constraints suffered by users. The three most voted attractions by the users were the Museum of Contemporary Art,[10] MAC-quinho,[11] and one of UFF's campuses.

None of the users chose one of these museums: Solar do Jambeiro, Antônio Parreiras museum, and Ingá museum. To visit these three venues, permission is needed, and they did not have good memories from previous experiences when trying to enter. People who have been living on the streets longer than others have a kind of aversion to closed spaces. It is as if the walls and doors do not comfort them anymore. In addition to that, they are constantly in motion, causing them not only a sense of autonomy and freedom, but also an "identity crisis" (Frangella 2004, p. 192). This could be noticed in the statements of some users who claimed they were used to living on the streets and would not like to leave anymore.

One of the goals of the partnership between UFF and Centro Pop is to collaborate with new possibilities and expand the horizons of homeless people, allowing them to be protagonists of their own lives and paths in the city. We believe that social tourism is a way to democratize living in the city by different social groups.

The relationship between homeless people and other tourists

Reflecting on the encounter between homeless visitors and regular tourists is challenging, because the organization of tourist attractions/equipment requires such visitors to adapt to certain invisible and symbolic rules of coexistence. The first one is appearance, which, according to Mattos and Ferreira (2004), is an inseparable trait of the man or woman who lives on the streets. The authors claim that:

> the hygienist discourse that labels and propagates the stigma of homeless people is always associated with the dirt that must be swept under the rug. However, what surprises us and should be highlighted is that the majority of individuals who live on the streets do not share these attributes.
>
> (Mattos & Ferreira 2004, p. 4)

The "dirt" associated with those people influences the idea of removing them from the city streets (Mattos & Ferreira 2004). There is a belief that anything that is not beautiful should be hidden from sight. Tourism is also used as justification for the removal of those people, since seeing them "depreciates" the city's attractions. According to Sposati (1995, p. 89), the city's motto in this case is: "Let's remove people, let's bathe them, let's take the dirt away".

A female street dweller helped by Centro Pop reported that she does not feel bad when someone is afraid of her: "We go around carrying bags, we have dogs that are sometimes dirty, and we do not wear pretty clothes". The same woman told us, comparing herself to another user who usually carries a backpack and some bags (which called attention and probably made other tourists judge her during the visit to the Sugar Loaf), that she preferred to leave her "stuff"[12] at Centro Pop. She took a shower and wore clothes given by the social workers: "I am even wearing make-up, you see? Nobody is giving me a dirty look". This statement illustrates the reason why Centro Pop prepares them before the tours organized by UFF's Social Tourism project. On the tour days, users were asked to arrive early so they could shower and change into the clothes chosen by Centro Pop's employees. One of the social workers reported that not all the users needed clothes, but they provided guidance and "adequate" clothes for them.

All this prejudice related to the appearance of homeless people is a strong form of violence. It is not only physical aggression, but also symbolic, moral, silent, and hypocritical. Society justifies such violence, claiming that this group is a social threat, and thus it deals with them with "total indifference, showing repulsion or even using physical violence against them" (Mattos & Ferreira 2004, p. 51).

During the visit to the Museum of Contemporary Art (MAC), one of the users was severely reprimanded by another visitor, who seemed to be a teacher guiding a group of five students. That situation occurred in the exhibition gallery where several covers of vinyl albums by famous Brazilian artists from the 1970s and 1980s were displayed, and there was a record player playing one of the albums, which perhaps made that user think he could choose another album to be played as well and that he could change it. However, at the moment he was about to take the cover of another album that was hanging on the wall, the other visitor (the possible teacher) addressed him rashly: "*You cannot touch that, man!*" This story describes an example of verbal violence that a visitor who theoretically does not fit the social patterns of consumption of a museum can suffer from conventional visitors.

Nonetheless, the contact with general tourists was not always jarring. During the tour to the Sugar Loaf, the homeless joined other tourists in the cable car, in a closed and moving environment. The short time the two groups shared the same space brought two important and paradoxical reflections to the investigation. The first one concerns silent violence, since it was possible to observe women holding their bags closer to their bodies (due to fear of being robbed). They were apprehensive and looked at the homeless visitors strangely and also whispered. The second perception brings the group of homeless people closer to the conventional visitors, as the dazzle, excitement, and phrases of enchantment when seeing the landscape were similar, no matter whether those who expressed them were a national/foreign tourist or a street dweller. This demonstrates the relative equality of both groups, in the condition of tourists, when living and discovering something new.

The first tour (MAC, MACquinho and UFF campus) happened in places that receive fewer tourists than the second one (Sugar Loaf). In the former, the cost of admission for visitors is usually low or free, whereas in the latter it is higher. Thus, in the second experience, there was more contact between the group of users and tourists of different cultures and social classes – it is common for people who have good financial conditions to feel uncomfortable when mixed with the homeless as visitors/tourists. This could have caused the users of Centro Pop to be inhibited, which fortunately did not happen. During that visit, they were having a great time with the tourist experience, interacting within the group itself, and mainly enjoying the stunning view. In a conversation with three users, they reported they loved the trip to the Sugar Loaf because they had always admired it from the streets below it, imagining they would never be able to access that attraction. They had wondered since their childhood what it was like "to be there on the top of this famous tourist attraction where only rich people go."

Milton Santos (1987), taking into account the spatial perspective of poverty, stated that citizenship is largely influenced by the territory where someone is. According to him, citizenship in developing countries is constantly threatened, increasingly limiting individuals' mobility within the territory. However, he argued that it is by means of the construction of citizenship that individuals can have access to places and have the right to mobility, thus reducing social inequalities. Giving it another analysis, we wondered whether, without the "hygiene" provided by Centro Pop before the tour, the homeless people would have been equally tolerated at those attractions. It is not possible to predict what the relations between Centro Pop users and other tourists will be like during the tours. Although members of the group were watched and supported by workers from Centro Pop, and despite wearing clean clothes and having taken a shower, there were situations of discrimination, causing tensions and requiring constant attention from the mediators.

The relationship between homeless people and Centro Pop

In the opinion of the psychologists and social workers interviewed, Centro Pop provides users with a strong family and affectionate relation, in which that institution and workers are the closest idea of housing and family they may have. Centro Pop's objective is to create solutions and help raise awareness in the adult street population instead of having them as frequent users of the institution's services. Qualification workshops, psychological counseling sessions, drug addiction support groups, celebrations, educational and cultural events, and occasionally a bath and food are some of the services of the organization. Nonetheless, Centro Pop's coordinator in Niterói reported an internal difficulty in "cutting the ties" with some users. According to her, some users feel so welcomed and beloved there that they find ways to make it be part of their daily life.

Centro Pop is a place that provides sociability and meetings for different groups of homeless people. Therefore, its users feel respected and feel the institution cares about them. Due to the lack of a home and traditional family, the users themselves become references for one another; they teach and learn with the others. Survival on the streets depends on sharing experience with other street dwellers, i.e., life on the streets has visible and invisible rules and borders, which are shared by those who have been in this condition for a longer time (Magni 1995).

Escorel (1999) explains that social relations within a group, although necessary for survival, are composed of conflicts that often result in violence. An example of conflict observed during the research happened at the meeting before the first tour. Every time one of the users pointed to a photo among the options of places to visit, two others interfered, trying to dictate the choice. The others were uncomfortable with this interference, showing lack of respect for the leadership of the former. However, the intervention of a social worker was necessary, and after that, some users felt more comfortable to talk about the places they wanted to visit.

According to the coordinator of Centro Pop, conflicts within the group are common, and they generally happen when there is a new member. When there is somebody new, coming from another city or who has been living on the streets for a short time, the group itself investigates "who he is" and his behavior, especially if he has committed a crime. The stereotype that homeless people are criminals does not fit them and is defended by Centro Pop's users and workers, who repeated several times: "Homeless people are not criminals". Centro Pop's workers constantly try to change the negative image associated with the homeless population. Obviously, a few of them have committed crimes before, but this is not unique to street people.

The relationship between homeless people and the members of UFF's project

None of the members of UFF's Social Tourism project was used to spending time with street dwellers. There was unease, a collective feeling of being unfamiliar with the situation when the members did not know how to act, behave, what to talk about, how to come closer to them. In spite of that, little by little, UFF's students and the coordinator felt more comfortable and integrated. Ethnographic activities, one of the methods of the project, were useful at Centro Pop. During these activities, students talked freely about their feelings and perceptions, eliciting debate and reflection. This evaluation process occasionally happens at Centro Pop after some activity with the mediation of psychologists and social workers without the preparation and previous reading of a report. A change of attitude could be noticed in the testimonials of some students, who bumped into the users on the streets of Niterói. They reported that unexpectedly, these meetings brought mutual recognition, a smile, conversations, or just a friendly look without prejudice.

The members of UFF's Social Tourism project seemed happy with the results. All of them expressed the same satisfaction: "*Now we are engaging in real social tourism*". This statement, sometimes followed by a smile, made us think that the experiences we witnessed during the research could help the development of public policies that combine urban mobility, leisure, and social work at the same time, having the principles of inclusion of homeless men and women as citizens who belong to the urban area where they live. Thus, when we reflect on the experience of tourism from a social and democratic perspective, having homeless people as the focus of our research was a challenge that encouraged us to change an unfair and unequal reality. Therefore, it is important that further research be carried out to analyze the complex relations of homeless people regarding the tourist's experience, citizenship, and rights.

Notes

1 We are grateful for financial support from FAPERJ (Research Support Foundation of the State of Rio de Janeiro), Brazil, which provided funding for this study.

2 An architectural complex built in 1872 by Portuguese merchant Bento Joaquim Alves Pereira to serve as his residence. Currently it is a cultural center of the Municipal Secretariat of Culture of Niterói (Cultura Niterói 2013).
3 The purpose of the Social Tourism project is to offer free or low-cost tours to UFF's workers and/or students, as well as for partner institutions, with the aim of democratizing access to the tourist experience for groups at risk of social exclusion. The project has five scholarships granted by UFF's Department of Student Affairs (Proaes) to students engaging in the project as well as a college fund to pay for expenses. Moreover, after a careful process of analysis by Proaes, scholarships are offered to socially vulnerable students, who can choose one of the several projects of the program to take part in. The Social Tourism project has five spots for these students. All the students granted have the following tasks: extension practices and research. Students majoring in different subjects, such as tourism, social service, languages, economics, history, and cinema, are part of the project, which makes it interdisciplinary.
4 Centro Pop is directly linked to the Specialized Reference Center for Social Assistance of Niterói, which works with individuals who have lost their rights. That institution is not a shelter for overnight or longer stay; it serves exclusively to support the reintegration of users in society, offering services, workshops, psychological counseling, and so on. Most of Centro Pop's employees are social workers, but there are also psychologists, educators, and trainees from the undergraduate courses mentioned before.
5 The way homeless men and women who use Centro Pop are referred to.
6 At the end of the tours, a free lunch is served to all participants at the university restaurant. From conversations with Centro Pop's workers, it was possible to observe that the meal is the main motivation for the users to take part in the tours.
7 Created on June 7, 1963, in Brussels, ISTO is an international philanthropic association. Its purpose is to promote social tourism and be a source of exchange of ideas and development for national policies regarding that phenomenon.
8 A private institution, maintained and administered by businessmen, that carries out projects in the public interest. Sesc is directed to workers in the commercial sector and their families, providing healthcare services, education, leisure, and social activities.
9 Located in the neighborhood of Urca, the Sugar Loaf is one of the main tourist attractions of Rio de Janeiro. The hills are connected through cable cars, and its peak is 396 meters above sea level. It has attracted tourists since 1912, when the first cable car started to operate. According to data from RioTur (a department of the Rio de Janeiro's Secretary Office of Tourism), 40 million people have used the cable cars since 1912 (Riotur 2018).
10 The Museum of Contemporary Art in Niterói.
11 Similar to MAC, it was designed by the famous architect Oscar Niemeyer. It is located on a hill called Morro do Palácio and is the headquarters of the Urban Digital Platform, a project of Niterói's Secretary Office of Education, Science and Technology.
12 Although they do not have a house, homeless people have objects that they take with them wherever they go, as if their objects were almost an integral part of their body. Metaphorically speaking, they "carry their homes on their backs". When this woman said she had left her "stuff" at Centro Pop, she probably referred to the bags and backpacks she carries with her daily.

References

Arendt, H. 1989. *Origens do totalitarismo*, translated by Roberto Raposo. [e-book] São Paulo: Companhia das Letras. Available at: https://archive.org/details/ArendtHannahOrigensDoTotalitarismo1989 [Accessed on June 3, 2018].

Bureau. 1996. *Declaração de Montreal*. Bureau International du Tourisme Social.

Carta de Viena. 1980. *Estudios Turísticos*, 68, pp. 217–219. Madrid.

Cheibub, B. & Eugenio, J. 2018. *Turismo social e a população em situação de rua*. 15th World Leisure Congress [data?]. São Paulo: Sesc.

Cultura Niterói. 2013. *Solar do Jambeiro: Histórico*. Rio de Janeiro, Cultura Niterói. Available at: http://culturaniteroi.com.br/blog/?id = 189&equ = solar [Accessed on May 30, 2018].

Elliott, A. & Urry, J. 2010. *Mobile lives*. London: Routledge.

Escorel, S. 1999. *Vidas ao léu. Trajetórias de exclusão social*. Rio de Janeiro: Editora Fiocruz.

Ferreira, H. C. H. 2010. *A dinâmica da participação na construção de territórios sociais e do patrimônio ambiental da Ilha Grande-RJ*. PhD dissertation. Rio de Janeiro: Universidade Federal Rural do Rio de Janeiro.

Frangella, S. M. 2004. *Corpos urbanos errantes: uma etnografia da corporalidade de rua em São Paulo*. PhD dissertation. São Paulo: Universidade Estadual de Campinas. Available at: https://pt.scribd.com/document/142033254/Resenha-Simone [Accessed on May 30, 2018].

Lefebvre, H. 1967. *Metafilosofia*. Rio de Janeiro: Martins Fontes.

Lefebvre, H. 1970. *Du Rural à L'Urbain*. 2nd ed. Paris: Anthropos.

Magni, C. T. 1995. Povo da Rua: um estudo sobre nomadismo urbano. *Coleção Cadernos da Cidade*, 2(4), June. Porto Alegre. Available at: www.academia.edu/401264/Corpos_Urbanos_Errantes_Uma_Etnografia_Da_Corporalidade_De_Moradores_De_Uma_Rua_Em_S%C3%A3o_Paulo [Accessed on April 9, 2018].

Mattos, C. L. G. 2011. A abordagem etnográfica na investigação científica. In Mattos, C, L, G. & Castro, P. A. eds. *Etnografia e educação: conceitos e usos*. Campina Grande: EDUEPB, pp. 49–83. Available at: http://books.scielo.org/id/8fcfr/pdf/mattos-9788578791902-03.pdf [Accessed on April 9, 2018].

Mattos, R. M. & Ferreira, R. F. 2004. Quem vocês pensam que (elas) sãos? -representações sobre as pessoas em situação de rua. *Psicologia & Sociedade*, 16(2), pp. 47–58. Available at: www.scielo.br/pdf/%0D/psoc/v16n2/a07v16n2.pdf [Accessed on May 26, 2018].

Melo, V. A. 2007. "Educação, saúde . . . por último, o lazer!". *Entrevista concedida ao Observatório Jovem*. Observatório Jovem. Niterói: Universidade Federal Fluminense, 2007. ISSN: 1981-0539.

Riotur – Visit.Rio. 2018. *O que fazer? Pão de Açúcar*. Rio de Janeiro: Visit.Rio. Available at: http://visit.rio/que_fazer/paodeacucar/ [Accessed on May 30, 2018].

Santana, V. S. & Castelar, M. 2014. A população em situação de rua e a luta pela cidadania. *Revista Baiana de Saúde Pública*, 38(2), pp. 357–369. Available at: www.researchgate.net/publication/273899625_A_populacao_em_situacao_de_rua_e_a_luta_pela_cidadania [Accessed on May 30, 2018].

Santos, M. 1987. *O espaço do cidadão*. São Paulo: Editora Nobel.

Sposati, A. 1995. Comentário sobre as formas de atuação com a população de rua. In Rosa, C. M. M. ed. *População de rua: Brasil-Canadá*. São Paulo: Hucitec.

Chapter 6

Vulnerabilities in movement

Experiences from the research project I Exist and Move

Camila Maciel Campolina Alves Mantovani and Sônia Caldas Pessoa

Introduction

In the beginning of 2017, a research group was created, as will be explained further, in the Federal University of Minas Gerais (UFMG) in order to bring together the discussions and the work that some researchers, including us, had been doing around the relationships between communication, accessibility, and vulnerabilities. Sustained by the epistemological framework proposed by the new mobilities paradigm and the affect theory, we developed a project called I Exist and Move: Experiences and Mobilities of People with Disabilities. The main idea was to invite people with disabilities to "walk" and "talk" with us about their displacement experiences in the university campus.

Among the participants in this study were students, university administrative staff, and faculty members. Each of them brought a different and enriching account of their experiences that reverberated in the already known physical barriers as well as in the behavioral ones.

These accounts are the essence of the discussion we will present here. We will start the chapter by introducing the concept of mobility that guides us and will follow by introducing the perspective of disability and vulnerability with which we work. Then we will share the reports and reflections that these reports evoke and finally some considerations and notes for future studies.

Possible interconnections between mobility and disability

The 21st century has witnessed an acceleration of movement: people, images, information, goods, everything seems to move around in a more dynamic and complex way. In this sense, several changes permitted such new state of mobility. Technological, cultural, and social developments occurring in transport systems, in mobile communication devices, in border demarcation and its control mechanisms, as well as in other mobility systems and artifacts, are changing the conditions and possibilities of movement and affecting individuals in a way never seen before.

Nevertheless, it is noteworthy to mention that mobility is perceived and experienced in different ways. While for some individuals movement is spontaneous, faster, and more frequent and allows them to cover increasingly larger distances, for others, movement is somewhat troubled due to "rugosities (wrinkles)" – each place's preexisting conditions (material resources, social, economic, and cultural organization), which interfere with this space of flows, as put so well by Milton Santos (2003).

> Nowadays, we live in a world of rapidity and fluidity. But it is a virtual fluidity, made possible by the presence of new technical systems, mainly informational ones, as well as effective fluidity, achieved when such potential fluidity is utilized in the exercise of an action by businesses and hegemonic institutions. Potential fluidity arises in people's imaginary and ideology as if it were a common good, a fluidity for all, when, in fact, only a few agents are able to use it, thus becoming the effective holders of velocity.[1]
>
> (Santos 2003, p. 83)

However, in relation to such "rugosities (wrinkles)", we would like to highlight those that are given as a condition of existence, more specifically those related to the lives of people with disabilities. For these subjects, the relation between fluidity and resistance (immobility) can be perceived in most different spheres of life, both in relation to the physical movement (where sometimes this condition can be felt in a more intense way) and in relation to those that occur in networks with and without wires.

The perspective presented here is based on the social model of disability, formulated by the World Health Organization (WHO), which considers disability in its social dimensions of complexity and dynamicity. This social perspective shares with society its implication and responsibility with the issue of disabilities. It is not a medical problem concerned only with the individual. On the contrary, the clinical and individualized approach is replaced due to the serious consequences that this kind of conduct had brought to the effective adaptability and accessibility of social facilities and structures for the mobility of people with disabilities.

Based on the notion of disability proposed by the World Health Organization (WHO), disability is "complex, dynamic, multidimensional, and questionable" (WHO 2012, p. 04). Therefore, disability is found within a social model framework. This means that the displacement of the individualized medical model for the structural and social model is acknowledged. Its rupture is not, though. According to this perception, persons with disabilities would be perceived by society because of their limitations and not because of their bodies, and we add, their minds, as reported by WHO.

> It must be highlighted that it is common for a person with disability to present health problems or become disabled due to a serious illness or an accident, which does not validate the idea of disability as a pathology. In other words,

> pathologies may be associated with disability, but the disability would not be configured as a disease.[2]
>
> (Pessoa 2018, p. 39)

To understand the social importance of disability, according to data from the United Nations, about 10% of the world's population live with a disability. From this amount, about 80% dwell in poor or developing countries (Pessoa 2018). In Brazil, based on the Census 2010 database, IBGE indicates a proportion of people with disabilities at 6.7%, way below the previous 24% that was publicized until 2018. The explanation for this is that Brazil now follows the recommendations and guidelines of the Washington Group on Disability Statistics (WG), linked to the UN Statistical Commission, constituted to address the need for cross-nationally comparable population-based measures of disability. The method uses several questions to evaluate the difficulty in seeing, hearing, or climbing stairs, from a scale that contains the following items: "not difficult", "somewhat difficult", "difficult", "very difficult", and "not able at all". In 2010, IBGE changed the way it was interpreted and created a new indicator. In the margin of the previous cut, people with disabilities were those who answered that they had some difficulty in at least one of the items. The current proposition only considers those who reported the tasks were "very difficult" or that they were "not able at all".

Given this context, our proposition here is to look at disability based on the theoretical and methodological contributions of the mobility paradigm and its developments, focusing on the experiences narrated by the subjects regarding the vulnerabilities felt and perceived by the condition of their disability.

As argued by Goggin (2016), although the discussions on the new mobilities paradigm and the disability studies are in the beginning, it is possible to realize the enormous potential of this reflection, since the interfaces between these studies can not only shed light upon central issues that arise for mobility research, but they can also contribute to broadening our understanding of disability as from the human dimension and its relations with others and with the environment.

In this discussion, our perspective on mobility originates in the field of Social Sciences and features the new mobility paradigm, developed by Sheller and Urry (2006), as its theoretical and methodological framework. Based on the theoretical development and progressively more numerous empirical analyses concerning the mobility phenomenon in the most diverse aspects of life, there is, in Urry's point of view, the emergence of a new way of conceiving the characteristics of economic, social, and political relations, which would point to a mobility turn in the social sciences (Urry 2007).

> Such a turn is spreading in and through the social sciences, mobilizing analyses that have been historically static, fixed and concerned with predominantly a-spatial "social structures". Contributions from cultural studies, feminism, geography, migration studies, politics, science studies, sociology, transport, and tourism studies and so on are hesitatingly transforming social science and

> especially invigorating the connections, overlaps, and borrowings with both physical science and with literary and historical studies. The mobility turn is post-disciplinary.
>
> (Urry 2007, p. 6)

By developing the mobility paradigm, Urry (2007) acknowledges and stresses the diversity of "views" on that theme. To him, issues concerning movement are at the core of attention by several segments of society due to the actions and activities they seek to improve, control, or even perform through movement. He even states that the notion of mobility in 2007 was in the air, actually referring to a new way of thinking about and perceiving the world and the things in it.

In the field of social sciences, Urry highlights the existence of theories and concepts that become connected, providing a basis for the construction of his mobility paradigm. Authors such as Georg Simmel, Walter Benjamin, Gilles Deleuze, Henri Lefebvre, Michel de Certeau, and Erving Goffman are identified by Urry as precursors of the early notions on mobility. He also sees currently successful theoretical development toward a "mobility turn" in the social sciences in Paul Virilo's *Dromology* (1997), in Michel Serres's "Angels" (1995), in Bauman's *Liquid Modernity* (2000), in Nigel Thrift's "spacial turn", as well as in Hardt & Negri's views about contemporary society (Empire 2000). In the author's words, "this paradigm examines how social relations necessitate the intermittent and intersecting movements of people, objects, information, and images across distance" (Urry 2007, p. 54).

The mobility paradigm is important for our study because of the status it confers on movement and, therefore, to immobilities. Putting oneself in movement, be it physically or through information, which circulates in mobile networks, is something that, for a certain social group, has become a lifestyle. But for other groups, like people with disabilities, the idea of movement is sometimes an unattainable demand due to the many constraints that these people face in their daily life, which present themselves in Brazil as a series of difficulties and impossibilities to access basic services such as transportation, education, and health.

When we look into our society from the perspective of mobility, one of the first things that comes to mind is the potentiality of connections. Since connections draw our awareness to the others – to their existence in a basic level, it can provoke many different engaging responses. One of the possible ways to analyze these responses/actions is based on the notions of approximation and detachment; within these notions a variety of categorizations of actions/interactions also apply.

In the perspective of approximation, we can have both a violent movement – an attempt to eliminate the other, or a more inclusive one, genuinely interested in this being that is the other. Also, from the perspective of detachment, we could act in a way that opens space to the existence of the other and lets them be free to be who they are, or we can totally ignore their existence and cause this other to be completely invisible and socially, politically, and culturally excluded.

Current global events seem to bring out this variety of connection types between individuals and societies. It puts us on alert about these more negative (or even destructive) kinds of connections in relation to both the perspectives of approximation and detachment. This leads us to think about the future and mostly about how we can build a more solidary future as we are confronted with this frightening scenario.

Discussing about future can be a very challenging and risky task at the same time that it is also necessary. The need to think about the future is not only a matter of planning or managing in a more strategic point of view, but thinking about the future can often be the only alternative for individuals (or societies) to resist in the present.

But what kind of future a resistance perspective can entail? Also, how can we engage the subjects – especially those considered by Santos (2003) as the disinherited, the underdeveloped, and the poor, that is, vulnerable subjects, in a discussion (or movement) aimed to this exercise of thinking about futures, so they could see themselves as a part of it?

Santos (2003) believes the future will be a combination of our awareness about the "kingdom of possibilities" and the "kingdom of willingness". In this way, utopia can be considered a very powerful or, in the words of the author, a relevant concept, because it is built from human values such as liberty, dignity, and happiness.

Another important thing is that we must deal with the conditions that the present gives us. Our present world is interconnected (as we mentioned earlier), so the material infrastructure that allows for the "unicity of technique, the convergence of moments, and the knowability of the planet"[3] (Santos 2003, p. 24) must be used in a transformative way. But how?

One possibility pointed out by Santos (2003) is to change the use of the technical basis created for the circulation of capital in order to convey human values, to allow an effective integration of distinct cultural ties that allow the construction of a "solidary happening". In the author's terms, one of the possible ways in which we can build solidarity is from the interaction between "the different". Then we can see the difference that allows us to perceive the individual, but since we are connected (together), we do not lose the capacity of thinking in a more collective way. So there may be conflict, but there is also the possibility of collaboration that produces new understandings and also a critical view about our existence.

Since we are talking about differences and coexistence, it is appropriate to reflect upon the issue of people with disabilities in Brazil. These people face discrimination and barriers that restrict them from participating in society equally to others every day. At this point, the concept of mobility justice developed by Mimi Sheller seems to be crucial to discuss it from the point of view of people with disabilities.

> Mobility justice is a way of thinking about the differential mobilities and thinking about the ways in which people's mobilities are interrelated, and that

> we have different capabilities for mobility and different potentials for mobility. It's not to say that being mobile is always good, or that it equates with freedom, because sometimes there are coerced forms of mobility and sometimes staying still is important – being able to remain in a place. So mobility justice is a way to talk about those different relations around mobility and that is a way to highlight the power differentials that come into play in any form of mobility, and the different affordances that different people are able to make use of, or appropriate, in becoming mobile or not.
>
> (Sheller 2014)

Turning to the research experience presented here, we consider vulnerabilities, considered in the plural form, through the very logic of a conception that is still being generated, in our view, as a natural consequence of complex and decentralized societies in which individuals and groups emerge, each mediated and aware of their civil rights. This media exposure and the appropriations they make are fundamental components to not only go through vulnerability situations but also to reveal how subtle and fragile these situations and processes can be or may be constituted.

Based on Butler's "Rethinking Vulnerability and Resistance" (2016) and also on Martha Fineman (2008), we deem vulnerabilities to be sets of sociopolitical and communicational relations engendered by modes of deliberate exposure to power in permanent negotiation in everyday life and social practices.

In this sense, we understand that we can all be vulnerable or be in situations of vulnerability not only in relation to the other but also because of the interdependence that would modify the ontological understanding of corporeity. This personal exercise of the researcher that works with vulnerability connects us to reflections upon equality, inequalities, social justice, socioeconomic conditions, and mobilities.

Human life is conditioned by vulnerabilities. Virtually human beings are exposed to physical and material conditions, physical illnesses, injuries, offenses, (im)mobilities, disabilities, and death, the finitude of life. All this depends on long-term care throughout life. Socially and affectively, we are subject to conditions of emotional and psychological vulnerabilities such as neglect, abuse, lack of care, rejection, ostracism, and humiliation. Socially and politically, we are vulnerable to exploitation, manipulation, oppression, political violence, and abuse of rights, amongst others. From the point of view of mobility, we can become vulnerable by the lack of public transport services, for example, or by the very conditions of the body in its most basic mobility conditions.

These discussions can also be related to the concepts presented by Kaufmann et al. (2004) about mobility and motility. By pointing out three interdependent elements of motility – access, competence, and appropriation – they reflect on how these elements are "fundamentally linked to social, cultural, economic, and political processes and structures within which mobility is embedded and enacted" (Kaufmann et al. 2004, p. 751).

This perspective alerts us to not to empty the discussions on vulnerability. Rather than putting ourselves in a comfortable place that says we all are, or we can be, vulnerable, we invite the reader to an exercise. If we think this way, we can understand vulnerabilities in a manner that is broad, unrestricted, and virtually impossible to identify, categorize, enumerate, or recognize, amongst so many other actions that are important in order to recognize them, even though it may be subject to raising many questions. This movement would indicate a certain "security" amid the instability of the concept itself, which could be a trap for the groups that need it from the point of view of recognition and guarantee of fundamental rights.

If we relate vulnerabilities directly with corporeity and, therefore, with mobility, it implies a broad, hospitable, and sensitive look at the body. But not only our body, but also the body of the other, their movements and everyday experiences. It means that it would be our gesture, as researchers, as engaged citizens, to recognize that the body goes beyond rules of normativity, whether related to heteronormativity, as Butler thought, or to corponormativity, or to its ability to move, to carry out activities, to become autonomous, and to act as a "player" rather than a performative body in the pursuit of citizenship, as is the case of Fiona Campbell, a lawyer and a researcher with disabilities at the University of Queensland, Australia.

Campbell (2009) had been warned of the importance of carefully looking toward people with disabilities without taking them as frail or incapable but recognizing that their capacities must be considered in full perspective, without assistance, paternalism, or pity. It is the idea that ableism brings together actions and relationships that consolidate the prejudice toward people with disabilities as nonnormal, inferior, minor, incapable, or worse, people not worthy of recognition in their citizenship.

Still in dialogue with Campbell (2009), we turn to Scully (2013), who moves toward a widely held view that people with disabilities are especially vulnerable and that their vulnerabilities have a different range than the vulnerabilities inherent in humans. Taking a socio-relational view of disability, she argues that vulnerabilities and dependencies of many people with disabilities are relative to a contingent of factors rather than any dysfunction/insufficiency and therefore not to a particularity of disability. Nevertheless, as she explains, deficiency is always or usually equated with dependency and corresponds to lack of autonomy, especially in relation to the various aspects of mobility.

If the vulnerabilities of people with disabilities are even more complex than those of other individuals, addressing these vulnerabilities adequately in a research perspective that is engaged and committed to social issues also becomes challenging.

Below, we will present the work of the Afetos research group and the methodological strategies developed by the researchers in an attempt to promote reflection on the issues of disability, vulnerability, and mobility.

Empirical experience: between vulnerabilities, mobilities, and disabilities

Sharing experiences of accessibility and mobility is one of the goals of Afetos (www.afetos.com), a Research Group on Communication, Accessibility, and Vulnerabilities, linked to the Department of Social Communication and the Post-Graduation Program in Social Communication of the Federal University of Minas Gerais (UFMG), located in Belo Horizonte, state of Minas Gerais (Brazil). The motivation for creating the group comes from the desire to think and make a real inclusion in academia, and it also comes from an ethical conviction about research and projects that can touch and sensitize society to the importance of a science that believes in more hospitable and less unequal worlds. Therefore, beyond the theoretical discussions, we are also concerned with the engagement of students, university administrative staff, and faculty members, with or without disabilities, in the research, thus allowing the appearance of multiple perspectives about mobilities and vulnerabilities. The research project I Exist and Move: Experiences and Mobility of People with Disabilities[4] is an example of this attempt. It intends to look at the subjects in the face of the vulnerabilities felt and perceived by their condition as a person with disabilities in the urban space. In the first phase of the project, people with disabilities narrated their experiences at the Pampulha campus of UFMG. It is important to highlight that since 2017, there is a law in Brazil that guarantees specific vacancies for the admission of people with disabilities to public universities in undergraduate and postgraduate programs. This legislation has modified the landscape of universities that, given the diversity of public, have been facing several challenges, ranging from the promotion of physical accessibility to spaces to the development of actions that seek to prevent and punish prejudiced and disrespectful behavior.

It is important to mention that the project is anchored in an affective dimension in order to allow disabled volunteers, as well as the students with and without disabilities who conducted the interviews, to manifest their modes of affection while walking on campus and to reflect on their own mobility and their disabilities. In this sense, the affective approach adopted in this study was that of Kathleen Stewart (2007), which states that "ordinary affects" are public feelings that circulate in our intimate lives. "They can be experienced as a pleasure and a shock, as an empty pause or a dragging undertow, as a sensibility that snaps into place or a profound disorientation. They can be funny, perturbing, or traumatic" (Stewart 2007, pp. 1–2).

From this perspective we ask ourselves some questions. How do they move? What are their difficulties and needs? Why are their rights to access public services and spaces not respected? These and other questions led to the accounts that gave rise to a series of in-depth interviews, conducted on the streets of the campus, and to a series of reports from which we selected some lines that we consider important.

The students of the Radio and Digital Media course of the Department of Social Communication of UFMG developed the series, available at www.afetos.com.

They walked, observed, and interviewed students, administrative staff, and teachers with disabilities. The experience resulted in nine programs that were released on the Web Radio "Terceiro Andar" ("Third Floor")[5] – a project linked to the group and aimed at enhancing students' affections for radio. The productions were also broadcasted on Rádio UFMG Educativa,[6] a partner of Web Radio Terceiro Andar.

The special reports were carried out under the supervision of the teachers Camila Mantovani, Sônia Pessoa, and Ângela Marques. The people with disabilities who volunteered to participate in the interviews also worked on the development of the reports. They have helped us perceive important elements of their daily life that are affected by the low accessibility conditions of the places where they circulate. In addition, they designed with us paths and constructed narratives mobilized by the encounters and the ways of experiencing space.

Abel Passos do Nascimento Júnior, who is visually impaired, is an employee of UFMG and works in the Visual Impairment Support Center at the libraries of Federal University of Minas Gerais.

> There are several difficulties that a person with disabilities, in my case visual impairment, finds: architectural barriers, attitudinal barriers, digital barriers and pedagogical barriers. These are basically the four axes. The architectural barrier concerns the physical space, the digital barrier concerns accessibility in relation to electronic equipment, computers and cell phones. Pedagogical accessibility refers to access to didactic material. For me, the most complicated of all is the attitudinal barrier. And that depends on the community, it depends on the people around you. And often people with disabilities are not qualified by their potentials. Because people usually focus much more on the disability than on the possibilities that the person has.[7]
>
> (translated by the authors)

The student Paulo Madrid, who has cerebral palsy, uses a poetic narrative to encourage people with disabilities to love their bodies.

> Love your limited, handicapped hand, because it was certainly one of the things that clung unconditionally to the meager 5% survival chance you had one day. Love all this weakened body, because it fought for you, survived for you, gave you a life. What good would it be to be as functional as most people and not have the opportunity to live? Never look a gift horse in the mouth. Live.[8]
>
> (translated by the authors)

The lecturer Michelle Murta was approved in the civil-service examination to work at the university and became the first teacher with hearing impairment to be hired by UFMG. She comments on how seemingly simple and mundane everyday situations can become a major challenge of mobility and communication for her.

> Sometimes a very simple thing that gives me quite a lot of fear, which I keep thinking, for example, is about my cell phone not working inside the elevator. Think with me: if one day I get stuck in the elevator, how will it be? How will I communicate with people if I'm alone? How can I tell someone that I'm stuck, that I'm feeling bad? How can I communicate? So this is my fear. A fear I have, a simple thing, but that afflicts me. Sometimes we may think that this is silly, but if you put yourself in the shoes of a deaf person, who has difficulty accessing and communicating, you would see that this fear is real. And there are other things as well that are gradually evolving and developing in the sense of improving the processes. We know that many deaf people can point things that need to be improved. That will happen. I, for example, have my desk, my office facing the door. I have to sit facing the door because I'm deaf. If I turn my back, I will not know what's going on. Maybe someone comes by and says hello and I do not even respond because I did not hear. And then the person thinks I'm rude. But it has nothing to do with it. These issues involving culture and interpersonal relationships within the university will be affected and adapted. This process is already happening in the direction of improvement.[9]
>
> (translated by the authors)

Romerito Nascimento, an employee of UFMG, highlights the importance of institutions and society in considering disabled people with active voice, as subjects that must be heard in the reflections on mobility.

> When I entered university, UFMG was a specialist in inclusion, that is, at the university they could talk about inclusion for others, but they did not practice inclusion within their facilities. After we went in and "fought" together, discussing and punctuating the issues, we found some sensible managers who were opening up to this new possibility, so we could change a few things. We have already changed the tools, procedures, forms of treatment, concepts. But we still cannot change the physical, real world. And I think it's because of the lack of consultation with people with disabilities, they are seen only as recipients, which adversely affects the process. If you do not see me as someone who can contribute, you will always do what you think is good for me. Then it will never be good, because it will never meet our needs.[10]
>
> (translated by the authors)

From the speeches of the participants, we can see that the daily challenges for people in situations of vulnerability, especially people with disabilities, are multiple. Each of them, from their bodies, feel, experience, and understand the experiences in a way. Thus, in the face of this brief experience, it is clear that the experiences of people directly affected by these experiences is essential for us to advance conceptually and methodologically in disability and mobility studies.

Final remarks

From the narratives presented and also from an attentive and careful look at the processes that constituted the first stage of this study, we are able to say that conducting collaborative research is something that opens us to the multiple possibilities of the scientific work.

Making the research subjects, in our case people with disabilities, fundamental participants in the process sets us in the face of multiple challenges as we seek to sustain a kind of corporeality that is neglected, unrecognized, invisible, and having differentiated mobilities. However, we believe that such corporeities are important indicators of the diverse inequalities that are present in the lives of these people.

From the point of view of mobility, reflecting on the challenges that come to those who need to move through and between physical and virtual places is something that demands the availability of the researcher to also get moving. This movement is not limited to a physical dimension but is linked to an affective one. Moving along with a person with disability, even if it does not allow us to feel how they feel, this is something that always obliges us to imagine ourselves in someone's shoes. It makes us reflect on the complexity of a differentiated movement that comes from this corporeity.

In the case of people with disabilities, the act of moving creates, even in known environments, such as the university, which is a place of work for some and study for others, everyday affections that tell us about a confrontation between these impediments brought about by corporeality itself and by the architectural and attitudinal barriers. The mobility of people with disabilities, before being a desire, is a necessity to guarantee their daily living in a world in which physical, mental, and social vulnerabilities are not contemplated in their specificities.

Walking and talking, as carried out at this stage of the project, enables people with disabilities and us, the researchers, to make a methodological reflection on possible social interventions that could minimize the impact of unfriendly societies to people in situations of vulnerability due to limitations in their movements. Perhaps it is not too much to reflect in order to advance critically. Inspired by Santos (2003), we dare to say that the recognition and confrontation of (im)mobility of some people are a necessary step for a future that effectively ensures freedom, dignity, and happiness for all in their singular modes of existence. Is that utopia?

Notes

1 Hoje, vivemos um mundo da rapidez e da fluidez. Trata-se de uma fluidez virtual, possível pela presença dos novos sistemas técnicos, sobretudo os sistemas da informação, e de uma fluidez efetiva, realizada quando essa fluidez potencial é utilizada

no exercício da ação, pelas empresas e instituições hegemônicas. A fluidez potencial aparece no imaginário e na ideologia como se fosse um bem comum, uma fluidez para todos, quando, na verdade, apenas alguns agentes têm a possibilidade de utilizá-la, tornando-se, desse modo, os detentores efetivos da velocidade (translated by the authors).

2 Ressaltamos ainda que é comum uma pessoa com deficiência apresentar problemas de saúde ou se tornar deficiente como consequência de uma doença grave ou um acidente, o que não valida a perspectiva da deficiência como patologia. Em outras palavras, patologias podem estar associadas à deficiência, mas a deficiência em si não se configuraria como uma doença.

3 . . . unicidade da técnica, a convergência dos momentos, a cognoscibilidade do planeta. . . .

4 The project I Exist and Move: Experiences and Mobilities of People with Disabilities is financed by the following sectors and agencies: PROBIC/FAPEMIG, Accessibility and Inclusion Center of the Federal University of Minas Gerais (UFMG), in partnership with the Office of the Dean for Undergraduate, Student Affairs, Extension and Research Departments (PIPA Funding), in addition to scholarship funding: ADRC/PRPq.

5 https://radioterceiroandarufmg.wordpress.com/eu-existo-e-me-movo-experiencias-e-mobilidade-de-pessoas-com-deficiencia/

6 https://ufmg.br/comunicacao/radio-ufmg-educativa

7 São várias as dificuldades que uma pessoa com deficiência, no meu caso deficiência visual, encontra: barreiras arquitetônicas, barreiras atitudinais, barreiras digitais e barreiras pedagógicas. São basicamente os quatro eixos. A barreira arquitetônica diz respeito ao espaço físico, a barreira digital diz respeito à acessibilidade em relação aos equipamentos eletrônicos, computadores e celulares. A acessibilidade pedagógica diz respeito ao acesso o material didático. Para mim, a mais complicada de todas que é barreira atitudinal. E aí depende da comunidade, depende das pessoas que te cercam. E muitas vezes as pessoas com deficiências nãos são qualificadas nos seus potenciais. Porque as pessoas geralmente focam muito mais na deficiência do que nas possibilidades que a pessoa tem.

8 Ame a sua mão limitada, porque certamente ela foi uma das que se agarrou incondicionalmente aos míseros 5% de chance de sobrevivência que você teve um dia. Ame por inteiro esse corpo debilitado, porque ele lutou por você, sobreviveu por você, deu-lhe uma vida. De que adiantaria ser tão funcional quanto a maioria das pessoas e não ter a oportunidade de viver? A cavalo dado não se olha os dentes. Viva.

9 Às vezes, uma coisa muito simples que me dá bastante receio, que eu fico pensando, por exemplo, é sobre o meu celular não funcionar dentro do elevador. Pense comigo: se um dia eu ficar presa no elevador, como vai ser? Como vou me comunicar com as pessoas se eu estiver sozinha? Como vou avisar que estou presa, que estou passando mal? Como vou conseguir me comunicar? Então isso é um medo meu. Um receio que eu tenho, uma coisa simples, mas que me aflige. Às vezes a gente pode pensar que isso é uma bobagem, mas se você se colocasse no lugar de um surdo, que tem dificuldade ao acesso e de comunicação, isso mostraria que esse receio é real. E há outras coisas também, que aos poucos vai caminhando e se desenvolvendo no sentido de melhorar os processos. Nós sabemos que muitos surdos podem pontuar coisas que precisam ser melhoradas. Isso vai acontecer. Eu, por exemplo, tenho minha mesa, meu escritório de frente para a porta. Eu não posso ficar de costas para a porta porque sou surda. Se eu ficar de costas não saberei o que está acontecendo. Pode ser que alguém passe e me cumprimente e eu nem responda porque não vi. E aí a pessoa pensa que sou mal-educada. Mas não tem nada a ver com isso. Essas questões que envolvem a cultura e o relacionamento interpessoal dentro da universidade serão afetadas e adaptadas. Já está acontecendo esse processo no sentido de melhorias.

10 Quando eu entrei na universidade, a UFMG era especialista em inclusão, ou seja, ela conseguia falar de inclusão para os outros, mas não praticava a inclusão dentro dela mesma. Depois que entramos e "brigamos" juntos, discutindo e pontuando as questões, nós encontramos alguns gestores sensíveis e que foram se abrindo a essa nova possibilidade, então pudemos mudar algumas coisas. Já mudamos as ferramentas, procedimentos, as formas de tratamento, os conceitos. Mas ainda não conseguimos mudar no físico, no real. E acho que seja por falta de consulta às pessoas com deficiência, vendo-as somente como receptoras, o que prejudica bastante o processo. Se você não me vê como alguém que pode contribuir, você vai sempre fazer aquilo que acha que é bom para mim. Daí nunca será bom, pois nunca vai atender as nossas necessidades.

References

Butler, J. 2016. Rethinking vulnerability and resistance. In Butler, J., Gambetti, Z. & Sabsay, L. eds. *Vulnerability in resistance*. Durham and London: Duke University Press.

Campbell, F. K. 2009. *Contours of ableism: The production of disability and abledness*. London: Palgrave Macmillan.

Fineman, M. A. 2008. The vulnerable subject: Anchoring equality in the human condition. *Yale Journal of Law & Feminism*, 20. Available at: https://ssrn.com/abstract=1131407 [Accessed on March 2018].

Goggin, G. 2016. Disability and mobilities: Evening up social futures. *Mobilities*, 11. Available at: http://dx.doi.org/10.1080/17450101.2016.1211821 [Accessed on February 23, 2018].

Kaufmann, V., Bergman, M. & Joye, D. 2004. Motility: Mobility as capital. *International Journal of Urban and Regional Research*, 28. Available at: https://doi.org/10.1111/j.0309-1317.2004.00549.x [Accessed on March 6, 2018].

Pessoa, S. C. 2018. *Imaginários sociodiscursivos sobre a deficiência: experiências e partilhas*. Belo Horizonte: Selo PPGCOM.

Santos, M. 2003. *Por Uma Outra Globalização: do pensamento único à consciência universal*. Rio de Janeiro: Record.

Scully, J. L. 2013. Disability and vulnerability: On bodies, dependence, and power. In Mackenzie, C., Rogers, W. & Dodds, S. eds. *Vulnerability: New essays in ethics and feminist philosophy*. New York: Oxford Press, pp. 204–221.

Sheller, M. 2014. Mobile justice. *Wi: Journal of Mobile Culture*, 8. Available at: http://wi.mobilities.ca/mimi-sheller-mobility-justice [Accessed on May 12, 2018].

Sheller, M. & Urry, J. 2006. The new mobilities paradigm. *Environment and Planning*, 38, pp. 207–226. doi:10.1068/a37268

Stewart, K. 2007. *Ordinary affects*. Durham: Duke University Press.

Urry, J. 2007. *Mobilities*. London: Polity Press.

World Health Organization (WHO). 2012. *Relatório mundial sobre a deficiência*. Available at: http://whqlibdoc.who.int/publications/2011/9788564047020_por.pdf [Accessed on June 1, 2018].

Chapter 7

The use of geographic information system (GIS) for the promotion of citizenship through the improvement of the conditions of accessibility in urban spaces

An application of the Project *Ponto Certo*

Macello Medeiros, Rita Vieira and Elton Andrade

Introduction

Accessibility is a subject that encompasses several sectors of society. In Brazil, the Federal Constitution of 1988 was remarkable in the protection of the rights of people with disabilities or reduced mobility when it sought to promote greater insertion of those people in the legislative issues of the country (see also Marinho in this book). Since then, some progress in that regard has been made. The 2000s represented a milestone in the conquest of rights with the publication of Federal Acts 10048 and 10098. The former ensured priority service for people with disabilities or reduced mobility, and the latter established physical accessibility to public places and buildings, means of transport, and communication. In 2004, Federal Decree 5296, which regulates the two acts mentioned, given its importance, became known as "the accessibility decree". In 2009, with the publication of the Convention on the Rights of Persons with Disabilities, the political struggle of these people was consolidated, and above all a new phase was created to change paradigms.

Brazilian legislation defines accessibility as the "condition for the use, with total or assisted security and autonomy, of spaces, urban equipment and furniture, buildings, transportation services, and devices, systems and means of communication and information, for people with a disability or with reduced mobility" (Federal Decree 5296/2004). In order to enable a disabled person to fully perform their daily activities with autonomy and security, a set of measures with respect to buildings, the urban environment, transportation, communication, and information is necessary. These measures together with the concepts of accessibility and universal design result in a broader concept of "accessible route", an important concept in this work.

This concept is defined in the Brazilian Association of Technical Standards (ABNT in Portuguese) in the NBR 9050 standard, dated June 30, 2004 (revised and republished on October 11, 2015), which deals with accessibility in buildings, furniture, spaces, and urban equipment, such as being:

> Continuous, unobstructed and signaled path that connects the external or internal environments of spaces and buildings, and that can be used in an autonomous and safe way by all people, including those with disabilities. The accessible external route can incorporate parking lots, lowered sidewalks, pedestrian crossing lanes, ramps, etc. The accessible internal route can incorporate corridors, floors, ramps, stairs, elevators, and so on.[1]
>
> (NBR 9050/04)

Data from 2010 in the Demographic Census conducted by the Brazilian Institute of Geography and Statistics (IBGE in Portuguese) attest that about a quarter of the Brazilian population has at least one type of disability, which represents an amount of around 45 million people who self-declared as disabled. However, the social participation of these people still does not take place in an effective way, since the urban spaces are not meant nor thought to attend their true necessities. It is necessary to recognize the great advances already achieved in Brazilian legislation, but it is also necessary to point out that there is still a great distance between what is standardized or what obeys the rules and its currently application in the daily life of society.

IBGE also projects that life expectancy for Brazilians in 2050 will jump to 81.3 years. The increase in this expectation, generated mainly by advances in medicine and the reduction of birth rates, will contribute to a society with an increasing number of elderly people. This reconfiguration of Brazilian society shows that problems that will arise from handicaps or physical limitations will be part of the lives of an ever-increasing number of people who still have full intellectual capacity. That can spawn physiological disorders, such as depression.

In addition to the elderly, pregnant women, obese people, young children, and persons with temporary disabilities (those who have suffered an accident and are in physical rehabilitation), all of them experience the same limitations and challenges that people with permanent disabilities do on a daily basis. This outspreads the issue of accessibility to a universal domain, becomes an increasingly visible and present demand in society, and deserves the utmost attention by the public authorities as a necessary condition for improving the quality of life of the population in the cities.

This way, the primary goal of the Project *Ponto Certo*, withdrawn from this work as an example of the use of geographic information system (GIS) to promote citizenship, is to give visibility to the accessibility conditions of the bus stops in the city of Salvador by using georeferenced data gathered in the field from technical inspections. Therefore, we adopted some methodological procedures (described later), among which is the mapping of bus stops using geolocation platforms such as Google Earth, the georeferencing of data gathered in the field, and others, which seek to rank these bus stops according to accessibility conditions. The information produced by *Ponto Certo* can become a significant tool in helping the public administration, because through them, it is possible to verify what and where the problems faced by people with disabilities or reduced mobility are. Furthermore, all this information can be used as a reference to lead the actions to enable the necessary improvements to the urban infrastructure regarding the normative parameters predicted at law and in technical specifications.

This chapter is divided into three parts. Firstly, we will consider other aspects related to the right to the city of persons with disabilities or reduced mobility, highlighting issues regarding urban mobility and citizenship, focused in their autonomous and safe displacements in urban spaces. Secondly, we will demonstrate the importance of geotechnologies, in particular the GIS Web as an auxiliary tool in promoting the improvement of accessibility conditions. Finally, we will present the results obtained, as well as considerations about the next steps of *Ponto Certo* and other future prospects of GIS applications in urban intelligence.

Accessibility and the right to the city

We cannot discuss accessibility without taking into account other fundamental dimensions such as income, race, and gender. Although the Brazilian population lives predominantly in urban areas, much of the population does not enjoy the qualitative and equitable benefits of urbanization, considering that these are distributed in most cases directly proportionally to the income of inhabitants. When it comes to people with disabilities or reduced mobility, we perceive situations in which the right to the city is much suppressed due to the lack of accessibility in the urban space but also due to the income of less affluent people,[2] who live in suburbs, characterizing a kind of uneven mobility.

Simple daily activities can be a great challenge for these people, considering the existence of urbanistic barriers of different orders in the places where they move, whether for leisure or for work, for example the misinformation about bus lines and schedules in stops. It is known that access to information on the urban transport system and the conditions of mobility in a city is guaranteed by law to every citizen in Brazil (see the Urban Mobility Act 12587/2012), which corroborates what Henri Lefebvre (1996) contends is one of the political forms of "the right to the city". The adequacy of these accessibility issues is discussed all over the world by the International Organization for Standardization (ISO), which is responsible for the dialogue among the various entities dealing with standardization issues in the world. In the case of Brazil, it is up to the Brazilian Association of Technical Standards (ABNT) to establish normative technical standards, providing the necessary basis for Brazilian technological development.

Three technical standards were essential during the development of the Project *Ponto Certo*, namely, NBR 14022/2011, which deals with accessibility in urban vehicles for transportation of public passengers; NBR 9050/2004 (revised and published in 2015), which establishes criteria and technical parameters to be observed when designing, constructing, installing, and adapting buildings, furniture, urban spaces, and equipment for accessibility; and NBR 16.537/2016, which addresses tactile paving, based on guidelines for the elaboration of architectural projects and facilities aimed at accessibility standards, specifying parameters of how to implement the directional tactile paving to identify points of departure and the location of bus stops.

Population expected, therefore, that public policies were articulated in order to ensure the right to universal accessibility, since it permeates all other rights and is directly related to the application of the rules. By doing so, it prompts people to not give up on the right to the city, to work, to education, and to life, and to not let themselves become socially invisible. In a practical way, laws and norms do not guarantee accessibility in the urban space as expected. For a while, discussions concerning the theme are progressing in a practical reality that concerning the scale of the buildings (physical sense), or immediate accesses: ramps, tactile floors, furniture and urban equipment; on the other hand, this discussion still seems distant when it comes to planning the city or region.

Urban mobility and citizenship

In a broad sense, urban mobility is understood as the easiness of displacement of people in the city, using different means and manners, which, in other words, allow people to make use of all urban infrastructures. A city with good urban mobility is one that provides people with comfortable and safe travel in a reasonable time (Almeida et al. 2013). In fact, when we look more closely at the road infrastructures and public spaces in the cities, what can be observed are precarious conditions of accessibility for people in general and more aggravating conditions for those with some disability or reduced mobility, such as wheelchair users, the visually impaired, the deaf, elderly people, pregnant women, and so on (see also Mantovani and Pessoa in this book).

One of the biggest challenges for metropolises is the organization of public transport systems aimed at attending to the right of coming and going of the population, which is guaranteed by the Brazilian constitution and more specifically by the Urban Mobility Act 12587/2012. In Brazil, most development policies are focused on increasing the road infrastructure to benefit the circulation of private cars and cargo vehicles, including national and regional investments that do not take into account nonmotorized vehicles, which are also known as active transportation (pedestrian and bicycles).

In relation to the modes of transportation, the term "public transport", according to Ferraz and Torres (2008) is used to designate the displacements of population, that is, exclusively the transportation of passengers. Within the public transportation system, we can spot a series of driving vehicles (bus, metro, train, trolleybus, and so on), which are generally defined as being easy-to-use, efficient, clean transportation options that provide the users with the conditions to get where they want in a short time and with minimal wear for the passengers.

Also according to Act 12587/2012, which deals with the National Policy on Urban Mobility (Brasil, 2012), PNMU, more specifically in Chapter III, Article 14, item IV, it is everyone's right "to have a safe and accessible environment for the use of the National Urban Mobility System".[3] Among the principles that underpin the PNMU are those related to universal accessibility, sustainable development of cities, socioeconomic and environmental dimensions, equitable use of the public space of circulation, streets, and public places and access to public transportation; fair distribution of benefits and onus in the use of different modes; and efficiency, effectiveness, and functionality in urban circulation.

All of these principles serve to demonstrate how important urban mobility is in the organization of the city and how the right of the people to come and go is constrained in many cases due to the high price of tickets, deprivation of access to public transport services, and the uneven conditions of urban mobility to the majority of the low-income population, which reinforces the phenomenon of inequality of opportunities and spatial segregation that socially exclude people living in suburbs or away from the city center.[4]

In practice, this is the reality of what we can see daily in large Brazilian cities, particularly in Salvador: a low-quality public transport that is very scarcely accessible to the general population, particularly offered to the low-income population. Aimed to mitigate these inequalities, some public policies are created to provide subsidies for the use of public transport, and also to the planning and use of the land associated with urban mobility, thereby improving the conditions of accessibility through more adequate distribution and that is planned in the urban space in concomitance with the economic and social activities that are developed in the city.

Although accessibility apparently relates exclusively to the physical environment, it can be considered a determining factor for people to exercise their rights fully. If the physical environment and its urban elements constitute barriers, they will certainly hinder people having access to the places and tools that guarantee the exercise of their rights and duties. In this case, the "immobility" imposed implies the absence of participation of people with disabilities or reduced mobility in the life of the city.

The analysis of the urban circulation system is directly linked to consumption. Eduardo Vasconcelos (2011) proposes that this reading be made from two aspects: if on the one hand it is important to understand how the individual appropriates the collective means of consumption established in the context of economic and social relations, on the other hand, it is fundamental to evaluate how the circulation space is configured in the urban scenario. For the author, the distinction between structures of production, circulation, and reproduction helps analyze the transport system, although it is known that they are strongly imbricated structures. For example, public power must guarantee a minimum of security, accessibility and quality in the enjoyment of the services offered to the public, for better efficiency, effectiveness, and functionality in the urban circulation and equity of access to the transport service.

GIS and citizenship: the Project *Ponto Certo*

The Project *Ponto Certo* began to be developed in 2014 with the support of the National Council for Scientific and Technological Development (CNPq), by the Universal Call MCTI/CNPq/MEC/CAPES No. 43/2013. Initially, urbanization students from the State University of Bahia (UNEB) were divided into two teams of three members and mapped the existing bus stops within a 10 km radius from the Sarah Kubitschek Hospital in Salvador, in the neighborhood called "*Caminho das Árvores*". This route was chosen considering that it is an area where there is a huge flow of people with disabilities under permanent or temporary treatment in this reference hospital. The bus stops were catalogued by gathering their geographical coordinates and location references, using geolocation software, such as Google Earth and Google Maps.

After this mapping stage, we began to prepare a form with 12 criteria of analyses that would be used for the technical inspections *in loco*. To do so, we took as a reference a report produced by the Workgroup of Accessibility, Urban Mobility, and Citizenship of the Regional Council of Engineering and Agronomy of Bahia (CREA/BA) during a technical visit to the bus stop that is located in front of the Sarah Kubitsheck Hospital. The 12 accessibility criteria extracted from the report were the access to the bus stop, shelter, and seating, floor, ramp, sidewalk around it, platform to access, crosswalk to access, tactile floor, identification of the bus stop, identification of lines, and identification of the street.

Taking into account the technical inspections in the field, the accessibility status of each bus stop was then classified as "Critical" when they do not meet the criteria; "Acceptable" when they partially or inadequately meet the criteria; and "Favorable" when the criteria are totally and appropriately met. After the collection, the data were inserted and visualized in a digital map available at www.pontocerto.org (see Figure 7.1), which has each bus stop appear in three colors that correspond to its final classification: Red Bus Stop is "Critical", Yellow Bus Stop is "Acceptable", and Green Bus Stop is "Favorable". In addition, it is possible to access the classification by clicking on the bus stop on the map.

After CNPq's support ceased in 2015, the project was registered in UNEB's Pro-Rectory of Extension, and it entered into an instrument of technical cooperation with UFRB, the Federal University of Reconcavo of Bahia. As of such date, the scope of action of the project was expanded, collecting data from bus stops in the city of Salvador beyond the 10 kilometers initially proposed in the project in 2014. In this new stage, we consolidated the methodology, which was very similar to the former (mapping, georeferencing, and classifying the bus stops), including theoretical discussions during the meetings with students (monitors and volunteers). We considered that they should be aware of the importance of the project as a citizenship tool, especially in the perspective of "the right to the city" regarding the accessibility of people with disabilities or reduced mobility within the current urban mobility landscape.

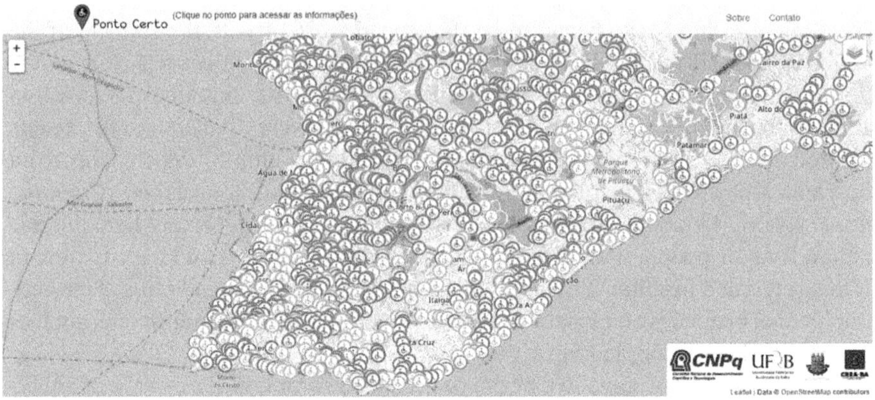

Figure 7.1 Interface of Project *Ponto Certo's* webpage.

Source: www.pontocerto.org.

As the second stage of the project started, we began mapping with the use of geolocation software as the main tool, which allowed the visualization of the bus stops in a cartographic map and generated the geographic coordinates of latitude and longitude. As we did in the first stage, these data about the bus stops were transferred to a spreadsheet that helped identify the stops, which contributed to the technical inspection *in loco* when the form was used to check the status of the bus stops in the city of Salvador based on the criteria mentioned above. In the second stage, there was a considerable increase in the number of bus stops (221 to more than 2.000). So we decided to divide the inspection teams considering the three collective transport basins of Salvador: Middle, Periphery, and Center-Border.

During the three years of the project, we had to deal with the various changes in the inspection teams. It is important to emphasize that from the students involved in the project, only one was a monitor, that is, he/she received a monthly grant to cover his/her expenses. All the others students participated in the project as volunteers, which contributed to constant changes in the groups, and as a consequence, several trainings were held to explain the methodology as well as the instructions about the technical inspections, such as the handling of the GPS device and the process of data insertion in the digital map system.

The Project *Ponto Certo* also provides for implementations of different tools to enhance the participation of citizens in the project. One of them is the possibility of inserting comments about the status of the bus stops from the engagement of the citizen to involve other users, which makes it more inclusive. Consequently, we could create a mechanism to monitor these bus stops with regard to updating their status. In case they suffer any changes to their accessibility conditions, a crucial aspect of the project, it will enable citizens to be engaged in the discussion and to know the problems that affect their environment. Thus, we can promote the clarification on issues of accessibility and urban mobility, assuring the legal security of these issues in the promotion of citizenship.

An important characteristic of this project is the use of collaborative tools, such as the Open Street Map (OSM), a crowd mapping platform, which allowed us to create a digital map composed of specific data collected in the field during technical inspections and based on the criteria that evaluate the accessibility status of bus stops. For the development of this map, we used the tools of GIS Web, whose framework was built from the connection of a database in PostgreSQL (QGis DBG) and a Django system developed in Python for the insertion of the data collected in the field during the inspections. The system is simple and consists of a home screen with buttons to register the stops and insert evaluations, in which the students insert the data of the inspected bus stops.

Beyond collecting and systematizing information, this project aims to contribute to the elimination of social, economic, and urban barriers, as well as to generate changes directly connected with the promotion of accessibility. Once these needs are met by the public administration, they ensure that people who have some kind of disability can be autonomous and exercise their citizenship when they enjoy the urban space without any challenges.

The project got to its final phase, and the results obtained so far evidence the low concern of the public administration with issues such as accessibility at bus stops in a tourist and important city as Salvador (the third-most-populous city in Brazil). Since there is no official record of the total number of stops in the entire city of Salvador due to its dynamic layout, which causes them to change frequently, it is essential to update the data so as to maintain the quality of the information provided. The last stage of the project ended in October 2018, reaching 2250 bus stops that have been inspected and evaluated. We can see a small amount of bus stops with a "Favorable" status. From the total of evaluated stops (see Figure 7.2), only 28 were considered favorable to people with disabilities or reduced mobility. It corresponds to approximately 1% of the total, which is much lower than the desirable minimum. On the other hand, bus stops with critical

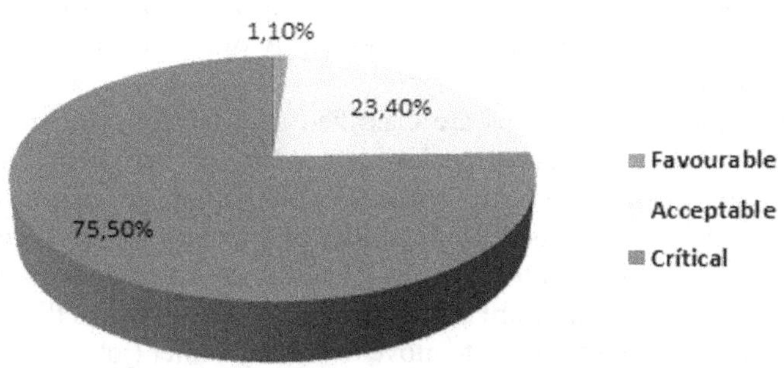

Figure 7.2 Results of bus stops status.

Source: Produced by the authors.

Figure 7.3 Bus stops with "Favourable" status.

Source: www.pontocerto.org.

status amount to 76%, which corresponds to 1748 bus stops that do not meet any criteria of accessibility.

Regarding the position of the bus stops in Salvador, we observed that 90% of those considered Favorable are in the Center-Border basin, concentrated in the "noble" areas of the capital located near the coast (the neighborhoods of Barra and Pituba, for example), and their urban infrastructure has been renovated recently, such as the surroundings of Lapa Bus Station and Orlando Gomes Avenue. Only 10% of those are located in the Middle and Peripheral basins of Salvador (see Figure 7.3), which reinforces our assertions regarding improvements in the accessibility conditions in regions where low-income populations live.

Bus stops classified as "Acceptable" represent around 23% of the total, concentrating predominantly in the areas of the city center of Salvador, where there is good transport service, as well as infrastructure and equipment services, because it is a traditional and historical area of the city. However, they still need proper adjustment to fully meet the criteria of accessibility of the city's bus stops in this area (see Figure 7.4).

The vast majority of the stops are classified as "Critical", which represents about 76% of the total inspected, mainly located in the Peripheral and Middle basins of the city, areas where lower-income populations are concentrated through spontaneous occupations, considered by critics of urban theory as a decisive factor for the few investments in these areas. Although considered less attractive by the public administration, they are exactly the urban spaces where the population uses public transportation the most to move to the city center (jobs and leisure, for example), and they need, therefore, better infrastructure to allow a better use of such spaces (see Figure 7.5).

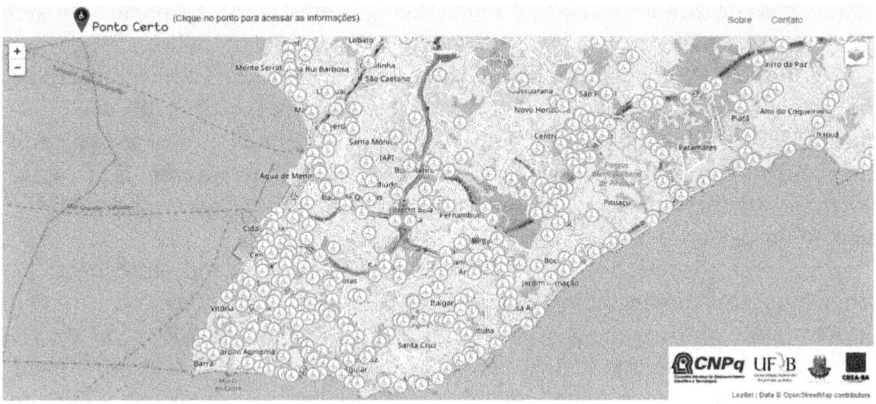

Figure 7.4 Bus stops with "Acceptable" status.

Source: www.pontocerto.org.

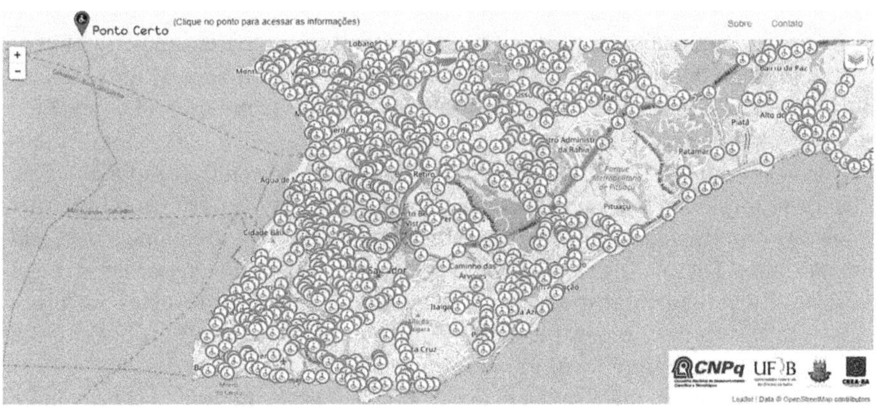

Figure 7.5 Bus stops with "Critical" status.

Source: www.pontocerto.org.

As mentioned earlier, the project is moving towards the end of the second stage with the completion of the latest technical inspections in the field and the inclusion of the data in the digital map system. Thus, we started to plan the next steps, which will consist of transferring the data to a project's own server that will be managed by software developed to allow the inclusion of other urban equipment for the visualization of information and classification. Once this platform is created (named Gindex temporarily), we hope to apply this methodology to any city in the world.

One of the main contributions to the concretization of this project is the creation of a database capable of assisting in the decision making of the population and public management, as well as the implementation of public policies. This way, we believe that we are contributing to an effective form of engagement regarding the participation of the population in the discussions about accessibility and urban mobility in Brazil and the world. However, we still see very low engagement of the population in these discussions, often not due to indifference but because we lack tools for citizen participation that would give them an active voice and bring them to the center of the discussions.

In this sense, we believe that with the end of the project and subsequent dissemination of the information regarding the conditions of the bus stops, we will be able to offer citizens the possibility of urging the public administration to offer better quality of displacement in the city, because it will allow them to evaluate the bus stops that are in better condition within their route, and, in addition, to have arguments based on a concrete dataset to demand the improvements that they so badly need.

Considerations

There are great challenges on the way to building an egalitarian society. Moreover, there is no doubt that one of them is the promotion of accessibility. Accessibility and the rights of people with disabilities are the expression of a new kind of citizenship, which was conquered in the world by people and organizations that deal with the issues of people with disabilities and reduced mobility in an attempt to ally other concepts such as equality, diversity, equity, mobility, right to the city, citizenship, democracy, participation, autonomy, social inclusion, and human rights. Therefore, this work has sought to highlight this important issue of accessibility in public transportation with attention to the inefficiencies and problems of infrastructure, and its focus is to point out the problems of the bus stops in Salvador with a geographic information system (GIS).

In the last decades, the issue of accessibility and urban mobility has been more debated in the area of urbanism, since citizens are looking at cities with more concern to create pleasant and sustainable spaces in search of better quality of life and reduction of inequalities between its inhabitants. Social barriers can only be eliminated to the extent that they are deconstructed, and for that it is essential to develop actions that cause society to change its view in relation to the right to the city of people with disabilities and reduced mobility. Moreover, what did the data show? In the face of all the collected data, it is necessary to take some urgent action to improve the conditions of the bus stops. The proposition of adequate solutions will only be possible with the amplification of research and studies in the attempt to understand deeply the problems in the transportation system and, therefore, we will have a more feasible system that will improve the quality of life of its users.

This is what really matters: finding efficient and effective solutions with regard to ensuring accessibility in the urban space. In this sense, the investment in research and different projects in the area of urbanism that applies new technologies, such as urban informatics, become increasingly important in the global scenario in which we live. Therefore, the implementation of the Project *Ponto Certo* seeks to make its contribution to create conditions for other projects to emerge and to follow parallel paths to promote the accessibility and rights of people with disabilities and reduced mobility in other cities in Brazil and in the world.

Accordingly, universal accessibility and urban mobility are urgent and challenging issues of this century, since these issues have a major impact on people's economy and quality of life. Thinking about the urban space more efficiently with regard to social, economic, and environmental issues should be aligned with innovation and technology, because together they can find more effective solutions to solve current problems.

Notes

1 "Trajeto contínuo, desobstruído e sinalizado, que conecta os ambientes externos ou internos de espaços e edificações, e que possa ser utilizado de forma autônoma e segura por todas as pessoas, inclusive aquelas com deficiência. A rota acessível externa pode incorporar estacionamentos, calçadas rebaixadas, faixas de travessia de pedestres, rampas, etc. A rota acessível interna pode incorporar corredores, pisos, rampas, escadas, elevadores, etc" – Translated by the author.
2 In this work, we will not dig into the discussion about purchasing power x accessibility or new mobilities paradigm, but it is possible to verify how these issues – such as (in)accessibility – are interwoven when comparing the Project *Ponto Certo* with the maps on the social organization of the territory and urban mobility available in the book *Salvador: transformações na ordem urbana*, https://repositorio.ufba.br/ri/bitstream/ri/17348/1/Salvador%20-%20Transformac%CC%A7o%CC%83es%20na%20Ordem%20Urbana%20%28Ebook%29.pdf
3 "ter ambiente seguro e acessível para a utilização do Sistema Nacional de Mobilidade Urbana" – Translated by the author.
4 Some data about this issue involving income and planning of urban spaces can be accessed in the work cited above, *Salvador: transformações na ordem urbana.*

References

Almeida, E. P. & Giacomini, L. B. 2013. *Mobilidade e Acessibilidade Urbana.* In 2° Seminários Nacionais de Construções Sustentáveis. Passo Fundo/RS: IMED. Available at: https://www.imed.edu.br/Uploads/Mobilidade%20e%20Acessibilidade%20Urbana.pdf.

Associação Brasileira de Normas Técnicas (ABNT NBR 14022). 2011. *Transporte – Acessibilidade à pessoa portadora de deficiência em ônibus e trólebus, para atendimento urbano e intermunicipal.* Brasil: Associação Brasileira de Normas Técnicas.

Associação Brasileira de Normas Técnicas (ABNT NBR 9050). 2015. *Acessibilidade a edificações, espaço, mobiliário e equipamento urbano.* Brasil: Associação Brasileira de Normas Técnicas.

Associação Brasileira de Normas Técnicas (ABNT NBR 16537). 2016. *Acessibilidade. Sinalização tátil no piso. Diretrizes para elaboração de projetos e instalação.* Brasil: Associação Brasileira de Normas Técnicas.

Brasil. 2012. *Política Nacional de Mobilidade Urbana.* Brasília: Ministério das Cidades.

Ferraz, A. C. P. & Torres, I. G. E. 2008. *Transporte Público Urbano.* São Paulo: Editora Rima.

Instituto Brasileiro de Geografia e Estatística (IBGE). 2010. *Censo Demográfico.* Available at: www.ibge.gov.br/estadosat/temas.php?sigla = rj&tema = censo demog2010_defic [Accessed on June 5, 2017].

Lefebvre, H. 1996. *Writing on cities.* Cambridge: Blackwell Publishers.

Vasconcelos, E. A. 2011. *Transporte Urbano, espaço e equidade: Análises das políticas públicas.* São Paulo: Editora Annablume.

Chapter 8

Urban mobility and citizenship in Brazil

Advances in the legal framework

Filipe Marino

Introduction

In recent years, Brazil has seen a new type of crisis in its cities, especially in those of large and medium size: the urban mobility crisis. At the heart of this crisis are elements such as the socio-spatial segregation resulting from the accelerated and unequal[1] process of urbanization that characterizes the Brazilian territory, lack of consistent planning policies, and low investments in urban mobility by the public authorities.

According to *Instituto Brasileiro de Geografia e Estatística* (IBGE; Brazilian Institute of Geography and Statistics, 2010),[2] more than 20% of the Brazilian population spends more than 1 hour commuting to work. This means that one-fifth of the population spends more than 2 hours in daily commute to meet an average eight-hour journey. Data from *Instituto de Pesquisa Econômica Aplicada* (IPEA; Institute of Applied Economic Research, 2013)[3] indicate that trips carried out by low-income workers are, on average, 20% longer than those of the wealthiest, and that the number of hours spent in these commutes has been increasing year by year for all income layers:

> The *Índice de Bem-Estar Urbano* (IBEU) [Urban Welfare Index] developed by *Observatório das Metrópoles* [Observatory of the Metropolises] (Ribeiro 2010) demonstrates the increase in the commuting time to work in the 2000s. . . . But what has been observed in the metropolises over the 2000s, based on the PNAD data,[4] is that the rate of mobility has decreased; that is, there are more people in the metropolitan regions spending more than one hour in their daily commute, which allows us to say that commuting time and mobility conditions tend to worsen and compromise the welfare conditions in the metropolises.
>
> (Ribeiro et al. 2011, p. 200)

Therefore, the precariousness of urban mobility and spatial segregation are two issues that have been directly affecting the quality of life in Brazilian cities and have worsened over the years. Despite the increase in income and employment, since 2003, urban growth in Brazil has created citizens who are "deprived of the city", in the words of Raquel Rolnik (2013). In the same sense, Ermínia Maricato (2013) points out that mobility is a central question of the urban issues faced by the Brazilian metropolises, culminating in the large protests of June 2013, known as "June Journeys". According to the author,

> It is the condition of transport that demands the greatest deal of sacrifice from the residents of the city. While the worsening of mobility is general – that is, it affects everyone – it is from the lower income layers that mobility will charge the highest price for immobility. The average commute time in São Paulo was two hours and 42 minutes in 2007. For one third of the population, such time exceeds three hours, that is, a part of life is spent in transportation, whether it is a luxury car or a bus or an overcrowded train – which is more common.
> (Maricato 2013, p. 41)

Although it is a more acute issue for the lower classes, immobility impacts everyone, therefore the urgency of addressing urban mobility in Brazil from a new perspective. Such an approach has been already endorsed, for example, by the Universal Declaration of Human Rights when it pointed out the relationship between mobility and social welfare. In Article 13, the document establishes that people have the right to freedom of movement. It states that "many studies accept the axiom that the increase in spatial mobility reflects the process of democratization and freedom of movement, and by extension, the increase in social mobility and equality in general" (Kaufmann & Montulet 2008, p. 38). The increase in freedom, social mobility, and equality relates inextricably to the increase in mobility qualification.

Although it is directly related – since to increase mobility does not necessarily mean to increase equality altogether – the expansion of urban rights permeates the expansion of the right to mobility. This right is indeed a possible but not unique way to a more democratic and inclusive city (and society), and consequently a more equal one. For Herce (2009, p. 15), urban mobility has become so fundamental these days that it has transcended the urbanistic discourse and has formulated the "territorial articulation and economic development" of cities.

Because it currently represents a major challenge for Brazilian society, this chapter has the general objective of relating urban mobility and citizenship, showing the evolution of Brazilian legislation in relation to urban mobility and transportation. The time covered by this chapter goes from the establishment of the Federal Constitution, dated 1988, until its change that resulted from Amendment 74 in 2015, which made urban mobility a *social right* (Brasil 2013). In this way, a descriptive survey was carried out with data collection from a bibliographical investigation. In addition to this introduction, the chapter is structured in three more sections: "Mobility and citizenship: a new social right", which addresses the theoretical reference on mobility; "Urban mobility in the Brazilian law", in which it presents the evolution of the laws supporting urban mobility in Brazil; and finally, "Conclusions".

Mobility and citizenship: a new social right

The relationship between urban mobility and citizenship in Brazil is recent. Although Brazilians have been supported by the Federal Constitution since 1988, only in 2015 did the right to transport[5] become a social right, with the approval of the Constitutional Amendment 74, dated 2013 (Brasil 2013). For Marshall (1967), citizenship is called a "tripod of rights" that comprises political, civil, and social rights:[6]

> Citizenship requires a link of a different nature, a direct feeling of participation in a community based on a loyalty to a civilization that is a common heritage. It understands the loyalty of free men, imbued with rights and protected by a common law. Its development is stimulated both by the struggle to acquire such rights and by their enjoyment once acquired.
>
> (Marshall 1967, p. 84)

Civil rights, regulated through legislation, "are the fundamental rights to life, freedom, property, equality in law". These are the rights that "unfold in the guarantee of coming and going, choosing the work, manifesting thought, organizing oneself. . . . Its touchstone is individual freedom" (Carvalho 2002, p. 9). Political rights are those that organize citizens' lives through political representation, which in Brazil is made through voting.

Social rights are those that allow the population to participate in the collective wealth beyond individual income. Collective wealth is herein considered in the sense of the assets of the city and its infrastructure available to all, where access to the collective assets in an equitable way is a premise of citizenship and may directly be related to the concept of "right to the city" (Lefebvre 1967; Harvey 2012), or to what Milton Santos (1987) named "right to the surroundings": "Social rights allow politically organized societies to reduce the excesses of inequality produced by capitalism and ensure a minimum of welfare for all. Their central and supporting idea is social justice" (Santos 1987, p. 10).

To Carvalho (2002, p. 10), "the full citizen would be the holder of the three rights. Incomplete citizens would be those who had only some of these rights. Those who did not benefit from any of the rights would be non-citizens". At its core, citizenship assumes that the assimilation of the importance of a particular social aspect, such as mobility, needs to be recognized and effected. This is how the current relationship between urban mobility and citizenship is established.

At the same time that under the concept of citizenship, civil rights limit the state's duty to ensure the protection of citizens, social rights establish what must be done to ensure the population's welfare from the social understanding of the fundamental issues of a society. In this sense, the transformation of urban mobility into a social right has been a great achievement.

François Ascher (1995, p. 5) believes that understanding the history of the contemporary period means to understand it as the period of urban mobility so that "it is not a simple movement in space. It is an ongoing process, which begins at the level of economic structures and ends at the level of social relations". Therefore, urban mobility has, among its components, the apprehension of social right, which corroborates the claims by Marshall (1967) and Carvalho (2002).

To these authors, the expansion of social rights is fundamental for reaching a "general reduction of risk and insecurity" so that we can seek equality:

> The expansion of social services is not primarily a means of equalizing income. In some cases, it can do it, in others it cannot. The issue is not of much importance; it belongs to a different sector of social policy. What matters is that there is a general enrichment of the concrete substance of civilized life, a general reduction of risk and insecurity, an equalization between the more and less favoured at all levels – between the healthy and the sick, the employee and the unemployed, the old and the active, the bachelor and the father of a large family. Equalization does not refer to both classes and individuals comprising a population that is considered, for this purpose, as a class. Equality of status is more important than equality of income.
>
> (Marshall 1967, p. 94)

The importance of social law is highlighted as an instrument of equalization in the sense of collective participation. In the Brazilian case, where inequality is large and territorialized, to address mobility means to address citizenship in order to enrich the "concrete substance of civilized life". The idea of equalization deals with the possibility that mobility has to confer a certain equity on such disparate territories. Creating opportunities that will provide access to leisure equipment, services, and culture is the first step to take so that citizens residing in places where there is no such equipment might enjoy them.

In this sense, urban mobility deals with the connection and approximation of the places of absence to the places of abundance, and sets itself as a kind of retraction that goes beyond the idea of the workers' commuting to their workplaces. Such retraction symbolizes a counterpart of social justice in the increase in mobility and allows people that suffer more due to their position in the social space (income, education, etc.) and in the physical space (the place where they live) to have broader access to the whole city, its assets, its surroundings (Santos 1987), culminating in a greater right to the city, that is, the right to full citizenship.

However, just *having* access is not enough. It is also important to pay attention to the qualitative aspects of mobility. Mobility should be regarded as citizenship in a general way, beyond physical movement. This includes safety, comfort, appropriate tariffs, speed, efficiency. In other terms, motility itself (Kaufmann 2004).

Therefore, the unequal mobility in the territory creates barriers to the extension of citizenship for all, since mobility restrictions of the less fortunate in addition to the unequal and poor distribution of infrastructure across the territory interfere with the social right of all, causing some people to be considered less of a citizen than others.

In his works *O espaço dividido* [*The Divided Space*] (1979) and *O espaço do cidadão* [*The Citizen's Space*] (1987), Milton Santos investigates the "mobility" category, relating it to the territory and the financial and social possibilities of individuals. Poorly located and low-income individuals are threatened by immobility, or in the words of José Murilo de Carvalho (2002), they become "non-citizens". Santos (1987) states that one of the most striking characteristics of citizenship, and also one that is mostly concealed is its relationship with the territory and with the valuation of individuals according to their spatial location. In a clear way, Carvalho explains the importance of place in relation to the matter of mobility:

> The value of each person depends on the place he lives: his worth as a producer, consumer, citizen depends on his location in the territory. His worth changes incessantly for better or for worse depending on the differences in accessibility (time, frequency, price), regardless of his own condition. People with the same potential, the same training, even the same salary are valued differently depending to the place where they live: the opportunities are not the same. Therefore, the possibility of being a full citizen or less than the average citizen depends, in a large proportion, on the point of the territory where the person is.
>
> (Carvalho 2002, p. 107)

To the extent that income, class, and place value individuals according to their spatial location, another relationship established from the perspective of the territory stands out: men, as producers, consumers, and citizens. This aspect often surpasses the idea of place by considering parameters of global scale, although citizenship is not a deterritorialized value, as are production and consumption. In summary, "dwellers who have the means to move around have, thus, easier access, and those whose mobility is limited or void should locally pay a higher price, and sometimes, as a consequence, renounce their use" (Carvalho 2002, p. 116).

By corroborating the disadvantages of bad location and precarious access to transport systems, "geographical distance doubles due to the political distance" (Carvalho 2002, p. 118), so that information is economic and territorialized, that is, it is geographically concentrated. Having information is also fundamental for mobility and, consequently, for citizenship, something that the poorest lack.

Therefore, the direct relationship between urban mobility, constituted as social right and citizenship herein, allows a broader look at the importance of the legal framework that guarantees urban mobility in the Brazilian State. Although recent, the new laws aim to establish urban mobility in a concrete way as a central right in social justice. This is what will be shown next.

The urban mobility in the Brazilian law

After the period of democratic recession caused by the dictatorship in Brazil (1964–1985), in 1988, the Brazilian Federal Constitution was promulgated. This document, called Citizen's Constitution (Contituição Cidadã), states today the actions of the state in the most diverse aspects of national urban life. As regards urban mobility, the Federal Constitution is not very specific and mostly mentions the term "urban transport" to address mobility. The text contains 26 occurrences of such term and only one occurrence of the term "mobility". Such realization helps understand both the historical relevance of the term "transport" to refer to commutes of all kinds, especially the urban ones, as well as the novelty attributed to the term "mobility" within the field of urban studies these days. According to *Associação Nacional de Transportes Urbanos* [National Association of Urban Transport] (2017),

> The Constitution of 1988 brought in its core the elimination of censorship, equality of rights between men and women, racism as a crime with no right to bail, property as a social function, the establishment of the guidelines of urban policy, the creation of *Sistema Único de Saúde* (SUS) [Unified Healthcare System], the definition of the environment as a public good and the recognition of the Municipality as a federal entity and, in this case, it brought the seed of the municipalization of almost everything, especially traffic, which is today fully recognized by Brazilians. The years following the Constitution have seen an increase in the creation of ordinary laws giving life to the texts of the new Constitutional Charter and the same was also expected to occur in the context of transport, traffic, and mobility.
>
> (ANTP 2017, p. 7)

First, the most important highlight within the Federal Constitution in the field of urban mobility is to address the right to transport (Art. 6) as a social right from its revision in 2015, alongside the right to education, health, and food. Presented in December 2013, the proposed Constitutional Amendment (PEC 090-A/2011) was approved, and access to urban transport became a social right. According to the author of the amendment, Luiza Erundina,[7]

> people depend on public transport to access other rights, such as health, education, culture, and the right to the city itself. Surely the action will put the theme on society's agenda and will become a priority to the federal, state, and municipal governments.
>
> (O Globo 2013)

On the other hand, for the project rapporteur, Nilmário Miranda,[8] "when mobility becomes a social right, the State is almost obliged to work to universalize it. If the focus is changed, it will no longer be a sector regulated only by the market" (O Globo 2013).

Both the author and the rapporteur's words comprise two important ideas: the first is that the State "is almost obliged" to universalize urban transport through its recognition as social right. In this sense, there is a conflict with the very definition of "essential service" guaranteed by the same document.[9] This is because, by treating transport as an essential right in 1988, at least in theory, the state was already obliged to provide it as a service. Therefore, the main modification brought by the new perspective was to endorse that commuting must be seen beyond the sole necessity of locomotion. By doing so, the Federal Constitution ratifies mobility as a matrix of urban life.

The second idea deals with the awareness of the power of the market in transport regulation, which also denotes the subservience of the state in the selective concession of that right. Since Brazilian public transport is carried out almost entirely by private companies, turning it into a social right can lead to a new approach to mobility in various spheres, from the social structuring level of cities to public transportation tenders.

As mentioned earlier, this shows that the understanding of urban mobility as a right, and no longer as a service achieved when public transportation is provided is new to Brazilian society. This idea differs from Articles 21 and 22, dated 1988, which provides for the obligation of the Federal Government to organize railway, road, maritime, and air transport in Brazil, as well as to establish the guidelines of national transport and traffic policies.

In addition, the recent inclusion in the Federal Constitution in the year 2014 of the terms "road safety" and the sole appearance of the term "mobility" are remarkable in Article 144:

> Public security, a duty of the State and a right to, and responsibility of, all is exercised to preserve public order and the safety of individuals and properties, . . . comprises education, engineering and traffic surveillance, in addition to other activities provided for in the law, which ensure the citizen the right to efficient urban mobility.
>
> (Article 144, Brazilian Federal Constitution)

This inclusion highlights an important shift in the social understanding that "efficient urban mobility" is established through public security.

Two other articles are very relevant to urban mobility: Articles 182 and 183. While not dealing directly with transport and mobility, they set out the basic guidelines for urban policy on which the City Statutes are based (Brasil 2001). It was established 13 years after the enactment of the Constitution in the Federal Act 10257, dated July 10, 2001.

In turn, a few years earlier in 1997 the Brazilian Traffic Code (Brazil 1997) that structured the urban traffic organization "through the 'municipalization' of traffic placed the local authorities at the core of the planning and management of traffic" (ANTP 2017, p. 9). This new set of laws organized the rights and duties of drivers and structured the training and supervision of drivers.

The City Statutes (Brasil 2001) are considered until today the most prominent document in the sense of the organization of urban rights in Brazil. It determines the obligation to order and control the use of land, in addition to ensuring full access to transport supply according to the interests and needs of the citizens:

> The Federal Urban Policy Act – the City Statutes – passed in 2001 after 12 years of intense discussions and negotiations in the National Congress. Since then, the Act has been internationally acclaimed, to the extent that Brazil has been included in the Honor Roll of the United Nations (UN – HABITAT) in 2006 just for having approved it. Openly praised by public policy makers and urban managers from various countries, the City Statutes has been repeatedly promoted by the Cities Alliance, an important international initiative, as the most appropriate regulatory framework for providing solid legal bases for government and socio-political strategies committed to the promotion of urban reform.
>
> (Fernandes 2013, p. 214)

Besides the avant-garde content that its guidelines present to the Brazilian society, another fundamental issue is that the City Statutes (Brasil 2001) are the product of great debate with civil society, organized by *Fórum Nacional da Reforma Urbana* (National Forum of Urban Reform):[10]

> The approval of the Federal Act in 2001 was largely the result of a broad national process of socio-political mobilization that clamored for the promotion of urban reform in Brazil. The City Statutes regulated the original chapter on urban policy that had been approved by the 1988 Federal Constitution.
>
> (Fernandes 2013, p. 214)

One of the greatest innovations of the City Statutes was to make the Master Plan[11] compulsory for cities with more than 20,000 inhabitants. As regards urban mobility, it has forced cities with more than 500,000 inhabitants to draw up an Integrated Urban Transport Plan, which should be "compatible with the master plan or inserted therein" (Brasil 2001).

Another pressing question set up by the Statutes is the compulsory participation of civil society in the process of drafting the Master Plan and the Urban Transport Plan. Social participation, taking into consideration that this law was passed only 16 years after the resumption of democracy in Brazil, is certainly one of the greatest advances not only in the field of urban mobility but in all Brazilian urban law.

That is an inflection in the relationship of urban mobility with citizenship. Social participation, by becoming compulsory in decision-making processes, allows civil law, which is basic for existence, to be accessed by direct political law – that is, the right of choice. In no other time in Brazilian history has urban mobility been so democratic.

In 2005, the name *Plano Integrado de Transporte Urbano* (Integrated Urban Transport Plan) was changed to *Transport and Mobility Master Plan* by resolution no. 34 of *Conselho das Cidades* (Council of Cities; Brasil 2006).[12] According to Neto and Galindo (2013, p. 1), the resolution also established the minimum content of the Transport and Mobility Master Plan, which, among other aspects, predicted the observance of the various modes of transport, respecting the local specificities, the prioritization of the collective over the individual transport, nonmotorized modes, and pedestrians.

It can be said that the definitions of the resolution would form the basis of the National Urban Mobility Policy (Brasil 2012), which started to be enforced as law in 2010. That is evidenced by the focus given to sustainable urban mobility in the Guidelines for Municipal Managers, which previously treated mobility as public transport.

The addition of the term "mobility", which is a broader and more current term in the urban debate, already indicates that the subject will be addressed by the public authorities. In the statutes, there are six occurrences of the term "transport" and two of the term "mobility", and only one refers to urban mobility itself. It is noteworthy that the term "mobility" is broader and appropriate to encompass the dynamics of urban commute and has bypassed the term "transport" in urban studies from the 2000s (Marino et al. 2017).

After the approval of the City Statutes in 2001, Brazil experienced great economic growth allied to the lack of investment in public transport that was consistent with the increase in commuting, which aggravated the crisis of national urban mobility. In response to this crisis, *Política Nacional de Mobilidade Urbana* (PNMU) [National Urban Mobility Policy] was approved in 2012, establishing the parameters for urban mobility in the national territory. The aspects advocated in such policy were universal accessibility, efficiency in commuting, integration with urban development policies (sanitation, housing, etc.), reduction of inequalities, and democratic management. Thus, in theory, the policy created an institutional environment conducive to the promotion of urban mobility through the elaboration and implementation of mobility infrastructure projects in Brazil.

Some of the objectives of such act are to reduce inequalities and promote social inclusion; to promote access to basic services and social equipment; to provide improvement in the urban conditions of the population; to promote sustainable development; and to consolidate democratic management as an instrument and guarantee of the continuous improvement of urban mobility.

The National Urban Mobility Policy structures mobility through the prioritization of nonmotorized modes over others, besides the inclusion of the legal possibility of creating restrictions to the use of cars by the municipalities, in a clear appreciation of public transport. It also undertakes the mandatory development of the Transport and Mobility Master Plan for cities with more than 20,000 inhabitants, which modifies what had been established by the City Statutes and poses it as a major challenge for the Brazilian cities.[13] In this sense, in terms of urban mobility, PNMU is the greatest legal advancement in the establishment of rules and guidelines at the federal level. Since the 1980s, urban mobility has undergone developments in the federal sphere, as summarized in Table 8.1.

Table 8.1 The legal evolution of urban mobility in Brazil

LEGAL INSTRUMENT	*YEAR*	*ACTION*	*ACQUIRED BENEFITS*
Federal Constitution	1988	Creation of Law	Organization of the Brazilian law It obliges the Federation to organize transport Basic guidelines of urban law
Brazilian Traffic Code	1997	Creation of Law	Organization of traffic rules Municipalization of urban traffic
City Statute	2001	Creation of Law	Obligation of the Urban Transport Plan for cities with more than 500,000 inhabitants. Participation of the civil society
Article 34 of the Council of Cities	2005	Change of Law	Change of the name *Urban Transport Plan* for *Transport and Mobility Master Plan*
Urban Mobility National Policy	2012	Creation of Law	Prioritization of non-motorized transportation PDTM for more than 20000 inhab. Appreciation of Public Transport
Urban Mobility National Policy	2015	Change of Law	Recognition of urban mobility as a central component of citizenship

After the transformation of urban mobility into a social right in 2015, Brazil is considered to have become a well-equipped country in legal terms regarding urban mobility laws, better than it was before.

Conclusions

This chapter investigated the relationship between urban mobility and citizenship, presenting the evolution of Brazilian legislation on the subject of urban mobility and transport.

The conception of urban mobility, taken as an instrument of social equity toward more democratic cities, has undergone a major breakthrough in recent years, evolving from a civil right to a social right. From this perspective, the Brazilian State began to recognize the importance of urban mobility as a dimension that qualifies urban life.

The adoption of the term "urban mobility" replacing the term "urban transport" was also observed, which shows a more mature and consistent sense of the complexity it engenders. This adoption happens in parallel to the gradual conquest of rights on the matter, thus showing the maturity of the issue in our legislation.

But this complexity also shows, in a broader sense, compared to what is observed in Brazilian cities, that the potential movement of some entails the immobility of others, especially the poor. This matter comprises the importance of the urban mobility discussion on the Brazilian agenda, where the state, despite its policies, has been nonneutral when it comes to urban mobility practices.

On the basis of the construction of the laws that have come to guarantee more consolidated rules, it is evident that the themes of transport and mobility have been gaining space in the agenda of urban rights at least since the 2000s, although the legal text does not represent in itself a change in reality. However, this is a big step in terms of urban mobility for more equitable cities in Brazil.

Notes

1 According to Silva (2013, p. 9): "At the height of the urban expansion process in Brazil, the logics conceived to understand the transformations that occurred and the social inequalities that increasingly crystalized in space involved dimensions related to the exploitation, segregation, marginalization, exclusion, as the concepts of 'urbanization under the logic of disorder' and 'urban spoliation' coined by Lúcio Kowarick (1980)".

2 IBGE – Instituto Brasileiro de Geografia e Estatística. www.ibge.gov.br/censo2010.html. Accessed on May 5, 2018.

3 See Pereira and Schwanen (2013).

4 *Pesquisa Nacional de Amostra de Domicílios* (PNAD) [National Household Sample Survey]. Available at the IBGE website: www.ibge.gov.br/pnad.html. Accessed on May 4, 2018.

5 The Federal Constitution treats transport as a right, thus differentiating it from the idea of urban mobility, a broader term.

6 The author points out that the rights arose at different stages in modern societies: first, civil rights (18th century), followed by political rights (19th century), and finally social rights (late 20th century). According to Marshall (1967), citizenship only becomes a tangible concept as of the 21st century.

7 Former mayor of the Municipality of São Paulo and Congressman of the state of São Paulo since 1999 for five consecutive office terms. She was elected by *Partido Socialista Brasileiro* (PSB, Brazilian Socialist Party) and has been a member of *Partido Socialismo e Liberdade* (PSOL, Socialism and Freedom Party) since 2016.

8 He served as a Federal Representative between the years 2011 and 2015 as part of *Partido dos Trabalhadores* (PT, Workers' Party) for the state of Minas Gerais and was re-elected to the 2015–2019 term of office.

9 The right to public transport appears in the 1988 Federal Constitution as an essential service under the responsibility of municipalities (Article 30), and it is the responsibility of the states and the federal government to provide transport in metropolitan, interstate, and inter-municipal regions (Article 21).

10 At http: forumreformaurbana.org.br/. Accessed on May 2, 2018.

11 The Master Plan is a basic tool for the development and urban expansion policy of Brazilian municipalities.

12 *Conselho das Cidades* (Council of Cities; Brazil 2006) deliberates on the most diverse matters concerning the *Política Nacional de Desenvolvimento Urbano* (PNDU, Urban Development National Policy) and the actions and programs developed by *Ministério das Cidades* (Ministry of the Cities) through its resolutions, resulting from the political and technical debate carried out by the councilors. The objective of Public Resolution 34 was "To issue guidelines and recommendations to the minimum content of the Master Plan, based on the City Statutes".

13 By the rules of the City Statutes, only 36 cities were obliged to institute the Transport and Mobility Master Plan. With the changes proposed by PNMU, 1650 municipalities

are obliged to do so. For Neto and Galindo (2013, p. 12), "it is emphasized that this new cut equates the obligation provided for by the City Statutes for the master plans which, after a decade of the approval, has not yet reached all the municipalities".

References

Ascher, F. 1995. *Métapolis ou L'avenir des villes*. Paris: Éditions Emile Jacobs.

Associação Nacional dos Transportes Públicos – ANTP. 2017. *Mobilidade humana para um Brasil urbano*. São Paulo: Editora ANTP.

Brazil. September 23, 1997. *Lei n° 9.503*. Diário Oficial da República Federativa do Brasil. Brasília: Poder Executivo.

Brasil. 1988. *Constituição da República Federativa do Brasil*. Brasília: Senado Federal.

Brasil. July 10, 2001. *Lei n° 10.257 (Estatuto da Cidade). Diário Oficial da República Federativa do Brasil*. Brasília: Poder Executivo.

Brasil. 2006. *Decreto n° 5.790. Diário Oficial da República Federativa do Brasil*. Brasília: Poder Executivo.

Brasil. January 3, 2012. *Lei n° 12.587. Diário Oficial da República Federativa do Brasil*. Brasília: Poder Executivo.

Brasil. December 11, 2013. *Emenda à Constituição n° 74, 2013. Diário Oficial da República Federativa do Brasil*. Brasília: Poder Executivo.

Carvalho, J. M. 2002. *Cidadania no Brasil: O longo caminho*. Rio de Janeiro: Civilização Brasileira.

Fernandes, E. January/July 2013. Estatuto da Cidade, mais de 10 anos depois: razão de descrença, ou razão de otimismo? *Revista UFMG*, 20(1), pp. 212–233. Belo Horizonte.

Harvey, D. 2012. *Rebel cities: From the right to the city to the urban revolution*. Londres: Editora Verso.

Herce, M. 2009. *Sobre la movilidad en la ciudad: propuestas para recuperar un derecho ciudadano*. Barcelona: Reverte.

Jornal O Globo. December 4, 2013. CÂMARA APROVA PEC que transforma transporte em direito social. *Jornal O Globo*. Rio de Janeiro. Available at: https://oglobo.globo.com/brasil/camara-aprova-pec-que-transforma-transporte-em-direito-social-10972144 [Accessed on May 13, 2018].

Kaufmann, V. & Montulet, B. 2008. Between social and spatial mobilities: The issue of social fluidity. In Canzler, W. et al. eds. *Tracing mobilities: Towards a cosmopolitan perspective*. Hampshire: Ashgate Publishing Limited.

Kaufmann, V. et al. February 2004. Motility: Mobility as capital. *International Journal of Urban and Research*, 28(4), pp. 745–756.

Kowarick, L. 1980. *A espoliação urbana*. Rio de Janeiro: Paz e Terra.

Lefebvre, H. 1967. *O direito à cidade*. Reprint 2011. São Paulo: Editora Centauro.

Maricato, E. et al. 2013. É a questão urbana, estúpido! In *Cidades rebeldes: Passe livre e as manifestações que tomaram as ruas do Brasil*. São Paulo: Boitempo, Carta Maior, pp. 19–26.

Marino, F., Bastos, P. P. M. & Andrade, V. 2017. *Active mobility in Brazil: Advances in the scientific literature*, Text delivered in the Conference Mobile Utopia Pasts: Presents Futures. Lancaster: Lancaster University, pp. 24–25.

Marshall, T. H. 1967. *Cidadania, classe social e status*. Rio de Janeiro: Zahar Editores.

Neto, V. & Galindo, E. 2013. A Política Nacional de Mobilidade Urbana, os planos de mobilidade e os municípios brasileiros. *Revista Paranoá*, (9).

Pereira, R. & Schwanen, T. 2013. *Tempo de deslocamento casa-trabalho no Brasil (1992–2009): diferenças entre regiões metropolitanas, níveis de renda e sexo*. Rio de Janeiro: Instituto de Pesquisa Econômica Aplicada.

Ribeiro, L. C. Q. 2010. Índice de Bem-Estar Urbano (IBEU). Observatório das Metrópoles, s/p. Rio de Janeiro.

Ribeiro, L. C. Q., Silva, E. T. & Rodrigues, J. January/July 2011. Metrópoles Brasileiras: diversificação, concentração e dispersão. *Revista Paranaense de Desenvolvimento*, 120, pp. 177–207. Curitiba.

Rolnik, R. 2013. As vozes das ruas: as revoltas de junho e suas interpretações. In *Cidades rebeldes: Passe livre e as manifestações que tomaram as ruas do Brasil*. São Paulo: Editora Boitempo, Carta Maior, pp. 7–12.

Santos, M. 1979. *O espaço dividido*. Reprint 2004. São Paulo: Edusp.

Santos, M. 1987. *O espaço do cidadão*. Reprint 2007. São Paulo: Edusp.

Silva, E. T. 2013. *Estrutura urbana e mobilidade espacial nas metrópoles*. Rio de Janeiro: Letra Capital.

Chapter 9

Is it more 'Pokémon' than 'go'?

New mobilities paradigm in locative gaming

Luiz Adolfo Andrade

Initial thoughts

Pokémon GO is a locative game launched in July 2016 by the start-up Niantic Lab in partnership with Nintendo and Pokémon Company; it became a blockbuster in the U.S. within less than a week. In Brazil, the game was released in August 2016 at the same time of the Olympics in Rio de Janeiro. Nowadays it is available as a free application for Android and iOS operating systems, respectively from Google and Apple.

Ultimately, the locative game genre uses the geographical space as the support for players' interaction and mobility. In this way, *Pokémon GO* encourages the player to walk around the city looking for Pokémon by using a mobile phone, its camera, and the Global Positioning System (GPS). For instance, in the first year, Niantic published that the *Pokémon GO*'s players had walked 8.7 billion kilometres during the lifespan of the game, which accounts to more than 200.000 trips around the earth. In this case, if people shift their physical mobility from walking to flying in a commercial jetliner, it could take more than a thousand years to complete that (Weber 2016).

The game content follows the universe established by the game series developed in 1996 for Nintendo's Game Boy, a portable and mobile game console. Considering issues regarding mobility, *Pokémon GO*'s gameplay seems quite controversial when compared to the first generation of Pokémon games. Let's consider the case of challenging other players to a Pokémon battle. In this situation, in order to battle on the classic Pokémon game for Game Boy, the players had to meet physically to be able to connect the devices through a kind of cable called Game Link. On the other hand, in order to battle on *Pokémon GO*, i.e., raid or Gym battle, the players have to walk to specific locations in the geographical space labelled as Gymnasium (Gym) on the user's interface.

Since 2016, *Pokémon GO* has been appearing as the topic in some research papers, but actually anyone discussing the new mobilities paradigm could be interested in this locative game (see Sicart 2016; Hjorth & Richardson 2017; Colley et al. 2017; Luksac-Roesche 2017; Wong 2017; Licoppe 2017; Hung 2017; Henthorn et al. 2019). De Souza e Silva (2016) provides perhaps the closest study in mobility matters focusing on *Pokémon GO*. It was published in a special issue of the journal *Mobile Media & Communication*, which is a compilation of a set of short papers discussing *Pokémon GO*.

According to De Souza e Silva, *Pokémon GO* is an example of how locative games can encourage players' mobility through the city, which increases the potential to connect with other nearby players and causes people to experience urban spaces as hybrid spaces by overlapping physical and digital environments. She understands that, while the current version of *Pokémon GO* does lack a few of these characteristics, especially the sociability component, it surpassed all previous locative games in popularity and number of players, as the case of the famous geocaching and *Ingress*, another Niantic locative game.

However, De Souza e Silva does not present any data regarding issues connecting the new mobilities paradigm and the experience available on *Pokémon GO*. This way, we can address some questions such as: How can the levels of mobility, a core feature of the new mobilities paradigm, overlap in a *Pokémon GO* game session? Is this game more Pokémon than go?

This chapter aims to discuss locative games, particularly *Pokémon GO*, through the lens of the new mobilities paradigm. My hypothesis holds that *Pokémon GO* deals with the new mobilities paradigm by stimulating three levels of mobility (physical, informational, and imaginary) in the gameplay. Unlike previous locative games, *Pokémon GO* provides a special kind of imaginary mobility that can connect its gameplay to the universe provided by Nintendo and Pokémon Co. in the 1990s. Thus, the main fascinating feature on *Pokémon GO* could be a connection provided by imaginary mobility to the classic game, not the informational or physical mobility inherent to locative gaming. My choice then was to describe some data I have collected in *Pokémon GO* game sessions during the fall of 2018, which took place in the Copacabana neighborhood in Rio de Janeiro, Brazil.

As my research method, I use a mixed-method based on actor-network theory (ANT) and the methodological approach on computer games coined by Aarseth (2003), a reference in game studies. Aarseth proposes that 'playing the game' is the best way to understand the design, rules, and mechanics of the game, insofar as these are available to the player. The actor-network theory (ANT) in turn rises in the early 1980s as a subset of the social theory to describe its approaches to studies in scientific and technical innovation (Law 2007). Ultimately, the actor-network theory does not celebrate the idea that there is a difference between people on one hand and objects on the other; it refutes the idea that people are necessarily special. In this perspective, ANT focuses on the associations (agencies) between humans and non-humans (devices, rules, laws, machines, subsets, objects, and so on).

However, some scholars hold that the actor-network theory is, differently from what the name suggests, more a method than a theory (Fragoso 2017). A method is not a more or less successful set of procedures for reporting on a given reality; it helps produce realities (Law 2004). Thus, ANT could be useful as an attempt not only to report the reality enacted by locative games, but it could also be important to craft and understand the reality provided by *Pokémon GO* and the new mobilities paradigm.

To support the researcher in this work, the actor-network theory provides a specific compilation of terminologies that sets forth a proper kind of vocabulary. The first expression is actant, which through ANT's lens can be human or nonhuman and refers to anyone or anything that enables or causes others to act. The second term is mediator, used to describe the actant's role in the network; it is an entity that does things and makes others do things as well; with mediators, the incoming information is different from the outgoing. On the other hand, there are intermediaries, who convey meaning without transformation: defining inputs is enough to define outputs; they can be anything that circulates between actors and what helps define the relations between them as well (Latour 2005; Lemos 2013).

These relations – or agencies, according to ANT-related vocabulary – could be described in three different ways. The first one is translation, which consists in the process operated by mediators to transform and send the information to another actant. The second is delegation, which occurs when a mediator transfers the agency from another network to make an actant do something. The third kind of agency is inscription, which consists in the process where a designer embeds a special way the user must interact with the designed object, based on a script that was previously created, as is the case of laws, maps, codes, rules, and so on.

Network is another expression in the ANT's vocabulary that sounds different from the sense we commonly see in cyberculture studies: networks are understood as associations with varying degrees of stability, connected to other local actor-network nodes (Callon 1991). Bonner (2016) argues that this is where the hyphen between actor and network is critical: it does not hold actors and networks apart; rather, it stresses the interrelationship between the terms as defining each other in action.

The idea of controversy plays an important role in a description using actor-network theory. To ANT scholar Venturini (2010), controversies are situations in which actors disagree – or agree on their disagreement, to use Venturini's expression. Controversies begin when actors discover that they cannot ignore each other, and they end when actors manage to work out a solid compromise to live together. Venturini reinforces that the task is just to look at controversies and tell what you see; it is nothing more than observing and describing. Lemos (2013) goes even further and argues that a controversy makes the perfect situation to reveal agencies, mediators, and the formation of intermediaries and the relationships of power.

So the mixed-method used in this research consists basically in 'playing' *Pokémon GO*, following Aartseth's thoughts, as a way to understand the network, mediators, and agencies created by this locative game, and trying to understand the role of mobility and how the application of this method crafts a kind of reality. Basically, this is an alternative methodology approach for locative game research I have proposed in a previous work (Andrade 2018).

This chapter is structured in three sections. First, I present the idea of the new mobilities paradigm by splitting it into three levels of mobility to contrast some perceptions about movement and mobility in game studies. Second, I argue about the issue of space in games, focusing on a relationship called code/space as an attempt to discuss how locative gaming and the mobilities it provides can promote shifts in space. Finally, I present some data I have collected during the game sessions in the Copacabana neighborhood during the fall of 2018.

New mobilities and games

Since more than a decade ago, a new approach to the study of mobilities has been emerging across the social sciences involving research on the combined movements of people, objects, and information in all of their complex relational dynamics, which was called by Mimi Sheller and John Urry the new mobilities paradigm (Sheller & Urry 2006). According to Urry (2007), contemporary societies are organized around the movement of people, ideas, information, and objects rather than a static set of relations, structures, and institutions. In the same way, Mimi Sheller argues that

> Unlike the rich tradition of sociological study of social mobility, the new transdisciplinary field of mobilities research encompasses research on the spatial mobilities of humans, non-humans, and objects; the circulation of information, images, and capital, as well as the study of the physical means for movement such as infrastructures, vehicles, and software systems that enables travel and communication to take place.
>
> (Sheller 2014, p. 791)

At the same time, some scholars published approaches regarding these new features of the mobilities matters. Jansson (2005) presents the phenomenon called 'the spatial turn in media studies', which gave birth to the research field called 'Geography of Communication' (Jansson & Falkheimer 2006). Alongside a broad discussion that applies notions from Geography studies such as place and space to the communication process, Jansson points out three categories that summarize a range of spatial ambiguities: (1) mobility, (2) convergence, and (3) interactivity. Jansson understands that mobility can manifest itself as two related phenomena: mobility of people and mobility of media technologies. The saturation of media texts in everyday life, Jansson says, implies that a large share of them is consumed on the move.

Kellerman (2006) presents the terminology 'personal mobilities' as an attempt to put together corporeal self-moving such as walking, other physical mobilities extended by procedures such as the case of driving or riding a bicycle, and virtual mobilities through mobile telephones and the Internet. The Brazilian theorist Lemos addresses Kellerman's thoughts theoretically to coin what he called 'the culture of mobility'. In such work, Lemos (2009) divides the concept of mobility into three levels: 'physical/spatial', related to transport of body and things physically over the space; 'virtual/informational', which refers to spread of media and information by means of communication; and 'cognitive/imaginary' that labels the 'mental movement' provided by imagination, thoughts, dreams, and so forth.

It is possible to notice these kinds of mobility in *Pokémon GO*'s gameplay as an attempt to understand how each level can overlap the other. The physical dimension refers to the mobility of the player over the space; the informational level of mobility consists of the communication between the game app and the game servers on the Internet; the imaginary mobility appears in many ways, i.e., when the players elaborate their strategy on the game session or relate the content of *Pokémon GO* to the first generation of *Pokémon* for Nintendo's Game Boy.

The idea of motion, movement, and mobility appeared for the first time in game studies in the seminal work of Aarseth (1997) on cibertext and ergodic literature. To Aarseth, the concept of cibertext focuses on the mechanic organization of the text, which requires a physical effort to allow the user to transverse it. He calls this process of production of meaning ergodic literature, a term he borrowed from physics that derives from the Greek words *ergon* and *hodos*, which mean work and path, respectively. Aarseth provides some useful examples of ergodic literature considering texts from analogical supports, such as paper and coins as the case of *I-Ching* (the Chinese text of oracular wisdom), to digital media and hypermedia such as computer games.

Aarseth, Salen, and Zimmerman (2003) point out that playing is always a free movement, which is the power for mobility with more rigid structure. Walz (2010) goes even further and provides the concept of *kinesis*, also derived from the Greek, which means movement and motion connected to the ludic phenomenon.

> Kinesis refers to all movements, physical or virtual, that a player enacts to relate to a play-other, i.e., another player, a play object, or a play space. Without a play-other, there is no kinesis, and without kinesis, there is no play relationship. At its core, kinesis is a spatial activity because all play-movements imply space. And as opposed to a mere movement is an attempt to relate to someone or something else. Kinesis, thus comprises, for example, pointing, flicking, grabbing, holding, clicking, dragging, pulling, pushing, punching, constructing, manoeuvring, walking, running, jumping, stretching, sneaking, ducking, climbing, rotating, aiming, kicking, hitting, combating, assisting, and cooperating, as well as more verbal movements such as trading, bidding, bluffing, negotiating, and, always, imagining.
>
> (Walz 2010, p. 24)

Based on premises regarding the relationship between mobility and movement, such as 'an act of displacement that allows objects, people, ideas – things – to get between locations' (Cresswell 2004), 'human ability to move oneself in the sense of daily physical spatial mobility', or merely 'the movement is the power for mobility' (Andrade 2015), it is possible to realize that mobility relates to the idea of kinesis; in the same way, the list presented by Walz points out examples that corroborates the three types of mobilities provided by Lemos, as the case of imagining (cognitive/imaginary), walking, running, climbing (physical/spatial), and verbal movements (virtual/informational) mediated by information and communication technologies (ICT). Alongside issues on mobilities and movement, it is important to highlight that the idea of kinesis points to spatial matters as well. In the next section, I discuss the role of space in locative games, presenting some examples regarding locative gaming in Brazil.

Space and games

The idea of space has a broader meaning, and it can be used in many ways. For instance, some scholars often use the sense of geographic space to consider location matters; this notion takes the forefront in the communication process related to the ubiquitous computing technologies and in other proposals, as is the case of the aforementioned proposal of the 'spatial turn in media studies'.

On the other hand, the meaning of space sometimes is associated by scholars to practice, simulation, and representation, highlighting the concept of social space, provided by the Lefebvrian spatial triad 'perceived-conceived-lived spaces' (Lefebvre 1991) or the issue of the reassertion of space in social theory (Soja 1989). Thus, both comprehensions of space appear in locative gaming, as well as the support for players' interaction and mobilities (geographic space) or the product of these agencies (social space).

In game studies, Aarseth (2000) considers the space as an important issue for computer game analysis; he argues that games are essentially concerned with spatial representation and negotiation, and therefore a classification for them can be based on how they represent – or, perhaps, implement – space. To Flanagan (2009), locative games offer an ambiguous ambient game experience because the players explore both participation and space, particularly the space of the city, by combining physical and technological play. According to Leorke (2019), these games transform everyday locales and sites in spaces for play; in the process, they encourage players to explore new places.

Using this idea of space as a parameter to understand computer games, it is possible to oppose the locative game genre to the video game genre; while on video games the geographical space is a residual component with less importance in the interaction process, the space in locative gaming has a central role in the gameplay because it creates the support for players' mobility during the game session (Andrade 2016).

The platform for locative gaming is connected to the ubiquitous computing paradigm proposed in the early 1990s by Weiser (1995). It highlights a way to spread computer systems and networks over the urban space, settling pervasive microchips into everyday objects and environments that become connected by wireless networks. The ubiquitous computing paradigm gave birth to two important digital technologies that are currently available: wearable computers, which are developed to be used like headsets, glasses, watches, wristbands, and so on (Mann 1997; Randell 2005); locative media, which refers to the use and appropriation of location-based technologies, as the case of the GPS, wireless networks, smartphones, tablets etc.; and location-based services, such as maps, geotags, augmented-reality browsers, social networks that add geospatial information to the users messages, e.g., Facebook, Twitter, Foursquare, and so forth (Lemos 2010; Farman 2012).

The platform for *Pokémon GO* incorporates more than one ubiquitous computing technology: smartphones, which could be labeled as 'locative media' because they work according to the position of antennas; the game app, a location-based service that uses geotags, maps, among other resources in the gameplay settings; wrist devices, as the case of wristbands or watches that are conceived as wearable computers, because they are machines that users wear like clothing; wireless networks, also a kind of locative media, which connects the wearable computers to smartphones, and the game app on the Internet.

Pokémon GO's user interface basically presents a map supported by Google Maps's database and an avatar that shows the player's position. Then the player has to walk over the urban space, reaching geotags labeled Pokéstops and Gyms; while he or she is searching for these locations, some Pokémon will appear according to weather conditions and location, and the player has to capture them using a play object called Pokéball.

The game app for smartphones supports these agencies and others on *Pokémon GO*. However, the player can use a wearable computer in connection to the locative media, such as the *Pokémon GO* Plus and Go-tcha wristbands, or the Apple Watch. These devices simplify the execution of at least three interactions: hatching the eggs, a way to get a new Pokémon; spinning the icon available in a Pokéstop to get game items; notifying the player about nearby Pokémon and Pokéstop. The Go-tcha wristband goes even further: it automatically captures nearby Pokémon and spins nearby Pokéstop icons. It creates a kind of distributed platform introduced by *Pokémon GO* in locative gaming (Andrade 2019).

Thus, it is possible to notice that the use of wristbands and watches alongside smartphones can refashion the idea of the locative gaming platform due to these devices' support of the *Pokémon GO* game app. In this way, the game content goes from the mobile phone to the wearable device, which shows a flow of informational mobility provided by this kind of agency among ubiquitous computing technologies, that is, it converges physical and informational mobilities.

This feature on the *Pokémon GO* app corroborates a new kind of connection between space and software supported by the concept of code/space (Kitchin & Dodge 2011). It suggests that software alternatively modulates how space comes into being through a process of transduction, i.e., the constant making of a new domain in reiterative and transformative practices. Thus, code/space takes place when software and the spatiality of everyday life become mutually constituted; the spatiality is then the product of code, and the code exists primarily in order to produce a particular spatiality, i.e., a dyadic relationship exists between code and spatiality.

In a broader sense, the concept of code/space refers to the impact of the software on the space and its consequences to everyday life. Kitchin and Dodge mention the check-in area in airports as an example of code/space.

> If the software crashes, the area reverts from a space in which to check in to a fairly chaotic waiting room. There is no other way of checking a person onto a flight because manual procedures have been phased out due to security concerns, so the production of space is dependent on code.
>
> (Kitchin & Dodge 2011, p. 17)

Likewise, the example of the check-in area in airports, there is interesting occurrence of code/space in the case of Uber, a service of peer-to-peer ridesharing. It is an Internet application that connects vehicles and people (drivers and users), who are driving through the same route in the city. Then users can book a ride to any location by using an app for the mobile operating system. The first city were Uber became available in Brazil was Rio de Janeiro in 2014, a couple of days before the kick-off of the FIFA World Cup. In 2018, there were more than 500,000 drivers and more than 20 million users in Brazil (Darlington & Londoño 2017). As the case of the airport check-in area, if the Uber software crashes, the streets will become busy with cars, and it may culminate in a chaotic traffic incident that will affect everyday life and mobility.

In the same way, *Pokémon GO* presents a useful example of code/space in the Community Day; it is a monthly regular event in the game that seeks to encourage the players to play together everywhere. For just a few hours in previously defined location, the players have to meet and capture a special Pokémon. On April 15, 2018, there was a *Pokémon GO* Community Day that encouraged players to catch a Pokémon called Mareep. In Rio, some players used a Facebook group to meet and drive to outside areas such as the Copacabana neighborhood. A couple dozen players went to the location on April 15, 2018 to capture said Pokémon.

In this situation, the *Pokémon GO* app uses the informational mobility, i.e., the game content on the user's interface, to improve the players' physical mobility on the urban space, which causes some places to be crowded and noisy. However, if the software crashes, the consequence is quite different from the examples of the check-in area in airports and the Uber app. If *Pokémon GO*'s software crashes, the players will go home; in order to promote shifts in the space using physical and informational mobilities, this application has to continue working and not crash as with the check-in system or Uber application.

Considering the example of the check-in area provided by Kitchin and Dodge alongside the case of Uber and Pokémon, we can realize that they highlight different situations of how mobile media (smartphones and the application) can shift the space in everyday life. In the next section, I will present some data I have collected during the game session in Copacabana, which provides some insights regarding the role of mobility, space, and media in *Pokémon GO*.

Playing *Pokémon GO* in the Copacabana neighborhood: a list of mediators and agencies

As mentioned in the beginning of this chapter, there was a controversy at the starting point of descriptions using the actor-network theory, in this case, one regarding the reality enacted by the game sessions I played in Copacabana during the fall of 2018. Looking back to 1996, it is possible to realize a controversy in mobility matters between the gameplay of Game Boy's classic Pokémon game and *Pokémon GO*. Ultimately, both are designed for mobile devices – respectively Nintendo's Game Boy and smartphones. However, Game Boy improves informational mobility more than physical mobility because it forces players to stay static on the space while they are battling with another player. In this case, two players have to connect the mobile platform using a cable to start battling with their Pokémon.

As for *Pokémon GO*, physical mobility is a mandatory feature to the extent that the players have to drive themselves to the location pointed out by a Gym on the user's interface as a way to join battles. Unlike the classic Game Boy game, the player in *Pokémon GO* can do everything while they are performing physical mobility around the city. Controversially, both games were designed for mobile devices (Game Boy and smartphones), but the gameplay of *Pokémon GO* improves the physical mobility of the players and the platform alongside the informational mobility on the game app, while in the classic Pokémon game, the gameplay forces the players to stay physically static.

The notion of game mechanics could be useful in this discussion. In game studies, the concept of mechanics consists of everything that determines interactions between the game and its players; mechanics are methods invoked by agents, designed for interaction with the game state (Sicart 2008; Jørgensen 2013).

Walking could be considered the core game mechanic on *Pokémon GO*, because first of all the player should walk before performing agencies such as catching Pokémon, hatching eggs, or reaching Gyms and Pokéstops. Of course, this condition can shift in some sense. For instance, players can interact in Gyms or Pokéstops while sitting in a chair at home or while they are drinking something at a pub, but previously the players had to walk to reach these locations in the urban space. Another game mechanic performed on *Pokémon GO* is the 'first person perspective', which players often perform in battles or in an attempt to catch a Pokémon. Therefore, it is possible to realize that game mechanics of *Pokémon GO* such as walking and first-person perspective can update the sense of the ergodic activity seen by Aarseth in computer games in late 1990s.

Thus, game mechanics could be related to the players' physical mobility like running or walking and some mental efforts required from the player by the rules of the game as an attempt to solve puzzles in a ludic environment. In the same way, the game will imply several informational mobilities performed on the app, i.e., throwing Pokéballs, sending gifts to other players, walking to find Pokémon or to reach a Pokéstop, and so on.

This understanding of game mechanics can corroborate the concept of kinesis and the new mobilities paradigm because it refers to mental efforts such as imagining and all physical or informational mobilities that the player performs as an attempt to relate to another player, a play object, or the play space.

There is another interesting cognitive/imaginary mobility that links *Pokémon GO* and the Pokémon for Nintendo's Game Boy released more than 20 years ago, which will create a profitable relationship between the locative game, the player, and the universe provided by the classic game. The fans of the first generation of Pokémon could be attracted to *Pokémon GO* due to imaginary mobility. Perhaps it will encourage some players to download and join *Pokémon GO* to explore the city in search of Pokémon, Gyms, and Pokéstops.

In Pokéstops and gyms, the player can spin a tile to obtain some play objects such as Pokéball, fruits, and potions that could be used to restore the energy of a Pokémon. Specifically at the Pokéstop, the player can use an in-game tool called a lure module to attract more Pokémon to that location, and consequently other players. In this situation, by the agency of translation, the player becomes a human mediator that shifts the focus of the network to himself or herself. Consequently, their name appears on top of the Pokéstop during the lure module's effect.

In a Gym, the player can engage in battles that take place in two ways: (1) one or more players against up to six Pokémon placed in the same Gym; (2) from 1 to 20 players against a special Pokémon, stronger than the others, called raid battle. There is both physical and informational mobility in all these situations because the player has to use the game app to perform these interactions when they arrive physically at the location of Gyms or Pokéstops.

Based on the actor-network theory, it is possible to point out a couple of mediators and agencies that will help us toward a comprehension of the new mobilities paradigm in locative gaming. At first glance, the game app of *Pokémon GO* appears as the mediator that transforms by inscription the game's code into the content the player interacts with on the user's interface. Another mediator is the smartphone that transforms and sends this information by translation to the wrist devices, such as the watch or the wristbands. In the same way, the wrist device appears also as a mediator because it makes some actions easier and faster such as hatching the eggs or catching Pokémon, which modifies how the game session works. The agency here is delegation, since one device sends information to the other as a way to make each object operate in the game. In these movements as a whole, the wireless network plays the role of the intermediary that connects both devices (by Bluetooth) and the game app to the Internet (by Wi-Fi or 3G/4G).

Supported by the concept of code/space and an agency of translation, the game app is the mediator that modifies the space in which the game session of *Pokémon GO* takes place by attracting players to join battles or catch Pokémon. Other mediators in this *Pokémon GO* network are the game rules, which make the players do things that are the aforementioned game mechanics. Thus, the rules delegate some procedures to the players, modifying their action and consequently shifting the space. So we have another situation where the informational mobility provided by the game rules can modify the players' physical mobility. It is important to highlight that the game app is an actant; it is connected to other background networks, like the Google Maps database and *Ingress*, another locative game developed by Niantic, which provides the locations for Pokéstop and Gyms on *Pokémon GO*.

The urban space is another nonhuman mediator that can promote several impacts to the players' physical mobility because it provides streets, hills, buildings, everyday objects, and other spaces crowded with people, which can modify how the game session works. Depending on the features of an urban space where people are playing *Pokémon GO*, the game session could be easy or hard, because actually the space is the mediator that supports players' interaction and mobility. For instance, the Copacabana neighborhood provides a crowded space with people and vehicles alongside hills, favelas, level streets, and beaches.

Pokémon GO could reveal situations in which informational mobility overlaps physical mobility and vice versa, which were in our game sessions in Copacabana. For example, the perimeter of almost 20 squares between Nossa Senhora de Copacabana Avenue and the beach presents several Pokéstops and Gyms. In this way, the player can walk or use a bike to reach these geotagged locations. However, there is a complicated situation regarding public safety in Rio, and sometimes it could be risky handling a smartphone in Copacabana, especially at night. Thus, some players prefer to set small groups of five people and ride a car through these locations to spin the Pokéstop icon or to join a raid battle with the group at the Gym.

Sometimes, the player could take a prohibited action on *Pokémon GO* called GPS spoofing as an attempt to break the game rules and reach far locations over the geographical space without walking. GPS spoofing or using a fake GPS is a kind of procedure that allows users to cheat their position on the geographic space to reach locations anywhere. The procedure, which is informational mobility, happens by downloading a fake GPS app and connecting it to *Pokémon GO* using the mobile operating system. One of the most famous and iconic instances of GPS spoofing on *Pokémon GO* is related to an episode in mid-2016, in which some players from China took control of a Gym in Japan settled at the Yasukuni Shrine, and dropped a high-level Pokémon there nicknamed 'Long Live China' (Custer 2016).

In Rio, players sometimes use the GPS spoofing as a way to safely reach some distant Pokéstop. However, the players from Rio de Janeiro do not often reach locations by using fake GPS outside the city boundaries, as the case of the Chinese players. They usually prefer to play using the fake GPS close to their real location, perhaps as an attempt to stay connected to *Pokémon GO* servers in Brazil and avoid some risk of being banished from the game due to this illegal procedure.

The procedure using GPS spoofing apps can be considered a nonhuman mediator that modifies the game session by providing fake locations for the players. So there is an inscription agency between two mediators: the *Pokémon GO* app and the fake GPS software. This inscription allows the game to work according to the script on the GPS spoofing app and provides a kind of 'informational mobility' of the players that overlaps their physical mobility. Also, there is an intermediary at play here: the mobile operating system.

Final thoughts

At the end of this chapter, it is possible to support that *Pokémon GO* has a connection to the Pokémon universe established in the 1990s, which is provided by the concept of imaginary mobility. Considering the controversy between a more static and intimately connected interaction (*Pokémon* for Game Boy) and a mobile and remotely-connected interaction (*Pokémon GO*), obviously we can realize first of all that the second one improves the physical mobility of players more than the classic game. Also, there is informational mobility in the communication process between the game server and the platform used to play, including, in addition to the Game Boy or the smartphone, watches and wristbands. However, the imaginary mobility can link the experience available on *Pokémon GO* to the classic Pokémon game even in the case of two games created almost twenty years apart. In this way, we can answer the question asked in the chapter's title: Is it more 'Pokémon' than 'go'?

Acknowledgments

To Professor Espen Aarseth and other researchers from the Center for Computer Games Research for hosting part of this work during my position at IT-University of Copenhagen, Denmark; to the Coordination for the Improvement of Higher Education Personnel (CAPES/Brazil) and the State University of Bahia (UNEB/Brazil) for the financial support.

This work was supported by CAPES Postdoctoral Scholarship, process number 88881.119487/2016-01.

References

Aarseth, E. J. 1997. *Cybertext: Perspectives on ergodic literature*. Baltimore, MD: J. Hopkins.

Aarseth, E. J. 2000. Allegories of space: The question of spatiality in computer games. In Eskelinen, M. & Koskimaa, R. eds. *Cybertext yearbook 2000*. University of Jyväskylä. Available at: www.hf.uib.no/hi/espen/papers/space/

Aarseth, E. J. 2003. Playing research: Methodological approaches to game analysis. *Spilforskning conference*. Available at: www.bendevane.com/VTA2012/herrstubbz/wpcontent/uploads/2012/01/02.GameApproaches2.pdf

Andrade, L. A. 2015. *Jogos digitais, cidade e (trans)mídia: A próxima fase*. Curitiba: Appris.

Andrade, L. A. 2016. *Jogos locativos (locative games)*. Salvador: EdUFBA.

Andrade, L. A. 2018. Research method for locative games. *MedieKultur: Journal of Media and Communication Research*, 34(64), pp. 52–70. http://dx.doi.org/10.7146/mediekultur.v34i64.96926

Andrade, L. A. 2019. A tale of two screens: Space, ubiquitous computing and locative gaming. In Henthorn, J., Kulak, A., Purzycki, K. & Vie, S. eds. *The Pokémon GO Phenomenon: Essays in public play in contested spaces*. Jefferson, NC: McFarland.

Bonner, W. B. 2016. History and is – Broadening our view and understanding: Actor-network theory as a methodology. In Willcocks, L. P., Sauer, C. & Lacity, M. C. eds. *Enacting research methods in information systems*. London: Palgrave Macmillan, Cham.

Callon, M. 1991. Techno-economic networks and irreversibility. In Law, J. ed. *A sociology of monsters: Essays on power, technology and domination*. London: Routledge.

Code Runner [Locative Game.] 2011. Vancouver, Canada: Rocket Chicken.

Colley, A., Thebaut-Spieker, J. & Lin, A. 2017. *The geography of Pokémon GO: Beneficial and problematic effects on places and movement*. Available at: www.brenthecht.com/publications/chi17_geographyofpokemongo.pdf

Cresswell, T. 2004. *Place: A short introduction*. London: Blackwell.

Custer, C. July 24, 2016. *Why Chinese gamers are 'ruining'. Pokémon GO in Japan*. Available at: www.techinasia.com/chinese-gamers-ruining-pokemon-japan [Accessed on January 2, 2019].

Darlington, S. & Londoño, E. November 5, 2017. *Brazil becomes Uber's latest regulatory battleground*. Available at: www.nytimes.com/2017/11/05/world/americas/uber-brazil-regulation.html [Accessed on January 2, 2019].

De Souza e Silva, A. 2016. *Pokémon GO* as an HRG: Mobility, sociability, and surveillance Hybrid spaces. *Mobile Media & Communication*, 5(1), pp. 20–23. doi:10.1177/2050157916676232

Farman, J. 2012. *Mobile interface theory: Embodied space and locative media*. Boston: Routledge.

Flanagan, M. 2009. *Critical play: Radical game design*. Cambridge and London: MIT Press.

Fragoso, S. 2017. Os modos de existência do gameplay: Um exercício de aplicação com cities: Skylines. *XXVI Encontro da Compós*. São Paulo. Available at: www.lume.ufrgs.br/handle/10183/166205

Henthorn, J., Kulak, A., Purzycki, K. & Vie, S. 2019. *The Pokémon GO Phenomenon: Essays in public play in contested spaces*. Jefferson, NC: McFarland.

Hjorth, L. & Richardson, I. 2017. *Pokémon GO*: Mobile media play, place-making, and the digital wayfarer. *Mobile Media & Communication*, 5(1), pp. 3–14. https://doi.org/10.1177/2050157916680015

Hung, A. 2017. Beyond the player: A user-centered approach to analyzing digital games and players using actor-network theory. *E-Learning and Digital Media*, 13(5–6), pp. 227–243.

Ingress [Locative Game.] 2012. San Francisco, CA: NianticLabs, Inc.

Jansson, A. 2005. *For a geography of communication*. Paper från ACSIS nationella forskarkonferens för kulturstudier, pp. 13–15. Available at: www.ep.liu.se/ecp/015/040/ecp015040b.pdf

Jansson, A. & Falkheimer, J. 2006. *Geographies of communication: The spatial turn in media studies*. Götenburg: Nordicom.

Jørgensen, K. 2013. *Gameworld interfaces*. Boston: MIT Press.

Kellerman, A. 2006. *Personal mobilities*. London: Routledge.

Kitchin, R. & Dodge, M. 2011 *Code/Space: Software and everyday life*. Cambridge/London: The MIT Press.

Latour, B. 2005. *Reassembling the social: An introduction to actor-network theory*. Oxford: Oxford University Press.

Law, J. (2007). Actor network theory and material semiotics. Available at: http://www.heterogeneities.net/publications/Law2007ANTandMaterialSemiotics.pdf.

———. 2004. *After methods: Mess in social science research.* New York: Routledge.

Lefebvre, H. 1991. *The production of space*. London: Blackwell.

Lemos, A. 2009. Cultura da Mobilidade. *Revista Famecos*, 16(40), p. 28. doi:10.15448/1980-3729.2009.40.6314

Lemos, A. 2010. Locative media and surveillance at the boundaries of informational territories. In Firmino, R., Duarte, F. & Ultramari, C. eds. *ICTs for mobile and ubiquitous urban infrastructures: Surveillance, locative media and global networks*. Hershey: IGI Global.

Lemos, A. 2013. *A comunicação das coisas: teoria ator-rede e cibercultura*. São Paulo: Annablume.

Leorke, D. 2019. *Location-based gaming: Play in public space*. Singapore: Palgrave Macmillan.

Licoppe, C. 2017. From Mogi to Pokemon Go: Continuities and change in location aware – Collection games. *Mobile Media & Communication*, 5(1), pp. 24–29.

Luksac-Roesche, M. 2017. *Towards an understanding of the effects of augmented reality games in disaster management*. Available at: https://arxiv.org/abs/1702.06610

Mann, S. 1997. Wearable computing: A first step toward personal imaging. *Computer*, 30(2), pp. 25–32. doi:10.1109/2.566147

Pokémon GO! [Locative Game.] 2016. San Francisco, CA: NianticLabs, Inc.

Randell, C. 2005. *Wearable computing: A review*. Available at: http://citeseerx.ist.psu.edu/viewdoc/summary?doi = 10.1.1.60.7898 doi:10.1.1.60.7898 [Accessed on January 19, 2018].

Salen, K. & Zimmerman, E. 2003. *Rules of play*. Cambridge, MA: MIT Press.

Sheller, M. 2014. The new mobilities paradigm for a live sociology. *Current Sociology*, 62(6), pp. 789–811. doi:10.1177/0011392114533211

Sheller, M. & Urry, J. 2006. The new mobilities paradigm. *Environment and Planning*, 38, pp. 207–226. doi:10.1068/a37268

Sicart, M. 2008. Defining game mechanics. *Game Studies: The International Journal of Computer Game Research*, 8(2). Available at: http://gamestudies.org/0802/articles/sicart

Sicart, M. 2016. Reality has always been augmented: Play and the promises of *Pokémon GO. Mobile Media & Communication*, 5(1), pp. 30–33. https://doi.org/10.1177/2050157916677863

Soja, E. 1989. *Postmodern geographies: The reassertion of space in critical social theory*. London and New York: Verso.

Urry, J. 2007. *Mobilities*. Cambridge, UK: Polity Press.

Venturini, T. 2010. Diving in magma: How to explore controversies with actor-network theory. *Public Understanding of Science*, 19(3), pp. 258–273. Available at: http://pus.sagepub.com/content/19/3/258

Walz, S. P. 2010. *Toward a Ludic architecture: Framing the space of play and games*. Halifax, Canada: ETC Press.

Weber, S. December 21, 2016. Niantic reveals that *Pokémon GO* Players Have Walked a Far Enough to Pass Pluto. Available at: www.dailydot.com/parsec/pokemon-go-walking-stats/ [Accessed on January 2, 2019].

Weiser, M. 1995. The computer for the 21st century. *Readings in Human – Computer Interaction*, pp. 933–940. doi:10.1016/b978-0-08-051574-8.50097-2.

Wong, F. 2017. Influence of *Pokémon GO* on physical activity levels of university players: A cross-sectional study. *International Journal of Health Geographics*, 16(8). Available at: www.ncbi.nlm.nih.gov/pmc/articles/PMC5322678/

Chapter 10

Advertising discourse from the perspective of the new mobilities paradigm

Maria Alice de Faria Nogueira

Introduction

According to André Lemos (2009), the culture of mobility intertwines technological, social, and anthropological issues. In the case of communication, mobility is a central issue, since communicating is to put into circulation messages and information with all media ecology, such as devices, environments, and processes operating as strategies for displacing signs in a movement that affects our relationship with time and space (Lemos 2009, p. 28). In this sense, we cannot dissociate communication, mobility, space, and place, since when information is moved, communication produces meaning, subjectivity, and spatialization. Based on the perspective that communication is also mobility, this chapter deals specifically with the link between mobility and brand strategies from the perspective of the new mobilities paradigm, or NMP (Sheller & Urry 2006).

With special focus on brands' advertising discourse, this chapter aims to demonstrate how advertising has been appropriating the contemporary compulsion to mobility in order to promote new products and services by selling mobilities – social, symbolic, potential, and imaginative – as one of the most important features offered by goods. The basis of the theory of "consumption of (im)mobilities" that is used here as a contribution to think about the articulation between advertising and mobility in Brazil has been more deeply addressed in my PhD dissertation research (Nogueira 2015), and part of its results was published in the article "Consumption of (im)mobilities and discourse: mobility culture in the advertising of brands" (Nogueira 2016).

Nevertheless, it is worth pointing out that the concept of consumption of (im) mobilities was established based upon two fundamental premises that have given global advertising considerable prominence as an issue that must be studied for a better understanding of the mobility of cultural symbols and flows:

- first, that things in the world reach individuals regardless of their immobility, by means of objects, information, and images that circulate globally;

When focusing on how to reach the broadest audience, global brands plan their marketing strategies to put into circulation a realm of goods that need to be promoted in order to be sold. In this sense, advertising can be seen as a fundamental part of one of the five "interdependent mobilities" defined by Urry (2007, p. 47): the physical movement of objects. However, when we consider advertising communication as a marketing activity, it is possible to claim that, generally speaking, marketing strategies of global brands can also be seen as a point of intersection of various systems of mobility: from physical movement of objects to imaginative mobility of signs, all the way through the actual communicative travel of messages and the corporeal displacement of consumers (Nogueira 2015).

- secondly, that regardless of its commercial, persuasive, and selling character, advertising can also be understood as a cultural good that expresses the culture to which it belongs.

As has already been stated by a constellation of sociology and/or anthropology[1] authors, each one from their own perspective and context, consumption is a social activity that founds our entire cultural system, a new mythology of which the objects are a fundamental part, through which it is possible to understand how life is organized and represented in so many levels and different ways. For this reason, the discourse of advertising, seen here as an activity that enhances the visibility of consumption, can be understood as a product of the culture in which it is embedded, i.e., the culture of mobility that is characteristic of the mobile risk society (Kesselring 2008). This notion is based upon the assumption that advertising operates as "a transfer area" (McCracken 2003), as a "symbolic place" between the production and the consumption dimensions (Rocha 1985), within which objects become commodities after being symbolically embedded with cultural principles and social values through discourse.

The articulation of these two premises represents what Baudrillard (1970) claims to be the purpose of contemporary consumption: the motivations and consumption practices are translated into a life project that is ideally updated or resignified in the objects. Since mobility is regarded as a fundamental condition of the everyday life experience within the mobile risk society, the consumption of the (im)mobilities concept highlights Urry's idea that all objects, or "stuff" as Miller has stated (2014), are part of a network of interdependent mobility-systems by means of which they can move or block, resist or afford individuals' (compulsion for) movement, currently elevated as a life project: to be or not to be mobile.

In an effort to show how advertising discourse embodies the compulsion for movement, the objects of analysis presented in this chapter are printed advertisements released in Brazil on the occasion of the 2014 FIFA World Cup. The ads were published in a local weekly magazine called *Revista Veja* (*Veja* Magazine), whose circulation at the time was approximately 1 million copies per week. That period of time was chosen mainly because mega-events are one of the occasions when marketing and advertising of global brands potentializes the mobility of things, people, images, and information. According to Roche (2000), planned mega-events act as socio-spatial-temporal hubs that change and reorganize the global flows of people, because they not only produce intense moments of copresence, since they have the appeal to be seen "live", but they also generate robust global flows of goods, information, and images. Although Brazil had the opportunity to host a series of significant events throughout the last decade, the 2014 FIFA World Cup, alongside the 2013 FIFA Confederations Cup, was the one that had the largest commercial appeal to both global and local brands, since it was a nationwide event.

Mobility, motility, consumption

In today's world, mobility appears as a base, even if fluid at times, of new social dynamics, which together form a new way of existing in the world referred to as culture of mobility (Urry 2003). In the turn from the 19th to the 20th century, the notion of a culture based on the mobility of people, objects, information, and images is continuously growing in intensity and extension. As coined by Kesselring, mobility is a general principle of modernity (2008, p. 80).

The growth of spatial mobility and communication practices is an expression of these changes related to space-time compression, the speed of technique and the consequent death of distance. In this respect, what characterizes life on the move is the result but, at the same time, it is the cause of a life supported by complex and interdependent systems of mobility, with a focus on communication and transportation, which serves as a platform for the movement of people, objects, capital, information, and images.

In the context of several significant shifts in society that leads to new research questions and approaches, Sheller and Urry (2006) propose the new mobilities paradigm (NMP) by means of which the social sciences would become movement-driven. The so-called mobility turn of the social sciences emphasizes the fact that in this fluid social scenario, mobility becomes a paradigm in a sense that it establishes a theoretical connection between different ways of traveling, communicating, and moving goods, as well as people and information, and the multiple ways in which the economic and social life are performed and organized at different times and places in history. Also, according to the authors, all societies must deal with distance, and they do it by means of different processes, which depend on each other and include different discourses about movement. As stated by Urry (2007, p. 12), these processes originate from five types of mobility through which social life is organized from a distance: corporeal travel, imaginative travel, virtual travel, communicative travel, and the physical movement of objects, each one presupposing a range of interconnected systems that make movement possible in a predictable and risk-free way.

Especially in contemporary societies, the movement in this scenario is still maximized by new combinations between individuals and objects, and between these hybrids and systems, in various and different assemblages that demand new systems, which are (re)done and (re)organized while they are "intra-interacting". Moreover, by interacting and organizing themselves in movement, they create new paths and new possibilities that require new (re)forms and (re)organizations in a loop of shifts, changes, and (re)configurations that maximize the speed of the technique and the fluidity of the scenario and that requires new capabilities from the subjects as well as new kinds of potentialities from objects (Nogueira 2015).

These hybrids of people and machines are space-time interconnected in a multiple and complex way, creating a new range of situations where everything can happen, but not in a linear fashion. In this sense, the intensity of movement, circulation, and displacement of people, goods, images, and information operates as a trigger, which Kaufmann (2002, p. 6) calls the "liquid model" of social fluidification. As a fundamental actor of this social scenario, individuals are always changing, and interpersonal relations as well as the relations between people and their territory tend to disappear.

According to Giddens et al. (2012), this is the moment at which modernization reaches a certain stage, when it radicalizes itself and ends up by fluidizing their social macrostructures – which do not cease to exist but become incapable to operate with a solid basis for their own principles. These "Zombie categories", as put by Beck (2008), are all identified with the notion of a nation-state: a shared territory and national identity, as well as a common memory of the past and a taken-for-granted future. This new experience of life under the conditions of such uncertainty served as a platform for the emergence of a second modernity or reflexive modernization that configures a situation of auto confrontation of modernity and that highlights its own boundaries and fragilities.

In this sense, the transition to a reflexive second modernity not only changes social structures but also revolutionizes the very coordinates, categories, and conceptions of change itself. As stated by Beck et al. (2003, p. 2), "this meta-change of modern society results from a critical mass of unintended side-effects . . . more precisely, effects that were originally intended to be narrower in their scope than they turned out to be". Then the increased technical, economic, political, and cultural development of global capitalism gradually revolutionizes its own foundations, since it has broken the nation and the welfare state socially, politically, economically, and symbolically. "Reflexive modernization throws all of these basic social principles into flux"(2003, p. 2), Beck, Boss, and Lau claim.

Thus, under the conditions of reflexive modernization, a mobile risk society emerges based upon the idea of (im)mobilities of everything and everybody, which leads to a rise of new forms of risk, uncertainty, and insecurity. According to Kesselring (2008, p. 77), a mobile risk society is a society in which the structures become unstable and permeable and, consequently, the relationship between individuals and institutions is experienced in a variable and flexible way, as well as a free choice product. Life with no boundaries and affiliations opens up a series of possibilities for research in social sciences, which seek to understand life in contemporaneity, whose scope exceeds national issues and presents itself as a global phenomenon. In order to carry out this task, Beck (2008) proposes a kind of sociology that presents a more cosmopolitan than nationalist point of view and becomes a powerful tool for analyzing the social, political, economic, and cultural dynamics of contemporary life, in which global consumption of brands and their products, storytelling discourses, and lifestyle experiences have a huge impact.

For the studies on consumption and advertising from the NMP perspective, this cosmopolitan perspective of analysis sets up an important theoretical framework, because it proposes a shift in the point of view of the social analysis when placing at the same level, even though it does not deny their asymmetries, the global and the local. Moreover, from the research point of view, considering advertising from a cosmopolitan point of view, this investigation deals with the complexity of local-global marketing strategies, but also offers the opportunity to put together different contexts of analysis by articulating, on the one hand, authors from a global perspective and, on the other hand, local Brazilian authors, such as Gilberto Velho (2003), Everardo Rocha (1985), and Renato Ortiz (2003).

Returning to social scenario issues, from the moment that life happens in a scenario of uncertainty, ambivalence, and risk, there is a certain struggle for stability: individuals and groups are living in a constant process of building stability through affiliations and partnerships. Hannam et al. (2006) use the term "mooring" to express the idea that mobility does not exist without immobility. Beck (2008) coined the term "roots with wings" to emphasize the temporary and transitory nature of these affiliations – which may change, as stated by Velho (2003), due to the individuals' "set of possibilities" provided by their experienced social, political, economic, and cultural environment, within which people's projects and lifestyles are constantly (re)framed. However, above all, the concept of "roots with wings" draws attention to the fact that individuals in the mobile risk society tend to move, or more precisely, they have to move, but they do so while maintaining their roots or some fixity that ultimately produces some immobility.

Therefore, Kesselring states that "people need social benchmarks and stability cores to organize life in motion" (2008, p. 90). From the perspective of consumption studies, within the reflexive modernity scenario of ambivalence and uncertainty, goods (brands, products, services, places, celebrities, and digital influencers, among others), media (from media conglomerates to mobile technology devices), and messages (especially from global advertising discourse) are an important constitutive part of these benchmarks and stability cores. This proposition emerged from the notion that in contemporary society, consumption has become a means and/or a tool of self-identity that fits perfectly into the idea of a society of individualization, in which individuals perceives themselves as the owners of their lives and choices.

Going one step further, it is possible to affirm that in a mobile risk society, consumption surpasses its condition as operator of identity and emerges as a practice that supports some stability in a world in constant motion (Nogueira 2015). In fact, the core of the notion of consumption of (im)mobilities resides in the fact that when buying goods, individuals – ultimately consumers – are buying potential for movement as well, which will be ready to hand to be used (or not) as a tool to cope with the complexity and the new affordances of the contemporary social scenario with a focus on their personal projects and lifestyles. In other words, objects become instrumental to manage life in motion; objects [...] they empower individuals to "keep walking" (although it is not sure where the path will lead). In this sense, these hybrid entities formed by individuals and objects potentialize social human performance. This brings to the research another important theoretical framework used in the analysis: the concept of motility or potential for movement (Kaufmann 2002).

According to Kaufmann (2002, p. 37), motility can be defined as the capacity of a person to be mobile, not denying the structural or cultural dimension in which this capacity is embedded. By means of the notion of motility, the author emphasizes "the way in which an individual appropriates what is possible in the domain of mobility and puts this potential to use for his/her activities". The author also states that motility encompasses all the factors that define an individual's ability to be mobile: physical action, aspirations of fixation or mobility, accessibility to transport and communication technologies, spatial and temporal constraints, knowledge acquired, among other criteria. Motility consists, therefore, of elements relating to access, skills, and appropriation, and its intensity varies from person to person. Kaufmann (2002, pp. 38–39) further states that "motility is in fact formatted by the life course of those involved and by their financial, social and cultural capital, which together define the range of possible specific choices in terms of opportunities and projects". Considering that from a marketing perspective, objects can be seen as motility tools through which, depending on ready-to-handedness and on new affordances, they can (or cannot) support individual's everyday compulsion for (im)mobility with some stability and less risk.

Advertising agencies and marketing departments have already noticed the new social role of objects as motility tools and have begun to create new products or adjust the old ones to fit into this new consumption scenario, in which global consumers demand potential for movement. For this reason, new branding strategies and advertising campaigns are developed to put into circulation discourses by means of which mobilities are sold, as it has already been mentioned, as one of the most important features offered by goods, either symbolically or functionally. Hence, this is what consumption of (im)mobilities is all about: buying potential for movement as an attempt to achieve (but never accomplish) frictionless and risk-free life.

Rethinking advertising in a mobile risk society

Since the 1980s, especially after the release of Theodor Levitt's seminal article "The Globalization of the Markets" (1983), companies began to design their marketing strategies based upon the concept of homogenization, with emphasis on the idea that every target wants the same product since it shares the same needs and the same dynamic of goods appropriation, regardless of cultural differences that socially organize and regulate consumption activities.

Although this business vision failed for many reasons, it is not possible to deny the role of global brand advertising as an important tool for the so-called homogenization of markets. From the perspective of the marketing and business administration theory, advertising is understood as a communication activity that is part of the marketing communications mix. According to Kotler and Keller (2016, pp. 581–582), together with seven other major modes of communication – such as public relations and publicity, sales promotion, events and experiences, and mobile marketing, among others, advertising contributes to drive sales and increased brand and consumer equities. This business administration's pragmatic point of view emphasizes advertising as a tool for sales, neglecting its cultural role as a "banal form of cosmopolitanism". In Beck's words, banal cosmopolitanism refers to everyday cosmopolitanization in relation to cultural consumption and media representation, both put into circulation by consumption and advertising, besides the everyday travel and connection between distant places and people in the world.

According to Ortiz (2003), in this scenario of mobility of cultural symbols and flows, both textual and visual advertising discourse operates as an "international-popular memory",[2] i.e., as a cultural repository from which each individual from different cultures and backgrounds can recognized the world as a familiar place, establishing a cosmopolitan way to firm their identity: neither global nor local but personal. In line with Beck's cosmopolitanism, Ortiz presents the concept of "*world-alization* of cultures".[3]

In coining this term, Ortiz seeks to shed light on cultural exchanges made by social actors. Thus, cultural *world-alization* is a phenomenon of global society that is linked to the notion of diversity, not repetition or uniformity. In a world that has become a network of social relations through ever-increasing flows of information, people, and goods, the cultural *world-alization* means an intense intertwining of local cultures, as well as the development of new cultural manifestations without any limited territory.

Along with consumption, advertising emerges as the tool that gives visibility to these behavioral changes, since its discourse becomes also a cultural discourse, through which individuals can represent themselves and their identities. Thus, as an activity that gives visibility to consumption (Rocha 1985; McCracken 2003), advertising embodies in its practices the culture of mobility in appropriating individuals' compulsion for movement as a strategy of transformation of the product or brand into a particular consumer object, itself an object in circulation.

Therefore, in addition to its immediate commercial objective of promoting a product, the advertising discourse becomes instrumental in providing a potential for movement not only of goods but mainly of the targeted consumer. To put it another way, as a motility tool, advertising can be taken as the point of intersection of various systems of mobility: from physical mobility of consumers to imaginative mobility of signs, all the way through the virtual mobility of messages and images. Mainly, advertising potentializes the consumption and the actual movement of objects when its discourses are put into circulation.

With the mobility attribute of each object, advertising raises the potential for movement as its main discursive argument. About this aspect, advertising no longer just sells practical reasons for use, as in an industrial society, or only the status attained by purchasing a good, as in a consumer society. Instead, it sells motility, i.e., potential mobility, necessary to account for life in a mobile risk society, within which a culture of mobility is always present.

As will be seen in the images that follow, the idea of a culture of mobility and the notion of (im)mobility consumption appear in the advertising communication discourse published in printed advertisements during the 2014 FIFA World Cup in Brazil. As already mentioned, Roche (2000) states that mega-events operate like a hub of mobilities since they simultaneously promote, on the one hand, standardized commodities and images of global brands and their products and services to "people in a vast range of societies around the world in an effective and routine way"; and on the other hand, tourism and touristic consumerism, in which "mass public routinely travel the world in search of escapist pleasure and (occasionally) exotic difference". Hence, mega-events can be seen as a two-dimensional activity: as a tourist event and, more important to this work, as a media event. From each perspective, according to Roche (2000, p. 27) "mega-events represent temporal and spatial 'localisation' of potentially globally relevant cultural economic activity flow". Thus, from 2007 to 2016,[4] Brazil has become a place where global companies focused their marketing efforts and branding strategies by launching new products and running new advertising campaigns with the intention to be known in a market that had potentially 200 million consumers.

However, since 2010, the Brazilian political and economic context had started deteriorating after a decade of growth and inaugurated an institutional crisis whose effects we can feel even today. In June 2013, slightly before the FIFA Confederations Cup, the Brazilian people took to the streets to challenge the money spent (cost, expenses) on the World Cup and the Olympic Games, in a cycle of protests known as "June Journeys" (see Duarte in this book). Even though most Brazilians were against the amount of money spent by the government on the mega-events, for the organizers and local media, the World Cup was a huge success as regards business. According to Facebook data, regarding digital media coverage, the 2014 FIFA World Cup in Brazil was the first in which mobile devices and social media were the main medium in the coverage. It was the "second screen" Cup (TV and mobile devices, like smartphones) as well as the "#hashtag" Cup. All advertising campaigns, from larger or smaller companies, from global or local sponsors, used digital and social media to promote their products and suggested in their advertisements special hashtags for comments and (information?) sharing. According to the Facebook report,[5] there were 1 billion interactions about the World Cup, not to mention Twitter, Instagram, YouTube, and all other social networks. As to the event organization itself, even after so many schedule delays and protests, FIFA gave the World Cup in Brazil a 9.25 mark and declared a revenue that exceeded the most optimistic expectations: US$4.5 billion, which represented US$1 billion more than what was expected with "The greatest World Cup ever!", as the event was known in the country.

Based on the idea of consumption of (im)mobilities, four print advertisements were chosen to demonstrate how contemporary compulsion for mobility has been

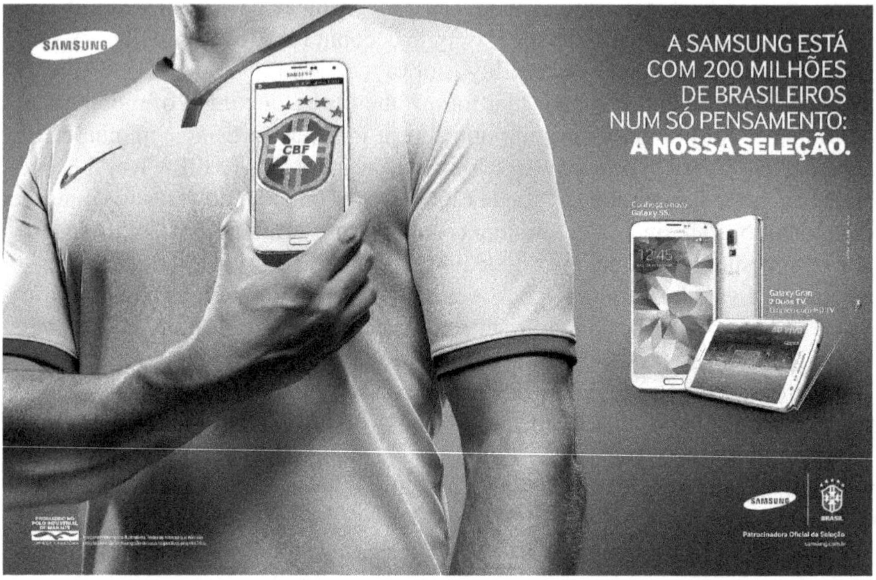

Figure 10.1 Samsung print ad. *Veja* Magazine, Issue 2378, June 18. pp. 46–47.
Source: http://veja.abril.com.br/acervodigital/home.aspx.

appropriated by advertising in at least two different ways: by the product or service announced, now seen as a hybrid assemblage used by individuals to better cope with their projects and life in motion; and by its discourse, now understood as a motility tool not just to the good – itself an object in circulation – but also to the consumers. As has already been said, all print ads were selected from *Revista Veja*, a Brazilian weekly magazine published during the 2014 FIFA World Cup.

As the official sponsor of the Brazilian team, (Figure 10.1) took advantage of the 2014 FIFA World Cup to launch a new smartphone that would allow people to watch the soccer games even when in transit. In this piece, the title refers to the population that cheered for the country during the World Cup: "Together with Samsung there are 200 million Brazilians, but just one thought: our national team", says the headline. What stands out in this advertisement is the clear representation of the hybrid assemblage as stated by Urry (2007): the mobile phone iconically takes the place of the heart of the Brazilian fans and expresses on their screen their love for the team. In his book *Mobilities* (2007), Urry presents the mobile phone and the pacemaker as examples of objects that would function as a "prosthetic" in their relationship with the individual. In this sense, nothing is more prosthetic than Samsung's smartphone as a fan's heart (or would it be a pacemaker?). Thus, the culture of mobility imposes itself on discourse, especially on the ad's nonverbal discourse, not only on the intrinsic use of the object for virtual or imaginative

Figure 10.2 Brasil Post website print ad. *Veja* Magazine, Issue 2378, June 18. p. 93.

Source: http://veja.abril.com.br/acervodigital/home.aspx.

mobility but also as the clear association of technology with the individual, which strengthens the notion of motility offered by the object to its user.

The next ad is from the (Figure 10.2). The piece was selected because it is the only one in the six *Veja* issues of 2014 used in the research that alludes to the June Journeys in its text: a photo of protesters is used as a background image; in addition, the 2013 demonstrations are the subject of messages exchanged by Twitter users portrayed on the smartphone, a key element of the visual discourse. Real-time, on-line, and on-the-move information exchange is the main argument of this ad, which has as its title the reinforcement of the concept of virtual mobility: "news generates conversations, conversations generate news". *Brasil Post*, from The Huffington Post group, and associated with Editora Abril, signs the ad, stating that "the future of journalism has arrived . . . on your tablet, smartphone, and social media". As stated by Urry (2007), in contemporary times, social, work, or family life, education, and political action can be experienced remotely or even during displacement, which determines new possibilities of life and enjoyment for the subject with their social groups and their objects of consumption. In this sense, the culture of mobility is present in the advertisement not only discursively but also due to the presence of the smartphone itself, a tool that organizes life in motion.

Over the last few years, especially in automotive brand campaigns, the idea of physical movement and technical innovation has been making room to the potential mobility offered by the car, having as an asset the connection to the Internet, via Bluetooth, for example.

In the case of the Mitsubishi print ad (Figure 10.3), it seems that the photo published on Instagram, as said in the headlines, was the result of all the trips made by the driver in his Pajero by crossing the most different and difficult ground and conditions. In this sense, all the power of the car, as a machine, is implied in the title: "The best postcards are those from your Instagram". It stays implicit in these lines that the driver does not stop at a tourist shop to buy a postcard of the place he/she has visited; he/she goes there, on the edge, takes a picture, and shares it on social media.

Discursively, both the culture of mobility and the idea of hybridity are present in the ad: the first one, by means of its image, which is pure movement, but also by means of the text that, when mentioning Instagram, leads us toward virtual or imaginative mobility. In the case of hybridity, the partnership between the car and the user is established by the idea that both of them make many trips together, and the object always empowers the individual in his displacement, which causes him or her to reach the top. As Urry states, "the cell phone and cars are the twins of late modernity" (2007, p. 174). To paraphrase McLuhan (1974): the car (or the medium) operates "as an extension of man" and drives individuals to travel, not only physically and geographically, but more virtually and imaginatively, amplifying their potential for movement.

In the case of (Figure 10.4), the text draws our attention to an issue dear to social sciences: it is not possible to talk about mobility systems without also

Figure 10.3 Mitsubishi/Pajero print ad. *Veja* Magazine, Issue 2382, July 7. pp. 20–21.
Source: http://veja.abril.com.br/acervodigital/home.aspx.

talking about the immobility systems that support the circulation and movement of people, things, information, and images. In this sense, in TIM's advertisement the argumentative line presents at the same time the culture of mobility, motility, and hybridity. The argument presented by the mobile operator company focuses on the potential for movement (social, professional, educational, economic), stressing the fact that by being a TIM customer, a "world without borders" will be possible the minute the customer walks through the blue door.

Moreover, it draws attention to the question of individuation in brand discourse, when the text plays with the idea of experience, "getting there", "living the moment", seizing the opportunities that "life gives you". The message, even if conveyed in mass media, is always directed to the individual's experience with the product, which, as already mentioned, will be used or not (ready-to-handedness) by the target audience in order to meet their lifestyle and personal projects.

Finally, it is interesting to remember that the fact that individuals use the connection, reversibility, and ubiquity of communication systems, such as in the case of the previously mentioned operator, does not necessarily mean that they are mobile. On the contrary: the ubiquity of technology offers the motility, which will (or will not) be transformed into real movement, based on the decision of an individualized action. The idea in this case is to be (potentially) mobile to be fixed, a good example of Beck's concept of "roots with wings".

Figure 10.4 TIM print ad. *Veja* Magazine, Issue 2379. June 25. pp. 4–5.

Source: Disponível em: http://veja.abril.com.br/acervodigital/home.aspx.

Final remarks

The four ads presented here are part of a group of 40 print ads that were analyzed for my PhD dissertation research regarding the ever-growing intense imbrication between mobility culture and advertising discourse. The biggest discursive changes noted were on advertisements of objects related to physical or geographical mobility. As shown, even the automobile, a major symbol of the idea of displacement and freedom in modern Western societies, has come to be promoted based not on its technical engineering and design features but on the individual's motility. This discursive change reinforces the idea that in the contemporary mobile risk society, the consumption of (im)mobility has been established based upon the idea that every object offer potential for movement for individuals to manage life in motion. For this reason, potential mobility is now discursively presented by the advertisement of global brands, regardless of the type of benefit or the commercial category of the good to be disclosed.

Finally, by confirming the hypothesis that the culture of mobility has been present in the discourse of global brands' advertisement, the notion of consumption of (im)mobilities strengthened the premise that advertising can be seen as a cultural product, worth studying as many other symbolic forms and cultural manifestations of contemporary society. Rethinking advertising, therefore, is also about understanding it from another point of view, realizing that the discursive nature of advertising allows the researcher to make an interesting socio-historical analysis of culture, not only limiting it to the villainous role of global capitalism but also understanding it as part of a larger cultural process involving sellers but also buyers in various new (re)configurations, in which potential mobility is just one among them.

Notes

1 Thorstein Veblen, Lévi-Strauss, Jean Baudrillard, Pierre Bourdieu, Arjan Appadurai, Marshall Shalins, Zygmunt Bauman, Colin Campbell, Grant McCracken, Daniel Miller, Néstor Canclini, and, in Brazil, Everardo Rocha, Livia Barbosa, Leticia Veloso, Claudia Pereira, Carla Barros, among others;
2 In Portuguese: "memória internacional popular". Translated by the author.
3 In Portuguese: "mundialização da cultura". Translated by the author.
4 The Rio 2007 Pan American Games; the Rio 2007 Parapan American Games; the Rio 2011 World Military Games; the 2013 FIFA Confederations Cup; the 2014 FIFA World Cup; the Rio 2016 Olympic Games, and the Rio 2016 Paralympic Games, without mentioning three editions of the global music festival Rock in Rio (2011, 2013, and 2015) and two Papal visits: Pope Benedict XVI for the 28th World Youth Day (2007) and Pope Francis (2013);
5 http://brasileconomico.ig.com.br/vida-e-estilo/esporte-clube/2014-06-10/fifa-fatura-mais-de-us-45-bi-com-copa-do-mundo.html. Accessed on October 2, 2014.

References

Baudrillard, J. 1970. *A Sociedade de Consumo*. Lisboa: Edições 70.

Beck, U. 2008. Mobility and the cosmopolitan perspective. In Weert, C., Kaufmann, V. & Kesselring, S. eds. *Trancing mobilities: Towards a cosmopolitan perspective*. Aldershot: Ashgate.

Beck, U., Bonss, W. & Lau, C. 2003. The theory of reflexive modernization: Problematic, hypotheses and research programme. *Theory, Culture & Society*, 20(2), pp. 1–33. London: Sage. Available at: http://tcs.sagepub.com/content/20/2/1.

Giddens, A., Lash, S. & Beck, U. 2012. Modernização Reflexiva. *Política, tradição e estética na ordem social moderna*. São Paulo: Editora Unesp.

Hannam, K., Sheller, M. & Urry, J. 2006. Mobilities, immobilities and mooring. *Editorial, Mobilities*, 1(1), pp. 1–22. Available at: www.tandfonline.com/doi/full/10.1080/17450100500489189.

Kaufmann, V. 2002. *Re-thinking mobility: Contemporary sociology*. Aldershot: Ashgate.

Kesselring, S. 2008. Mobility risk society. In Weert, C., Kaufmann, V. & Kesselring, S. eds. *Trancing mobilities: Towards a cosmopolitan perspective*. Aldershot: Ashgate.

Kotler, P. & Keller, K. 2016. *Marketing Management*, 15 Global ed. Harlow, England: Pearson Education Limited.

Lemos, A. 2009. Cultura da mobilidade. *Revista Famecos*, 40, pp. 28–35. Porto Alegre. Available at: http://revistaseletronicas.pucrs.br/ojs/index.php/revistafamecos/article/view/6314/4589.

Levitt, T. 1983. The globalization of markets. *Harvard Business Review*, 61(3), pp. 92–102. Available at: https://hbr.org/1983/05/the-globalization-of-markets.

McCracken, G. 2003. *Cultura & consumo*. Rio de Janeiro: Mauad.

McLuhan, M. 1974. *Os meios de comunicação como extensões do homem*. São Paulo: Editora Cultrix.

Miller, D. 2014. *Trecos, troços e coisas: estudos antropológicos sobre a cultura material*. Rio de Janeiro: Zahar.

Nogueira, M. A. de F. 2015. *Mobilidade em potência e discurso publicitário na sociedade contemporânea globalizada: Brasil, 1982–2014*. PhD dissertation – Centro de Pesquisa e Documentação de História Contemporânea do Brasil, Programa de Pós-Graduação em História, Política e Bens Culturais. Rio de Janeiro. Available at: http://hdl.handle.net/10438/13704.

Nogueira, M. A. de F. 2016. Consumption of (im)mobilities and discourse: Mobility culture in the advertising of brands. *Revista Comunicação, Mídia e Consumo*, 13(36), pp. 27–47. São Paulo.

Ortiz, R. 2003. *Mundialização e cultura*. Rio de Janeiro: Brasiliense.

Rocha, E. 1985. *Magia e Capitalismo: um estudo antropológico da publicidade*. 3rd ed. São Paulo: Editora Brasiliense.

Roche, M. 2000. *Mega-events and modernity*. London: Routledge.

Sheller, M. & Urry, J. eds. 2006. The new mobilities paradigm. *Environment and Planning A*, 38, pp. 207–226.

Urry, J. 2003. *Mobile cultures*. Published by the Department of Sociology, Lancaster University, Lancaster LA1 4YN, UK. Available at: www.comp.lancs.ac.uk/sociology/papers/Urry-Mobile-Cultures.pdf.

Urry, J. 2007. *Mobilities*. Cambridge, UK: Polity Press.

Velho, G. 2003. *Projeto e Metamorfose: antropologia das sociedades complexas*. 3rd ed. Rio de Janeiro: Jorge Zahar Editora.

Chapter 11

#Bhnasruas

Mobile journalism during the June Journeys

Fernanda da Costa Portugal Duarte

The June Journeys

Even though the June Journeys describe the events of June 2013, they are part of a broader context of protests that had been taking place in different parts of Brazil in the previous years. Most of the agenda set by the protests related to the implementation of urban policies that favored gentrification and urban development in favor of hosting mega-events, but it also includes more general protests against corruption.[1]

In June 2013, six Brazilian capitals hosted the FIFA Confederations Cup, an international soccer competition between the most recent winners of the six continental championships.[2] This was a "test event" for the upcoming 2014 FIFA World Cup. In order to host these mega-events, the Brazilian government committed to investing BRL 39.5 billion[3] in infrastructure, transportation, and stadiums, which would increase the federal budget deficit even more. According to Maricato et al. (2013), the protests in June 2013 erupted from a wave of dissatisfaction regarding these investments to the detriment of basic public services, such as health and education, as well as a lack of transparency concerning the expenses, fueled by ongoing accusations of corruption.

The protests gained greater traction when Movimento Passe Livre (*Free Fare Movement*) called for a public demonstration in São Paulo on June 6 and 7, 2013, against the 20-cent rise in the bus fare.[4] The *Free Fare movement*[5] was created in 2005 in Porto Alegre and defines itself as a nonprofit, autonomous initiative that advocates for urban inclusivity: people's rights to the city through free and effective public transportation. The first demonstrations gathered a few thousand people in São Paulo and shut down main avenues in the city. Some of the protesters adopted black bloc tactics[6] and faced a violent response by the police, who used tear gas and rubber bullets to disperse the crowds.[7] Hundreds of protesters were detained, and dozens were hospitalized in consequence of police brutality.[8] By June 13, the protests in São Paulo gathered about 20,000 people and had already spread to other capitals in the country.

In response to the rising protests, the Minas Gerais Court of Appeals prohibited political protests in the state capital, Belo Horizonte, for the duration of the

Confederations Cup. Belo Horizonte, one of the host cities of all three mega-events, was already undergoing major transformations. The installation of a bus rapid transit system (BRT) had already forced the removal of houses in the Mineirão stadium's neighborhood. According to the CPCMO, 2014 World Cup and 2016 Rio Olympics Committee for the People[9] (2013), since 2010, 150,000 families in different cities of Brazil had been forced to leave their houses in order to accommodate the designed changes in the urban landscape to host the mega-events. The hope for economic growth and job creation, expressed by the Brazilian government as justification for the expenses, was undermined by the implementation of legislation that prohibited all informal sales by independent street vendors and sales of any other merchandise not authorized by FIFA. Despite the court's prohibition, on June 17, the day of the first match of the Confederations Cup, more than 20,000 people had taken over the streets of Belo Horizonte,[10] marching from the city center toward the Mineirão stadium. By June 20, the protests had reached a peak with more than 1.4 million participants in 388 Brazilian cities.[11] Mottos adopted by the protesters, such as, "it's not about the 20 cents", "no education, no health, no patience", "down with PEC 33", (a proposal of constitutional amendment that would reduce the powers of the Supreme Court), and "no to gay cure", (regarding a proposal to validate sexual orientation conversion therapy), demonstrate the variety of demands that were incorporated into the June Journeys.

In Belo Horizonte, as in other parts of the country, the protests were met with police brutality. Protesters scheduled marches on the same days as the Confederations Cup matches and followed the same high traffic route as the soccer fans, from the city center to the Mineirão stadium. The avenues that provide access to the stadium also provide access to the campus of the Federal University of Minas Gerais (UFMG). On June 22, more than 125,000 people blocked the main avenues that surround UFMG's campus.[12] The protests were marked by street fires, Molotov cocktails, tear gas bombs, and reports of wounded and arrested protesters.

Between June and December 2013, 2,608 people were arrested in the 696 protests that took over Brazil. During the demonstrations, 837 people were wounded (117 of whom were journalists), and 8 people died during the protests in Brazil. During the last week of June, five protesters fell from an overpass close to the main entrance of UFMG's campus in Belo Horizonte, resulting in two deaths.[13] The federal and local governments' response to the protests was to freeze the bus fare prices in several parts of the country. Toward the end of the Confederations Cup, the intensity of protests had decreased but not entirely faded.

The rise of media activism during the June Journeys

The news coverage of the protests by broadcast media presented a challenge. The speed with which the protests took place, the lack of centralized coordination, and the diversity of agendas made it difficult for news media to interpret and describe the purpose of the protests. The first wave of news coverage emphasized the turmoil caused by the interruption of traffic and the destruction of property and described the protests as a threat to public safety and order (Silva 2014). *Black bloc* tactics, such as the destruction of the facades of banks and stores, were emphasized by broadcast media, who attributed the motivation of the protests to vandalism and erased the political intention of their actions. As noted by D'Andrea and Ziller (2014, p. 16), the rise of police brutality in response to these actions led to the construction of a media discourse that separates "peaceful protesters" from radical black bloc activists, depicted as a minority of vandals. The authors also mention other challenges faced by traditional news media channels. News reporters and photographers employed by them were often antagonized by protesters, given their allegedly biased editorial content and historical support for conservative political parties. D'Andrea and Ziller (2014) remark that the solution presented by the Brazilian broadcast media was to cover the protests from a distance, using helicopters and drones, and to remain behind police barriers that kept them separated from the protesters. While this strategy ensured the physical safety of reporters, it also prevented them from getting firsthand access to information in real time. Meanwhile, protesters ensured that information regarding the events was being broadcast immediately through social media. Alternative media collectives, such as *Mídia NINJA* and *BH nas Ruas*, broadcasted live images through mobile apps and smartphones and provided more immediate access to information as well as accountability regarding police activities. In this section, I focus on *Mídia NINJA* as an example of a nationwide media activist group whose *modus operandi* served as a blueprint for other collectives. In the next section, I discuss *BH nas ruas* as an example of a regional alternative media group composed by Journalism students, who experiment with mobile journalism as a strategy to create independent news reports.

Mídia NINJA defines itself as a collaborative and decentralized network of communicators who appropriate new technologies to produce and share information.[14] The acronym stands for Independent Narratives, Journalism and Action, and its mission is inspired by earlier initiatives such as Centro de Mídia Independente[15] (the Brazilian branch of the international Indymedia),[16] the nonprofit organization Intervozes,[17] and various free radio experiences. *Mídia NINJA* argues for its capacity to create "an ecology of content production that directly impacts the contemporary imaginaries in dispute, and therefore contributes to the achievement of social public interests".[18] It bases its action on collaboration and cooperation with other independent media organizations for the democratization of information in order to produce alternative modes of news production that are not compromised by established political and economic interests. In this sense, *Mídia NINJA* presents itself as a model for independent, alternative, and media activism in opposition to traditional media forms, which find themselves in a moment of economic and credibility crisis. Such traditional media crisis is discussed extensively by various authors (Castells 1996; Gillmor 2006; Deifell 2009) and relates to traditional media's inability to adapt their business and distribution models to the contemporary convergence culture (Jenkins 2006), to experiment with emerging technologies, and to develop innovative formats (Pereira 2016), as well as their questionable credibility due to ongoing accusations of editorial bias and their omission and manipulation of information to favor conservative political groups. A tweet posted during the protests exemplifies these beliefs: "We don't need partisan media, we have smartphones!" (Lorenzotti 2014).

The most common reporting provided by *Mídia NINJA* relies on live streaming on social media platforms. During protests, independent journalists and volunteers use smartphones to create multiple real-time "cathartic experiences of occupying the streets" (Malini & Antoun 2013). The livestreams reached a peak of 120,000 views per stream and more than 5 million accumulated views on Twitcasting, Twitcam, Google Hangouts, and UStream (Lorenzotti 2014). *Mídia NINJA* not only "hacked" the single narrative provided by traditional news outlets but also set the news agenda to discuss the dynamics of protests. Videos produced by amateur and independent reporters captured police brutality and police planting evidence against protesters. Videos were also used by police to identify individuals and were used by individuals to provide alibis against crime accusations.[19] Malini and Antoun (2013) say that the activities carried out by *Mídia NINJA* during the June Journeys in 2013 mark a turn for media activism in Brazil. They point out that "*midialivrismo* and media activism find themselves in a place of language experimentation and thus create another distribution of the sensible, an experience of flow in flux that invents time and space, a poetics of dyscontrol and of happening" (Malini & Antoun 2013, p. 15).

"Midialivrismo" is a term that originated in the 2008 I Fórum de Mídia Livre (Free Media Forum) that took place at the School of Communication of the Federal University of Rio de Janeiro. The agenda for a "Mídia livre" is defined in a manifesto[20] signed by more than 150 journalists, activists and communication professors who advocate for the democratization of communication as a human right through the mapping of ongoing alternative media initiatives, the diverse expenditure of public advertising budget (to include independent media outlets rather than exclusively traditional media conglomerates), and the creation of forums for discussion and content depository, such as open and free software, Wiki, and P2P platforms.

Parente (2014) points out that alternative media strategies shifted since the process of redemocratization of Brazil. During the military dictatorship (1964–1985), the censorship imposed on traditional news media outlets provoked the emergence of tabloids, zines, and informal publications authored by intellectuals and union workers that acted as instruments to denounce violent acts committed by the military regime. As the dictatorship ended, these oppositionist publications gave place to initiatives more focused on community communication and education. Costa (2011) adds that "*mídia livre*" initiatives organized in 2008, which acted as inspiration for the 2013 protests, differ from alternative oppositionist initiatives from the 1960s and 1970s because of their declared interest to work in partnership with governments to install federal legislation that ensures the application of free media principles.[21] The second edition of "*Fórum de Mídia Livre*" occurred in 2009 at the Federal University of Espírito Santo, and in 2012, the World Forum of Free Media was hosted by the School of Communication of the Federal University of Rio de Janeiro. This intense articulation between free media projects, the government, and communication schools demonstrates what Costa (2011) has pointed out as another characteristic of the media activism initiatives that took shape during the June Journeys: the professionalization of the activists. Communication departments, particularly in public universities,[22] became a locus of research, discussion, and engagement around issues that concern free media and the broader issues of social justice that were embraced by the June Journeys. The historical participation of students, staff, and faculty in social movements, such as UNE (National Student Union), ANDES (National Union for Faculty in Higher Education), FASUBRA (Brazilian Union for Staff in Higher Education), to name a few, and the recurring cuts to public universities' funding for research, teaching, and extension programs[23] have contributed to the politicization of university *campi* and deliberation around public expenditures in education (Costa et al. 1994; Campos 2017).

BH nas Ruas

On June 16, 2013, while the wave of protests took over Brazil, a group of Communication students at the Federal University of Minas Gerais engaged in an online discussion[24] about the media coverage of the events. They shared their dissatisfaction regarding narratives created by the press and expressed a desire to bring forth a testimonial, a first-person report of what was going on during the protests. Within a few hours, a group of students decided to cover the protests and created a Facebook page[25] (see Figure 11.1) and a Twitter profile[26] titled *BH nas Ruas* (*BH on the Streets*) (Oliveira et al. 2014). On the Facebook page description, the group states: "Collaborative coverage of popular demonstrations in Belo Horizonte. The revolution will be recorded by you. #bhnasruas. Email content to: bhnasruas@gmail.com".[27] A couple of days after the creation of the page, *BH nas Ruas* consisted of more than 200 collaborators and 20 page administrators and had accumulated more than 30,000 followers on Facebook (Silva & Ziviani 2018, p. 35).

According to Oliveira et al. (2014), students formed a network of collaborators with defined roles: reporting from the streets, checking information and validating sources, or editing texts, video footage, and photographs. All of these steps were mediated by mobile apps and platforms: Google Sheets was used to register, oversee, and manage the entire coverage process by assigning roles, shifts, and coverage locations among volunteers; WhatsApp was used to coordinate the different groups, specifically those on the streets; Facebook Messenger and Google Hangouts were used for remote editorial meetings; and Dropbox acted as a shared content depository. Volunteers who were not directly associated with the page also

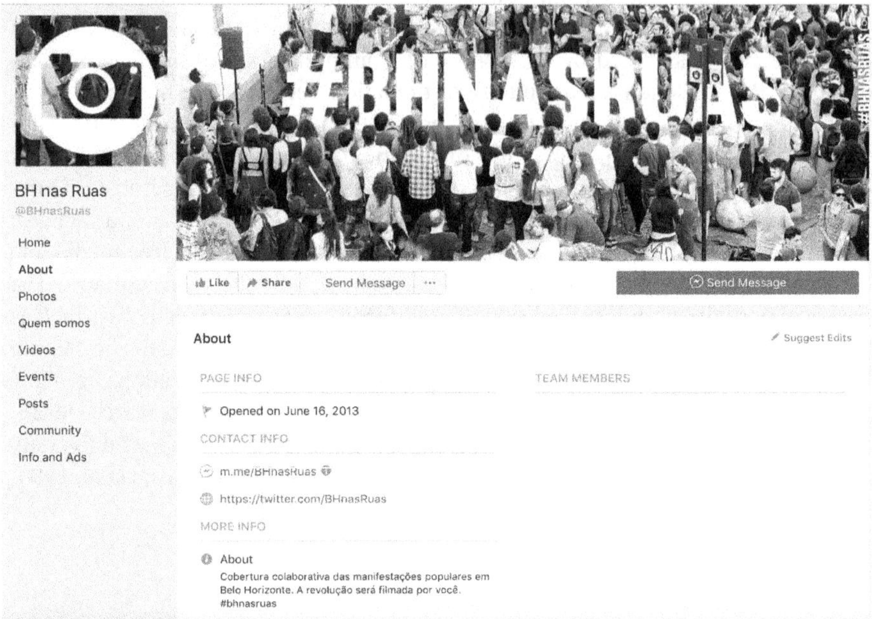

Figure 11.1 *BH nas Ruas* home page.

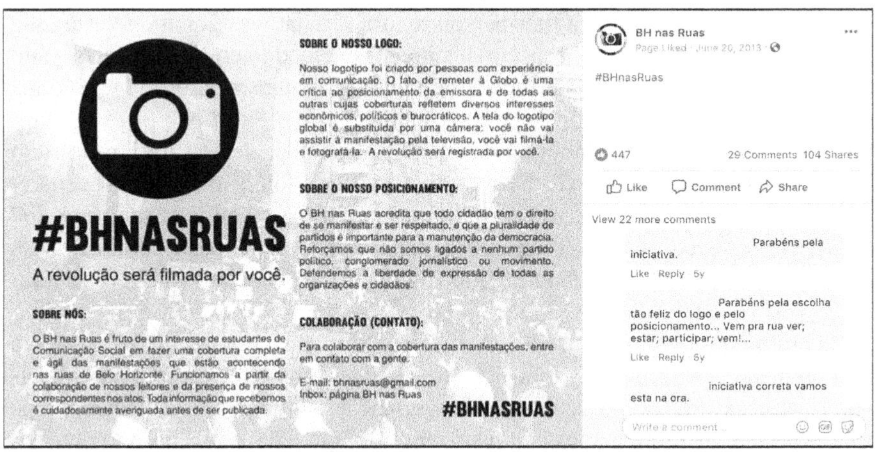

Figure 11.2 *BH nas Ruas* editorial page.

contributed to the coverage by adding #bhnasruas to their public posts or by submitting content to the page's email. *BH nas Ruas*'s editorial stance is defined as follows:

#BHNASRUAS. The revolution will be recorded by you.

> *About us:*
>
> *BH nas ruas* is an initiative by Social Communication students who are interested in the production of a complete and agile coverage of the public manifestations that are taking over the streets of Belo Horizonte. We work in collaboration with our readers and through our collaborators who are present in the protests. Every piece of information we receive is carefully checked before it is published.
>
> *About our logo:*
>
> Our logo was created by people with experience in Communication. Its resemblance to Globo's is a criticism to Globo's and other networks' editorial stances, whose news coverage is compromised by economic, political, and bureaucratic interests. The screen featured in Globo's logo is replaced by a camera in ours; you will not watch the manifestations on TV, you will film them and photograph them. The revolution will be recorded by you.
>
> *About our editorial stance:*
>
> *BH nas Ruas* believes that every citizen is entitled to express themselves freely and to be respected, and that the plurality of political parties is important for the maintenance of democracy. We reiterate that we do not associate with any political party, media conglomerate, or social movement. We defend freedom of expression for all organizations and citizens.
>
> *Collaboration (contact):*
>
> To collaborate with the protests news coverage, get in touch with us. Email: bhnasruas@gmail.com. Inbox. @Bhnasruas page

The logo for *BH nas Ruas* features a camera, recognized by the students as a symbol of the manifestation narratives, which were defined by the images captured by the protesters' cameras (Oliveira et al. 2014, p. 23). The use of the hashtag (#bhnasruas) in every post acts as a content aggregator as well as a demonstration of the collaborative intention of the coverage (Figure 11.3).

"What do you see?" is the initial question that guided the reports produced by *BH nas Ruas* (Oliveira et al. 2014, p. 21). The motivation behind the coverage was the pursuit of immediate information that would prioritize the factual aspects of the protests. Ferreira (2016) notices three recurring themes that characterize the page posts: (1) organization: the logistical coordination of actions regarding

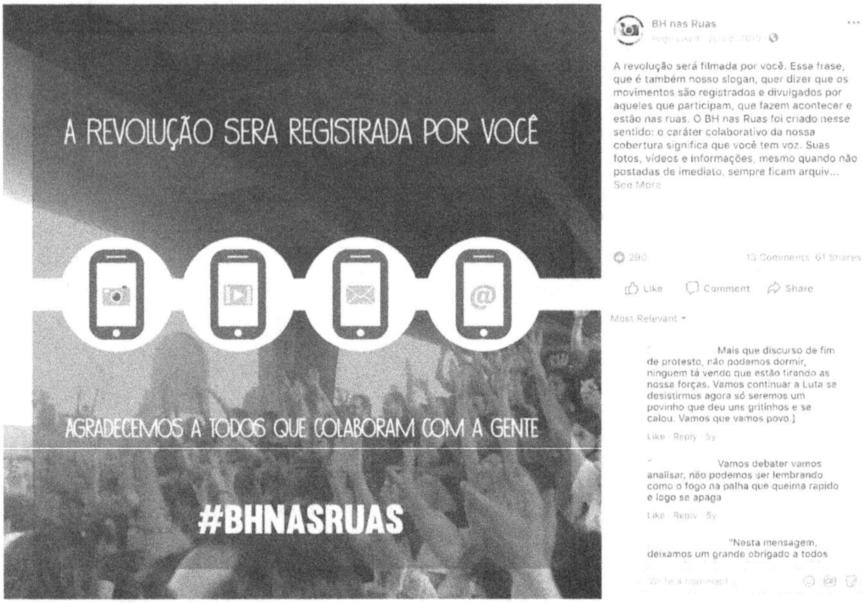

Figure 11.3 *BH nas Ruas* publishes a "thank you" note to the audience for submitting information, images and videos to the page and highlights their collaborative approach of news making.

the protests, i.e., traffic information and protest routes; (2) mobilization: calls for political participation and deliberation, i.e., invites for scheduled manifestations; and (3) display of personal actions: content that shapes an editorial identity for the page, i.e., when a post addresses the audience directly, for example, when the page grieved the death of a protester.

Although the news reports produced by *BH nas Ruas* were fast paced, they were not instantaneous, as were *Mídia NINJA*'s live streams. Their posts went through several steps before publication. Once information was gathered on the streets and via the Facebook page's inbox, it was verified by a group of fact-checking students. After the information checked out, a group of student editors worked on the text and image production for the story. Every post was collectively approved before being published on the page. At the end of the day, students would gather in a Google Hangout meeting to assess the coverage and plan for the next day (Oliveira et al. 2014, p. 34).

BH nas ruas covered all of the demonstrations that took place in Belo Horizonte during June 2013. Since the creation of the page until the end of 2013, 575 posts were published, which received 26,059 comments and 296,584 reactions.[28] The page averaged one post every 15 minutes during protest days. As of 2018, the page has accumulated 81,709 likes and an organic outreach of 417,290 people (Oliveira et al. 2014, pp. 62–64).

Mobile medialities, experimental genres, and a moving ethos

The appropriation of mobile technologies was fundamental to the implementation of *BH nas Ruas*. The first use of smartphones for journalism practices dates back to 2007, when Reuters News Agency (Silva 2015; Cameron 2009) assembled a toolkit composed of a Nokia N95 smartphone, a wireless keyboard, a solar battery, a tripod, and an external microphone.[29] This kit was distributed to select journalists to provide more dynamic, faster field reports, and it inaugurated mobile journalism, or *MoJo*. *MoJo* initially referred to the use of mobile devices as a tool to speed up the collection and broadcasting of information. Researchers in the field of mobilities studies (Farman 2012; de Souza e Silva & Frith 2012) call attention to the need to revise the centrality of agency assigned to technical devices and instead understand them as mobile interfaces that mediate social experiences in physical spaces, as well as enable power relations. In this sense, the mobile interface is not a surface of access or division between the user and the tool but an embodied space of social action. Moreover, as computing technologies become smaller, more mobile, and more pervasive to our everyday experiences, the social processes they mediate are more easily conflated with their technical capacities. More than the smartphone device itself, mobile technologies are cultural devices in which the interface is not a surface or a threshold that defines the limits of the human and the computational but a milieu of cultural practices encoded in digital form (Manovich 2001).

Embodied spatial actions mediated by mobile technologies are referred to by Sheller (2013) as mobile medialities. A mobile mediality is a new form of hybrid mediated spatiality created by current forms of urban mobilities, social interaction, and connections with places and technologies while on the move. It is not about a technological shift prompted by mobile technologies that grants greater speed to information exchange, as noted by early *MoJo* enthusiasts. Mobile medialities speak of the ecological aspect of the emerging practices of movement that engage and disengage people, things, technologies, and information. They can be exemplified by collaborative cartography, location-based games, and mobile news, such as *BH nas Ruas*, to name a few. The concept is particularly focused on how mobile and pervasive art changes mobility, spatiality, sociability, and traditional forms of power.

Silva (2015) acknowledges that journalism practices have historically dealt with information mobility: the movement of information from sources to newsrooms and then to newspapers' front pages. Lately, the wide appropriation of mobile technologies, such as wireless networks and smartphones, has shifted the space and time dimensions in which information is produced and shared. Social practices mediated through mobile technologies, such as live video streaming, social media mobile apps, automated location awareness, and hashtagged content production, create greater volumes of information, which are shared in real time. These emerging practices require reassessing the modes of production and circulation of news information. The medial relationships developed by the collaborators of *BH nas Ruas* spawned inventive forms of appropriation of mobile media technologies, such as apps, authoring, and publishing platforms. In consequence, *BH nas Ruas* experimented with journalism genres and techniques and discovered new tactics to negotiate information and audience participation.

To look at *MoJo* from a mobile perspective means looking at mobile practices as not merely enabled by smartphone devices but as mobile medialities that are enacted by the constant circulation of data and information. The challenge for *Mojo* and *BH nas Ruas* then goes further than mastering efficiency in delivering news but requires the invention of informational practices and news reporting genres while renewing a sense of legitimacy (*ethos*) that is bound to the audience's participation.

The adoption of mobile technologies and the experimentation with journalistic genres marked the narratives brought forward by *BH nas ruas*. Instead of privileging traditional journalism genres and formats, such as news reports, interviews, and chronicles (Marques de Melo & de Assis 2016), to name a few, *BH nas rua*s embodied the material organization of Facebook's interface to report in formats that are more in tune with modes of mobile production-consumption of information. During the coverage of the protests, collaborators published a great volume of posts that included short texts and photographs taken by members that accompanied the protests on site. Differently from *Mídia NINJA*, which live streamed many of the protests over social media platforms, *BH nas Ruas* never published a live video. However, narratives of the protests were built in an almost live fashion. As events took place, collaborators on the streets gathered images and wrote texts that were sent to editors via WhatsApp. Editors fact-checked the content before publishing it on the page. Even though not immediate, the quick mediation between editors, reporters, and *BH nas Ruas*'s followers that contributed with information or commented posts forged a collective narrative that was gradually built as the events unfolded on the streets.

The criticism against traditional news and the commitment to a "complete and agile", fact-checked coverage demonstrates an idealistic motivation behind *BH nas Ruas* that is in tune with the objective and impartial premises of informational journalism. Such premise is based on the understanding that journalistic narratives can act as accurate representations of reality. However, the ideal of producing independent coverage proved to be challenging, as *BH nas Ruas*'s followers questioned their political and editorial bias. For example, *BH nas Ruas*'s logo referred to a major Brazilian media conglomerate. Such resemblance was interpreted by commentators as a contradiction. Moreover, posts that describe destruction of property during protests generated controversial comments. Many commentators questioned the genuine political intentions of the demonstrations due to these acts, while others speculated that they were carried out by infiltrated militia groups whose agenda was to discredit the protest claims. The political aspects of the coverage are undeniable and inescapable, which makes the call for objectivity even more problematic.

Figure 11.4 *BH nas Ruas* showcases the conflict between protesters and the police during the Confederates Cup in Belo Horizonte and states that the streets belong to the people not to FIFA.

Furthermore, when *BH nas Ruas* proposes an entirety of representation by providing multiple accounts brought directly from the streets of Belo Horizonte, it initially fails to acknowledge the impossibility of such a task. This realization quickly hit the collective, which decided to acknowledge their ideological position. Posts that asserted the importance of freedom of expression, respect for the plurality of ideologies, calls for political manifestation, and praise for the collaborative nature of the coverage became more frequent on the page (see Figure 11.4).

Even though *BH nas Ruas* never affirmed its association with other media activism initiatives, the rhetorical tone of its posts and its Facebook page likes (*Mídia NINJA*, *Tarifa Zero BH*,[30] *Assembleia Popular Horizontal::Belo Horizonte*,[31] and *Salve a Rede Minas*)[32] demonstrates its validation for the political ideals of democratization of information argued by free media initiatives. Often editorial posts published by *BH nas Ruas* admins crossed the informative genre of traditional journalism and assumed a critical tone regarding the motivation that drove the protests and an educational approach to orient protesters to ensure their safety. The use of specific hashtags (#ogiganteacordou, #vemprarua, #primaverabrasileira)[33] clearly demonstrates *BH nas Ruas*'s support for the protests.

Howard Rheingold (2007) recognizes that the social practices tied to mobile technologies have paramount political effects. The notion of a collective intelligence that describes the contemporary networked condition of media infrastructure is updated to the notion of "smart mob", as the use of mobile connectivity to organize collective action in the social, cultural, economic, and political spheres increases. Citizen journalism, civic media, and recent *MoJo* experiments such as *BH nas Ruas* often includes bottom-up, grassroots, participative initiatives. The expectation behind peer-to-peer communication in contemporary mobile medialities is that they might allow for decentralized and equalitarian participation.

Conclusion

Similarly to previous political demonstrations, such as the anti-WTO protests in Seattle in 1999, the anti-Estrada movement in the Philippines in 2001 (Rheingold 2007, 2012), and later the Arab Spring in 2011, the June Journeys relied on a mobile communication infrastructure to mediate and coordinate the protests. The demonstrations materialized through the physical bodies of citizens that took over the Brazilian streets and through a massive amount of footage, posts, comments, and shares that mobilized traditional media and social media platforms. The 2013 protests and the modes of information production and sharing that emerged with them demonstrated that the public spaces of the streets and the symbolic arenas for public deliberation are not exclusively composed of co-present interactions. Mobile and pervasive technologies, along with the networked connections they bring, are an intrinsic part of our everyday experience of the city. New mobile medialities are creating new affordances for journalists to engage with emerging mobile technologies and urban spatiality and generate new forms of audience interaction. The notion of *mobile journalism* is reconfigured when the implications of information mobility reshape journalism professional practices for information sourcing, fact-checking, and bringing forth experimental genres for news coverage. While the development of mobile technologies and wireless infrastructure allows for intense information circulation, the implications of such mobile medialities are far more complex than a matter of efficiency in news production or increase of speed.

The motivation behind *BH nas Ruas* as a journalism collective in the context of the June Journeys in 2013 is the production of more immediate and legitimate information of the protests in the streets of Belo Horizonte. In this sense, it takes an epistemological effort to comprehend and further explain the political interests at play and the underlying social forces that characterized the protests. In doing so, the students of *BH nas Ruas* developed new tactics to collect, validate, process, and circulate information about the protests. The students experimented with journalistic formats and genres, developed new procedures to ensure information accuracy, engaged with audience collaboration, and negotiated a transparent and shifting editorial stance with the audience. Consequently, they also take on an ontological approach to mobile journalism as they are forced to reflect about how the changing regime of information requires them to revisit their social roles as journalists in training.

Throughout the coverage of the protests produced by traditional media outlets, *BH nas Ruas* was often the primary source of information for protesters and for media conglomerates' reports. In parallel, traditional media outlets are also provoked to reflect on how to adapt to emerging mobile medialities in an information ecology that favors audience participation. Such a call requires further consideration about the responsibility of media conglomerates and alternative media initiatives regarding how information is produced with and by the audience and its potential for social justice.

Notes

1 See www.facebook.com/BHnasRuas/. Accessed on September 2018.
2 See http://midiaNINJA.org/. Accessed on September 2018.
3 The actual investment amount by the Brazilian government is controversial. See https://goo.gl/2TCLGf. Accessed on September 2018.
4 For a comprehensive account of the protests, see the 2014 documentary titled *June* by João Weiner. www.youtube.com/watch?v=9qcrPve51qo. Accessed on September 2018.
5 See more information at http://tarifazero.org/mpl/. Accessed on September 2018.
6 According to Dupuis-Deri (2004), the expression *black bloc* was coined by the West German police in the 1980s to describe the squatters who would wear black clothing and use improvised weapons such as helmets, shields, wooden sticks, and projectiles to resist eviction. They were associated with a social movement titled *Autonomen,* composed of workers and young leftists who defended participatory politics, individual freedom, and equal rights, and positioned themselves against neo-Nazism. Black bloc tactics have been appropriated in contemporary protests since 1999, during the anti-WTO demonstrations in Seattle, and consist in preserving anonymity through wearing masks and black clothing, use of force, and strong positioning against capitalist symbols.
7 See https://goo.gl/JYqhs8. Accessed on October 2018.
8 See https://goo.gl/MVZgeR. Accessed on September 2018.
9 In Brazilian Portuguese, CPCMO stands for Comitê Popular da Copa do Mundo e das Olimpíadas do Rio de Janeiro.
10 See https://goo.gl/crtpcS. Accessed on October 2018.
11 See https://goo.gl/Dd6dC. Accessed on December 2018.
12 See https://goo.gl/a2tE3o. Accessed on December 2018.
13 See https://bit.ly/2ACjZ0I. Accessed on December 2018.
14 See more at http://midiaNINJA.org/perguntas-frequentes/. Accessed on December 2018.
15 See more at https://midiaindependente.org/. Accessed on December 2018.
16 Indymedia is a global collective of independent media organizations and journalists offering grassroots noncorporate coverage of news events. It originated in the 1999 anti-WTO protests in Seattle, and its political views advocate for global justice, against neoliberalism.
17 According to the Intervozes website (http://intervozes.org.br/quem-somos/ Accessed on November 2008), they are a Brazilian organization founded in 2003 that works for safeguarding freedom of expression and human rights in all forms of communication.
18 See http://midiaNINJA.org/perguntas-frequentes/. Accessed on December 2018.
19 On July 22, Bruno Ferreira Telles was arrested in a protest in Rio de Janeiro under the accusation of throwing a Molotov cocktail toward police officers. *Mídia NINJA* posted a video on its YouTube channel requesting that protesters uploaded videos that would show Bruno in the protest so evidence could be provided that Bruno was not involved in the explosion. After several videos were posted, the accusations against Bruno were dropped. See at https://goo.gl/ahX4Ah. Accessed on December 2018.
20 See the manifesto at www.consciencia.net/midialivre/fml_manifesto_final_2008.pdf. Accessed on December 2018.
21 Between 2009 and 2015, the Brazilian Ministry of Culture sponsored 82 free media projects. The list of awarded projects can be seen at https://goo.gl/fjQ1aY. Accessed on November 2018.
22 Historically, Brazilian public universities followed a European curriculum structure that privileged humanistic education. Journalism programs in the 1960s emphasized humanities coursework, such as philosophy, history, and literature. From the 1970s

onward, they entered a critical-reflexive period, focused on the development of Latin-American communication theories. For a more detailed account of communication programs in Brazil, see Dias (2015).

23 Since 2013, there has been a 28% reduction in funding from the Ministry of Education for research, teaching, and extension programs in the 68 Federal universities in Brazil. At the same time, enrollment has increased by 10%. See the numbers in detail at https://goo.gl/Kv6272. Accessed on December 2018.

24 See the thread at https://goo.gl/L24uNq and https://goo.gl/uqbGQJ. Accessed on September 2018.

25 At www.facebook.com/bhnasruas. Accessed on August 2018.

26 At https://twitter.com/bhnasruas. Accessed on August 2018.

27 At www.facebook.com/pg/BHnasRuas/about/?ref = page_internal. Accessed on August 2018.

28 Data extracted using the NetVizz application available for Facebook.

29 See more at https://goo.gl/2vs1pz. Accessed on June 2018.

30 Social movement for transportation as a human right. See at www.facebook.com/pg/tarifazerobh. Accessed on December 2018.

31 Page for a civil organization in Belo Horizonte that promotes public deliberation and the right to the city. See at www.facebook.com/AssembleiaPopularBH. Accessed on December 2018.

32 Page of a funding campaign for the Minas Gerais State Public TV Network. See at www.facebook.com/salvearedeminas. Accessed on December 2018.

33 #thegianthasawaken, #cometothestreets and #brazilianspring are literal translations of the original hashtags.

References

Cameron, D. 2009. Mobile journalism: A snapshot of current research and practice. *End of Journalism*. Technology, Education and Ethics Conference, Luton, UK.

Campos, D. A. de. 2017. A avaliação da educação superior diante de uma colonialidade do saber e do poder: a participação política discente. *Avaliação: Revista da Avaliação da Educação Superior (Campinas)*, 22(1), pp. 179–199.

Castells, M. 1996. The rise of the network society. In *The information age: Economy, society, and culture volume I (information age series)*. London: Blackwell.

Costa, J. B. da et al. 1994. Universidade: espaço institucional para o desenvolvimento político. *Temas em Psicologia*, 2(1), pp. 17–35.

Costa, R. 2011. Mídias livres: reflexões sobre a intervenção social na contemporaneidade. *Intercom*. Available at: www.intercom.org.br/papers/regionais/sudeste2011/resumos/R24-0905-1.pdf.

CPCMO, Comitê Popular da Copa do Mundo e das Olimpíadas do Rio de Janeiro. 2013. *Megaeventos e violações de direitos humanos no Rio de Janeiro. Dossiê do Comitê Popular da Copa e Olimpíadas do Rio de Janeiro*. Available at: https://comitepopulario.files.wordpress.com/2013/05/dossie_comitepopularcoparj_2013.pdf [Accessed on December 2018].

D'Andrea, C. & Ziller, J. 2014. BH: mídia e movimentos nas ruas da cidade. In Oliveira, A. et al. eds. *#BHnasruas. Uma experiência de cobertura colaborativa*. Belo Horizonte: Editora Livramento, pp. 9–20.

de Souza e Silva, A. & Frith, J. 2012. *Mobile interfaces in public spaces: Locational privacy, control and urban sociability*. New York: Routledge.

Deifell, T. 2009. *The big thaw: Charting a new future for journalism: A guide to the evolution of independent media*. Media Consortium. Available at: https://craig.typepad.com/thebigthaw.pdf [Accessed on January 6, 2019].

Dias, R. 2015. Comunicador Social ou Jornalista? A estruturação do conhecimento profissional o jornalista em cursos de graduação. *Revista Brasileira de História da Mídia*, 1(2). Available at: www.ojs.ufpi.br/index.php/rbhm/article/view/4023 [Accessed on January 6, 2019].

Dupuis-Deri, F. 2004. Penser l'action directe des Black Blocs. *Politix*, 17(68), pp. 79–109.

Farman, J. 2012. *Mobile interface theory: Embodied space and social action*. New York: Routledge.

Ferreira, M. A. S. 2016. #Bhnasruas: uma análise do confronto político contemporâneo a partir de páginas do facebook. *Revista Eletrônica de Ciência Política*, 7(2). Available at: http://revistas.ufpr.br/politica/article/view/48546.

Gillmor, D. 2006. *We the media: Grassroots journalism by the people, for the people*. Sebastopol: O'Reilly Media Inc.

Jenkins, H. 2006. *Convergence culture: Where old and new media collide*. New York: New York University Press.

Lorenzotti, E. 2014. *Jornalismo século XXI: O modelo #MídiaNINJA*. São Paulo: e-galáxia.

Malini, F. & Antoun, H. 2013. *A Internet e a rua: ciberativismo e mobilização nas redes sociais*. Porto Alegre: Sulina.

Manovich, L. 2001. *The language of new media*. Cambridge: MIT Press.

Maricato, E. et al. 2013. *Cidades Rebeldes: Passe Livre e as manifestações que tomaram as ruas do Brasil*. 1st ed. São Paulo: Editora Biotempo.

Marques de Melo, J. & De Assis, F. 2016. Journalistic genres and formats: A classification model. *Intercom – RBCC*, 39(1), pp. 39–54. São Paulo.

Oliveira, A. et al. 2014. *#Bhnasruas: a revolução será filmada por você*. Belo Horizonte: Editora Letramento.

Parente, R. E. 2014. *Do midialivrismo de massa ao midialivrismo ciberativista: uma reflexão sobre as perspectivas de comunicação alternativa no Brasil*. Available at: www.compos.org.br/biblioteca/trabalhos_arquivo_ASH2UVPTLL57IYK41IHX_23_3171_17_02_2014_14_05_48.docx.

Pereira, V. 2016. Understanding m.e.d.i.a. – media, entertainment, design, information and arts: The extensions of communication. *XXV Encontro Anual da Compós, Associação Nacional dos Programas de Pós-Graduação em Comunicação*. Available at: www.compos.org.br/biblioteca/compreendendoosmedia_comeciber_compos2016_3285.pdf [Accessed on September 2018].

Rheingold, H. 2007. *Smart mobs: The next social revolution*. Cambridge: Basic Books.

Rheingold, H. 2012. *Net smart: How to thrive online*. Cambridge: MIT Press.

Sheller, M. 2013. Mobile mediality: Location, dislocation, augmentation. In Witzgall, S. & Vogl, G. eds. *New mobilities regimes in art and social sciences*. London: Routledge, pp. 309–326.

Silva, F. F. da. 2015. *Jornalismo móvel*. Available at: https://repositorio.ufba.br/ri/handle/ri/18003 [Accessed on March 2018].

Silva, R. H. A., ed. 2014. *Ruas e redes – dinâmica dos protestos BR*. Belo Horizonte: Editora Autêntica.

Silva, R. H. A. da & Ziviani, P. 2018. "Temporalidades emaranhadas": desafios metodológicos da dinâmica dos protestos em rede de 2013 no Brasil. *Revista Crítica de Ciências Sociais*, 117, pp. 27–46.

Chapter 12

The Internet as a facilitator of mobilities in rural areas

Ariane Fernandes da Conceição and Sergio Schneider

Introduction

The image of the rural environment as an isolated and underdeveloped space becomes obsolete in view of the new features that can be ascribed to this space. These are activities and modes of occupation that affect social and cultural aspects, especially since the advent of access to new information and communication technologies (ICTs). Generally, rural areas have been assimilating the new means of communication and interaction – although in Brazil in a less extensive way – by gradually adopting the available ICTs.

These new technologies make communications easier and can be applied to facilitate production sales, as is the case of direct marketing on the Internet, improve access to markets, and, consequently, help redefine the relationships between producers and consumers. In particular, ICTs can leverage pluriactivity, as in agritourism, since the Internet serves as the gateway to consumers' cognizance of such initiatives.

Therefore, communication becomes an important way to enable new forms of organization or mobility in rural areas. Mobility is understood here as the possibility of a rupture with old paradigms, allowing at the same time the creation of new scenarios in which the actors have knowledge and power enough to lead processes of social transformation.

The reason is that information allows us to find out and employ new mechanisms that can promote culture and the development of society. Thus, the space, in this case the rural space, becomes socially differentiated, since some activities, especially those related to management and marketing, do not require physical presence. Therefore, the new mobilities paradigm allows us to analyze the possibility of creating new scenarios in which actors have the knowledge and power to conduct processes of social transformation (Urry 2003).

Means of communication have given rise to new opportunities and new forms of social, communicational, and economic interaction. Studies such as those carried out internationally by Nagel (2013), Rodrigues (2013), and Leeuwis and Ban (2004), as well as by Batalha et al. (2005) and Mendes et al. (2013) in Brazil (although, in this case, less detailed), show that besides broadening and facilitating interaction through social networks and other mechanisms, the Internet means a huge potential for rural enterprises to improve access to new markets and introduce new products and new inputs; moreover, it suggests a new form of rural extension focusing on communication.

The case study presented here features the initiative of family farmers from the municipality of Santa Rosa de Lima, located in the region of *Encosta da Serra Geral*, in the state of Santa Catarina, Brazil. Family farmers from this locality gained access to the Internet, when the municipal government made the signal freely available through the implantation and distribution of antennas throughout the municipality. To gain access, farmers must acquire a signal replication antenna for the signal to reach the property. Internet access is free, although it is up to the farmer to decide whether to pay a monthly fee to increase the available speed.

The reality of Santa Rosa de Lima in the state of Santa Catarina is in line with the World Bank's views suggesting that access to information and communication technologies (ICTs) in rural areas can represent an opportunity for family farmers to access knowledge and information, to create new socialization networks, and to improve access to markets. In this sense, the Internet represents a potential tool to enhance productivity and quality of life and to create new products and services, thus constituting a significant advance for rural development and for improvement and expansion of rural–urban interactions.

Studying this new reality becomes relevant, especially because communication and information technologies provide an expansion of possibilities for family farmers to make external contacts, thus making it easier to solve occasional problems, to meet the demands for more and better choices of access to markets, and chiefly to get in touch with more distant family members and friends. Thus, this study aims to analyze how the use of the Internet contributes to mobility in rural areas by demonstrating how it has assisted in the economic activities of family farmers, especially by fostering agritourism and the sale of organic products.

Information and communication technologies and the globalized mobility

Technological advancements engendered changes in society, and together with globalization, it gave rise to unprecedented forms of information exchange due to the facilities and mobilities that come with the technologies, more precisely digital communication technologies and the Internet. In this sense, Castells (1999, p. 330) explains that "New information technologies allow at the same time the decentralization of work tasks and their coordination in an interactive network of communication in real time, be it between continents or between floors of the same building".

As Thompson (2013, p. 197) points out, "the media produce a continuous intermingling of different forms and experience, an intermingling that makes the day-to-day lives of most individuals today quite different from the lives of previous generations." That is, there is a change in the standards previously experienced, which, for lacking connectivity, restricted in some way the contact with the new".

Access to various sources of knowledge directly impinges upon actors, and consequently, the way people interact also changes, which entails concrete results such as the building of new markets. Therefore, it should be taken into account that society has changed and tends to keep changing to become more and more reflexive. In a networked society, in parallel with such transformations, the standards followed by the actors also change (Brunori 2007; Brunori et al. 2010, 2012).

The emergence of new means of communication and information, such as the Internet, engendered substantial changes in the modes of communication and interaction between individuals. Martins and Nunes (2008, p. 135) point out that "the network society broke down frontiers and created a new economy, simultaneously becoming established as a global medium of communication between many people at once, a medium over which communication can be carried out in both synchronous and asynchronous ways" (Martins & Nunes 2008, p. 135).

Within this networked society, "virtual communities" emerge, which come to contribute to expanding information exchanges and which represent a new form of human common existence, thus engendering new possibilities for the construction of a shared experience of human interaction (Benkler 2006). In this sense, the Internet works as a vast space for global meetings, in which people can express and share their concerns and hopes through dialogue and accounts of similar and different experiences.

In a complex modern society, in which interaction is increasingly sought, or which, according to Urry (2003), is a society of new mobilities, communication emerges as an important way for information exchange, aiming to find out new mechanisms that can promote culture and development in the social context.

In the age of information, social practices can be materially sustained over long distances and can be maintained even outside their original local contexts. The space, therefore, becomes socially differentiated, while its functions continue to be performed without requiring physical proximity (Urry 2003). The Internet, thus, arises as an important tool for creating ample opportunities to enter the world of information, since it allows the exchange of knowledge in real time and the development of interest groups, which leverages alliances that serve as tools for building different kinds of knowledge, experiences, skills, and abilities.

Uses and information on the Internet

Communication, which in rural areas, in view of rural extension activities, was often connected to the presentation and incentive to the use of a new technology, to the use of agricultural inputs, and to new forms of production increase in the context of agricultural modernization, is now being differently incorporated into this scenario, mainly through the dissemination and proliferation of new information and communication technologies. That is, it begins to be observed with regard to the expansion of contacts and access to information and communication in general.

Rural development can be seen as a process of change, capable of producing conditions that allow actors/institutions to choose promoting better quality of life, as agents in this process (Conceição 2016). Therefore, the use of the Internet increasingly constitutes an opportunity for mobility in rural areas and even a tool that can provide new forms of social interaction, and it is up to the actors which path to choose.

According to the World Development Report published by the World Bank in 2016, more than 40% of the world's population has access to the Internet, with new users going online every day. Almost 7 out of 10 people have at least one cell phone. The report also points out that poorer households are more likely to have access to mobile phones than to toilets or clean water. These data provide an up-to-date picture of world reality, and given the incorporation of ICTs into the daily life of the world population, it is essential to pay greater attention to the changes occurring in contemporary society (World Development Report 2016).

Also, mobile phones and smartphones have been major means to access the Internet in recent years in Brazil. According to data from Cetic (2017), there was a considerable increase in the use of cell phones for Internet access, as can be observed in Figure 12.1.

In 2014, 76% of Internet users accessed it through cell phones, while 80% used computers to access the network. In 2016, a reversal was observed in this scenario, since 93% of users accessed the Internet through cell phones and 57% via computers.

According to data from a survey carried out in Brazil by Brazilian Micro and Small Business Support Service – Sebrae (2017), in the scope of the program

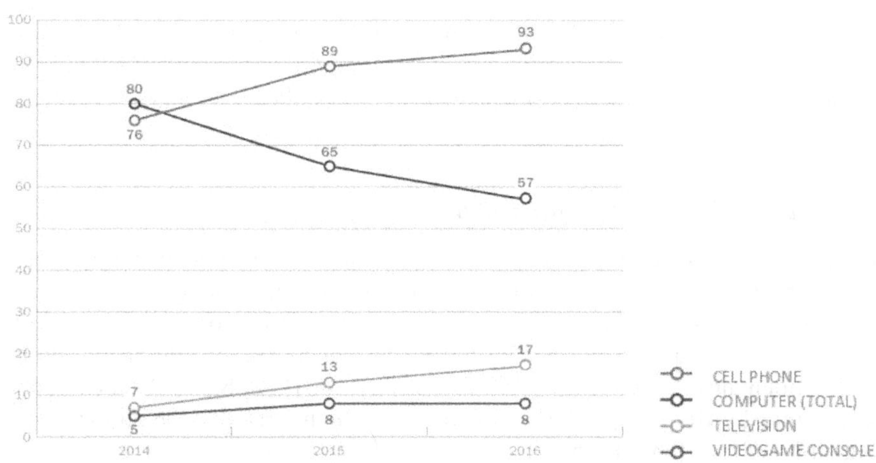

Figure 12.1 Internet users, per device used for individual access (2014–2016).
Source: Cetic (2017).

Information Technology in Agribusiness,[1] it was observed that farmers, although hesitant, have been using the Internet to manage their rural property. Sebrae interviewed 4,467 rural producers throughout Brazil. Among the states that presented the highest rate of Internet use in rural business management, on both computers and cell phones, we found Minas Gerais (21.2% of respondents) and Rio Grande do Sul (12.7% of respondents).

As to the use of Internet only via computers, it was observed that São Paulo (42.2%), Santa Catarina (40.2%), Rio de Janeiro (36.3%), Rio Grande do Sul (35%), and Minas Gerais (33.2%) are the states where most producers claimed to use digital tools that helped them manage their rural business.

According to data from Cetic (2017), the Internet Management Committee, 38% of households, whether rural or urban, in the Northern region had access to the Internet; 40% of households in the Northeast; 48% in the Center-West; 53% in the South; and 60% in the Southeast.

Farmers can make use of the Internet in several ways, both within their properties and outside. As Conceição (2012) points out, technologies can contribute to promote distinct cultures and to enhance capabilities aimed at social development and at new forms of human and commercial relationships. The Internet can also help individuals and groups form communicative bonds able to broaden public opinion and to bring new contributions to the debate on common-ground issues (Matos 2009).

The use of social networks and institutional websites has become increasingly necessary for visibility of enterprises. In rural enterprises it could not be different. Besides, we live in liquid times, when time-space notions and barriers are easily broken. The primary way of knowing about a given good, service, or situation happens to be the Internet, due to its promptness to give feedback most of the time.

Communication, leveraged by information and communication technologies, as a social interaction in rural areas, becomes an important ally in the construction of capacities that aim at rural development, since they allow individuals to expand their choices and to be agents of their own development.

The case of *Acolhida na Colônia*

The farmers' association *Acolhida na Colônia* is located in a region that is recognized for its prominence in Brazilian agritourism, the municipality of Santa Rosa de Lima, in the state of Santa Catarina, Brazil. The city is one of the smallest Brazilian municipalities. Located in the region called *Encosta da Serra* (slope of the mountain), the city was founded on May 10, 1962. Santa Rosa de Lima was formed by German and Italian immigrants who migrated to the region at the beginning of the 20th century.

According to data from the Brazilian Institute of Geography and Statistics, or IBGE (2010), the city of Santa Rosa de Lima has a population of 2,065 inhabitants, and 84.6% of the population live in the rural area of the municipality. The economy of the city is mostly based on agriculture and the services sector.

Santa Rosa de Lima became a national reference in the production of organic food, and as a result, it became a tourism route, especially following the establishment of Agreco (Association of *Encosta da Serra*'s Ecological Farmers). The association seeks to sell the produce of local family farmers. Then the need to provide accommodation to tourists that started going to the municipality attracted by the local organic production led to the establishment of the *Acolhida na Colônia* association. This association implemented an online reservation system, and currently the Internet represents a gateway and first contact between tourism consumers and the association.

The *Acolhida na Colônia* association is located in Santa Rosa de Lima and has 14 properties in this municipality, which began to offer online reservation of accommodation, which allowed tourists to interact through its institutional site and through international booking search sites, such as Airbnb and Booking.com, as well as through social networks such as Facebook. Contacts are available either through the official website of the association or through the hostel or the webpages of the associated family farmers.

Agritourism represents an example of pluriactivity in the rural areas and serves as an option to consumers who seek a peaceful space allied to a closer contact with nature. The Internet is an important channel for the distribution of rural tourism, since it constitutes a way for first contacts and first impressions for potential consumers of the offered services, besides facilitating the relationship between consumers and managers. It allows a prompt exchange of information and is a channel for suggestions and criticism.

In the case of *Acolhida na Colônia*, it is observed that the Internet, as well as other information and communication technologies, such as the telephone and more recently smartphones, became a necessity for rural areas, as much as it already was in large urban centers. It was observed that previous to the dissemination of such technology, it was possible to live in the rural areas without having access to it. However, with this new scenario and the growing demand for knowledge and information, access to the Internet became a necessity and regularly required. It is worth mentioning that the relationship between individuals as well as the time-space dynamic changes because of the Internet, that is, physical contact tends to be affected and even minimized and weakened.

The adoption of technology can be a very important and fundamental factor for implementing tourism activities in rural properties. It enables easier administration by farmers, since it allows to reconcile the requirements of their activities and the needs of the tourists. In this sense, even though some caution is needed as to the use of the Internet, new technologies can help match the interests of both farmers and tourists. It can be applied, for example, to analyze the rural tourism market in order to verify its importance and the kind of hosting in which it is worth investing.

It is worth mentioning that the use of the Internet from and for the property enables farmers to access information such as housing supply trends, climate, new forms of diversification of activities, and techniques to attract consumers' attention. Thus, it is helpful to rural properties, to its produce, to the tourists, and to the quality of life in the countryside.

The Internet helps through search websites and even through social networking websites, where the farmer can exchange information with peers and mobilize them for the cause. Ploeg (1994) praises the agency by family farmers, that is, their ability to act in social arenas. Thus, the Internet could empower family farmers and incite them to become agents of their future.

The Internet comprises an important distribution channel for rural tourism, since it is on the Internet that tourists are able to establish the first contact with the rural enterprise. According to a study carried out by Borges and Zaine (2007, p. 94), "the Internet has been used by most hotels for online bookings. . . . Thus, it facilitates the relationship between consumers and managers, and allows an agile exchange of information, and to promptly receive suggestions and criticism".

Access to the Internet provides a gateway to communication, information dissemination, and commercialization for family farmers who seek visibility for the enterprises in which they participate, through the most diverse contacts with their partners.

Final remarks

The Internet has proven to be an important factor for competitive advantage of family farmers in their properties, especially because it provides mobility and external contacts. The use of the Internet is more and more frequent in rural areas, mainly aimed to speed up the various activities that move such areas in the search of improvements for family farmers in their activities.

The Internet in rural areas is understood as an element that facilitates rural daily life, since it allows the establishment of new social relationships with suppliers and consumers. It then allows better control of productive, entertainment, and leisure activities and influences economic, social, political, and cognitive aspects.

Rural areas are generally integrated to this context of new forms of communication and media interaction, although less extensively in Brazil, and are gradually adopting the information and communication technologies locally available and suitable. New possibilities have, therefore, been presented, such as access to information, entry into new markets, differentiated forms of production, and to some extent, greater contact between producer and consumer.

Access to information and communication technologies (ICT) in rural areas can provide an opportunity for family farmers to access knowledge and information, create new socialization networks, and improve access to markets. In this sense, the Internet represents a potential tool to enhance productivity and quality of life and to create new products and services, which represents a fundamental advance for rural development and for the improvement and expansion of rural–urban interactions.

Note

1 Despite the name, Sebrae Agronegócio (Sebrae Agribusiness) is a program that also encompasses family farming, providing introduction to up-to-date rural management tools, seeking to improve capabilities of managing farming activities, and guaranteeing the livelihood of the rural families (Sebrae 2010).

References

Batalha, M. O., Buainaim, A. M. & Souza Filho, H. M. 2013. Tecnologia de gestão e agricultura familiar. In Batalha, M. O. & Souza Filho, H. M. de. eds. *Gestão integrada da agricultura familiar*. Vol. 1. São Carlos: EDUFSCAR, pp. 13–43.

Benkler, Y. 2006. Social ties: Networking together (Chapter 10). In Benkler, Y. ed. *The wealth of networks: How social production transforms markets and freedom*. New Haven: Yale University Press.

Borges, M. P. & Zaine, M. F. 2007. A Internet como canal de distribuição do turismo rural em algumas propriedades do estado de São Paulo: um estudo de caso. *Caderno Virtual de Turismo*, 7(3), pp. 90–99. Rio de Janeiro.

Brunori, G. 2007. Local food and alternative food networks: A communication perspective. *Anthropology of Food*, 1(2). Salleboeuf.

Brunori, G., Malandrin, V. & Rossi, A. 2012. Trade-off or convergence? the role of food security in the evolution of food discourse in Italy. *Journal of Rural Studies*, 29, pp. 19–29. New York.

Brunori, G., Rossi, A. & Malandrin, V. 2010. Co-producing transition: Innovation processes in farms adhering to solidarity-based purchase groups (GAS) in Tuscany, Italy. *International Journal of Agriculture & Food*, 18(1), pp. 28–53.

Castells, M. 1999. *A sociedade em rede*. Vol. 1. São Paulo: Paz e Terra.

Comitê Gestor De Internet – Cetic. 2017. *Pesquisa sobre o uso das tecnologias de informação e comunicação no Brasil*. São Paulo. Available at: www.cetic.br.

Conceição, A. F. 2012. *"Quem está online?" um estudo de caso sobre o uso e apropriação da Internet no meio rural de Estrela/RS*. 2012. Thesis (Master in Rural Extension) – Graduate Program in Rural Extension, Centro de Ciências Rurais, Universidade Federal de Santa Maria, Santa Maria.

Conceição, A. F. 2016. *Internet pra quê? a construção de capacidades e as TIC no processo de desenvolvimento rural*. PhD Dissertation, Universidade Federal do Rio Grande do Sul. Faculdade de Ciências Econômicas. Graduate Program in Rural Development. Porto Alegre.

Instituto Brasieiro De Geografia E Estatística – Ibge. 2010. *Censo demográfico 2010*. Rio de Janeiro. Available at: www.ibge.gov.br/home/estatistica/populacao/censo2010/ [Accessed on June 13, 2016].

Leeuwis, C. & Ban, A. V. D. 2004. *Communication for rural innovation: Rethinking agricultural extension*. 3 ed. Chichester: Wiley-Blackwell.

Martins, J. C. L. & Nunes, P. V. 2008. A Internet como factor de transformação social e das relações de poder. *Proelium: Revista da Academia Militar*, 9, pp. 135–158. Lisboa.

Matos, H. 2009. *Capital Social e Comunicação: Interfaces e Articulações*. São Paulo: Summus.

Mendes, C. I. C., Buainain, A. M. & Fasiaben, M. C. R. 2013. *Acesso ao computador e à Internet na agricultura brasileira: uma análise a partir do Censo Agropecuário.*

Proceedings of the 51° Congresso da SOBER – Sociedade Brasileira de Economia, Administração e Sociologia Rural, Belém, Pará, Brasil.

Nagel, J. 2013. Principal barriers to the adoption of ICTs in agriculture and in rural areas. In Rodrigues, M. & Rodríguez, A. eds. *Information and communication technologies for agricultural development in Latin America: Trends, barriers and policies*. Santiago: United Nations.

Ploeg, J. D. van der. 1994. Styles of farming: An introductory note on concepts and methodology. In Ploeg, J. D. van der. & Long, A. eds. *Born from within*. Assen: Van Gorcum, pp. 7–30.

Rodrigues, M. 2013. The evolutionary approach applied to ICT and agriculture technological systems in Latin America: A survey. In Rodrigues, M. & Rodrígues, A. eds. *Information and communication technologies for agricultural development in Latin America: Trends, barriers and policies*. Santiago: United Nations.

SEBRAE. *Serviço Brasileiro de Apoio às Micro e Pequenas Empresas. 2017. Tecnologia da Informação – Pesquisa Produtor Rural 2017*. Available at: www.sebrae.com.br/sites/PortalSebrae/bis/pesquisa-produtor-rural-2017,8f82e4188bb7d510VgnVCM1000004c00210aRCRD#0 [Accessed on March 25, 2018].

Thompson, J. B. 2013. *A mídia e a modernidade: uma teoria social da mídia*. Petropolis: Vozes.

Urry, J. 2003. *Global complexity*. Cambridge: Polity Press.

The World Bank. 2016. *World development report 2016: Digital dividends*. Available at: www.worldbank.org/en/publication/wdr2016 [Accessed on May 31, 2018].

Chapter 13

Why are we writing and speaking in English?

Coloniality of academic communication and its uneven mobilities

Leo Name

Nothing compares to you writing and speaking in English

Scene 1. I was at an academic event about the new mobilities paradigm (NMP) in one of the most important public universities in Brazil. There, master's and PhD students were going to present their work to specialists from Argentina, Belgium, Brazil, Chile, Germany, the United Kingdom, and the United States. The selection process had been arduous: they had to submit a written abstract and a video in which they talked about their ongoing research, both in English. I was one of the specialists who posed questions after the English-language presentations by a group of Brazilian and Argentinian researchers. Faced with a predominantly Brazilian audience, I said: "*I will ask them in Portuguese. But if the Argentinian students want me to ask them in Spanish, that's okay*". The students, seemingly relieved, answered the questions in their mother tongues. From then on, no one at the event knew which language they should speak. Moreover, those who chose to speak in English apologized.

Scene 2. You are holding the book *Brazilian Mobilities*, written by Brazilian scholars interested in the NMP. I imagine you are interested in the many aspects of mobilities in Brazil and that researchers, lecturers, students, institutions, and social movements from this country may want to access the texts. Nevertheless, there is no doubt: the ability to understand English will be demanded from any potential reader, which will drive some of these Brazilians away.

The two scenes show that, in Brazil, there is an academic interest in the NMP, whose origins date back to the conference at the Sociology Department of the Lancaster University and to the creation of the Centre for Mobilities Research (CeMoRe) in 2004 (see: Sheller 2018). This analytical field, however, brings together a geographically dispersed set of scholars, who investigate "the *complex interconnections* between physical, virtual, communicative, and imaginative mobilities, including the movement of people, objects, information, capital, and resources" (Sheller, p. 20, emphasis in the original). The scenes also exemplify the internationalization and broadening of scientific production circles and the dominance exerted by the English language over them – a question that is especially relevant to Brazil, the only Portuguese-speaking country in the Americas, and one which, although not exclusively related to the NMP scientific production, also affects it.

Luiz Paulo da Moita Lopes (2008), a Brazilian scholar of applied linguistics, states that communication is *performative* – and that includes scientific communication, one of the possible articulations between *writing* and *speech* and between *language*, *register* and the *sayable* (Pereira 2013, pp. 215–216). On the one hand, ideas travel – or not – through the movements of certain types of people (*scholars*) and through certain types of *writings* (essays, articles, monographs, reviews), acting upon certain types of *spaces for dialogue* (physical or virtual: books, scientific journals, conferences, seminars, roundtables) in which one can write or speak. On the other, they are not free from the dualism between center–periphery and the asymmetries of the modern-colonial world.

The NMP writings that are more focused on uneven mobilities (Freire-Medeiros and Name 2013; Cohen and Cohen 2015; Sheller 2016; Name and Freire-Medeiros 2017) point out that "some bodies can more easily move through space than others" (Sheller 2018, p. 24). With this in mind, I lead my inconclusive thoughts through the so-called Latin-American decolonial turn (Lander [2000] 2005; Mignolo and Escobar 2010; Ballestrin 2013), interested in showing what the Peruvian sociologist Aníbal Quijano ([2000] 2005) and the Argentinian philosopher Walter Mignolo ([2000] 2003) term "colonialities": power asymmetries that are constitutive of colonialism and its – still present – legacy. In the academic world, they manifest themselves decisively through the hegemonic propagation of English, interfering in the dialogue and movements of scholars, writings, and ideas, which I call the *coloniality of academic communication*.[1]

I will thus attempt to demonstrate in the first section that the smaller projection of Portuguese within the academic world cannot be explained by the number of its speakers but by linguistic ideologies surrounding a universal English (Moita Lopes 2008). In the following section, I will first list the English-language NMP writings that have been translated into Portuguese. Then I will outline the trajectories and part of the production and network of academic relationships of Bianca Freire-Medeiros and Thiago Allis – respectively, a sociologist and a tourism researcher at the University of São Paulo (USP), and probably the most prominent Brazilian scholars of new mobilities. I seek to outline their movements: first, toward a greater projection in Brazil of the NMP concepts and theories – a relevant analytical field, but with little global dominance and largely unknown in Brazil. Secondly, in order for their own production, and that of their network, circulate and gain greater attention and readership in academic spaces of dialogue.

Who runs the wor(l)d?

Like all other nation-states whose official language is Portuguese,[2] Brazil does not border any other country of the same language. It necessarily imposes alterities to the acts of writing and speaking – and, therefore, reading and listening – of those who move through any of the sides of its borders.[3] However, according to information from the Brazilian linguist Gilvan Müller de Oliveira (2013), there are around 250 million Portuguese speakers worldwide, with 80 percent of this total located in Brazil. Between 7 and 9 million people also speak Portuguese in the diasporas – especially in the United States and Canada, in different European countries, in Japan, South Africa, Paraguay, and Venezuela. These numbers put Portuguese in fifth place among the most commonly spoken languages in the world and third among the Western world, behind English and Spanish. Furthermore, following an increase in literacy in Portuguese-speaking countries, Portuguese is the fifth most commonly used language on the Internet, with more than 80 million users.

It is not, therefore, the small number of Portuguese speakers or their low circulation that explains its limited projection in academic communication. After all, the production, qualification, and legitimation of knowledge are not free from the power relations established in disputes over capital and territories – mobilized not only by nation-states but also by countless other agents (Name 2016, pp. 61–66). Thus, Mignolo ([2000] 2003) draws attention to the patterns of power that geo-historically disqualify cosmovisions and expropriate or discard knowledge or render it subaltern. He invites us to reflect upon the geopolitics of knowledge, i.e., the practices for conceiving, producing, transmitting, and disputing it based on "epistemological locations": we are *where* we think (Mignolo [2000] 2003, [1999] 2015).

The following move through academic circles: the *language* is the set of singular norms that are the substrate for the development and the translation of thought into word; the *register* is the functioning strategic arrangement of words, with specific particularities; and the *sayable* is the arrangements that, within each power regime, geo-historical context, and communicative situation, are authorized to enunciate thought (Pereira 2013). In directing the coloniality of academic communication, they aid in the control of writing and speech and join discursive performances that intend to be validated as a disembodied truth – with no subject. Likewise, they are based on expedients of universalization and generalness that hide their character as a situated knowledge (Haraway [1988] 1995).

Imperial disputes since the 16th century led French, English, and German to become the languages of the Enlightenment – imposed as the only ones capable of producing knowledge. Spanish and Portuguese, colonial languages previously dominant in the colonization of the Americas, and Italian, dominant during the European Renaissance, were assigned the role of just translating this knowledge. As for the other languages, not even that (Mignolo [1995] 2016) . . . The hegemony attained by the British Empire in the 19th century and the growing unipolarity of US power in the 20th century are two of some of the geo-historical conditioning factors that clarify the transformation of English from unimportant in 1600 to the planetary domination that it currently maintains: "globalized language of knowledge", "international university language" and "lingua franca of the information age".

In fact, for each of the circa 500 million native speakers of English there are three additional nonnative speakers. It is also used in 75 percent of all international written communication and 85 percent of the content available online (Scheyerl & Siqueira 2008). Such magnitude, according to Moita Lopes (2008, p. 314), is supported by linguistic ideologies (Woolard 1998). Founded upon economic interests but led by beliefs that permeate the world of work and commonsense views, they assign roles to English: inexorable requirement for professional success and unquestionable indication of all that is cosmopolitan and universal, for example.

In Brazil, scientific production is more concentrated in public universities. Several areas of knowledge have instituted rules that treat international diffusion as a determining factor in evaluations of courses and researchers. Even though French influence can still be perceived in the universities – largely due to their implementation process, in the early 20th century, during which academics from France were given important positions (Costa de Paula 2002) – there is an evident linguistic ideology surrounding English: it is tacitly accepted that, in order to increase the international relevance of Brazilian science, its communication must necessarily be carried out in forums and journals dominated by English. This is true despite the fact that indexation systems and indicators have been accused of being imprecise and unfair (Alperin 2013), although that there is no evidence that this broadens access to knowledge, either quantitatively or qualitatively (Goulart & Carvalho 2008; Gudynas 2017).

The hegemony of English actually reduces the circulation and the amount of academic communication in other languages, such as Portuguese. Consequently, it creates barriers that deny access to spaces for dialogue to many Brazilians, in addition to assigning discursive privileges to those for whom English is the mother tongue (or who speak it fluently). Therefore, it potentially naturalizes the idea that those who do not write or speak in English do not produce knowledge and consequently marginalizes countless scholars.

With regard to register, communicating in a language other than one's own can create difficulties for explaining local terms, situations, and contexts, which are often not limited to mere translation problems. Finally, there are effects on the sayable: if, on the one hand, it stimulates scholars from the peripheries, such as Brazilians, to research and publish subjects that are of interest to the U.S. and European scientific communities, on the other, it harms those who are interested in marginal subjects – in both cases, it reduces the number of those capable of writing or talking about urgencies of their place or community (Alperin 2013).

Facing these problems likewise requires that researchers from the Global South, such as Brazilians, act toward an academic world that is sweeter to them.

Sweet moves are made for this[4]

The journal *Mobilities*, created in 2006 in order to establish paths and update concepts in NMP-related research (Hannam et al. 2006), only publishes articles written in English. Additionally, in a quick search, I was able to verify that apparently not a single book by Mimi Sheller, Monika Büscher, Anthony Elliott, or Tim Cresswell has been published in Brazil. Among John Urry's writings, only the very first version of his work about the tourist gaze (Urry [1990] 1996), prior to the formulation of the NMP, was translated into Portuguese. In the same search,[5] I found Portuguese versions of his work in two books (Larsen and Urry [2011] 2014; Urry [2010] 2013). I also found a chapter from Elliott's *Identity Troubles* translated into Portuguese in a Brazilian journal (Elliott [2015] 2018). Lastly, I identified an article by Büscher on mobile methods with the Brazilian sociologist Letícia Veloso, specifically written in Portuguese for a dossier in the journal *Tempo Social* (Büscher and Veloso 2018). And that is all.

Thus, on the one hand, English is also the hegemonic language of knowledge produced by the NMP, affecting the register and the sayable of its communication. On the other, the paradigm seems not to interest Brazilian publishers and scholars who could translate it.

Given the aforementioned, Freire-Medeiros and Allis seem to perform four different moves. The first is defined by the persistent mobility of their own bodies: in search of dialogue, they travel the world – a great deal! – and also cause others to travel to them. The second is the creation of *new* spaces for dialogue: dossiers and collected works, interviews with important figures, reviews and events dedicated to the NMP. The third is the patient and insistent action in designing and conducting other subjects and methods in the mobilities research – not only writing about Brazil, Latin America, or the Global South but taking them as an epistemological location. Finally, the constant effort of publishing in more than one language – notably, Portuguese and English – is the fourth and final move.

It was around the year 2000 that Anthony King, Freire-Medeiros's PhD adviser at Binghamton University, New York, introduced her to Urry. His writings came to occupy a more central place in her academic work from 2003 onward: at this time, she was already back in Brazil, doing her pioneer research on tourist mobilities in the favelas – initially carried out at the State University of Rio de Janeiro (UERJ) and between 2005 and 2014 at the Getulio Vargas Foundation (FGV) (Freire-Medeiros 2009a, 2009b). In 2009, she went to CeMoRe as a postdoctoral fellow under Urry, where she met Büscher. Her interest in (im)mobilities also led her to the International Conference Unequal Mobilities in 2014 in Santiago, Chile, where she personally met Sheller and the Chilean sociologist Paola Jirón. The widespread diffusion of one of her articles on the *favela*'s tourist movements (Freire-Medeiros 2009b) led to an invitation in 2016 to be a Visiting Lecturer at the Teresa Lozano Long Institute of Latin American Studies (LLILAS – University of Austin, Texas). Similar invitations came from the Center for Migration and Development at Princeton University (2003); from the Florestan Fernandes Chair of the Colegio de México (2012); and from the Graduate Institute of Geneva (2018). In 2015, Freire-Medeiros migrated to the Sociology Department of USP, where she connected in the following year her networks to Allis's.

In 2016, three years after Allis had met Freire-Medeiros at the International Sociological Association Conference, he became a Lecturer at the School of Arts,

Sciences and Humanities (EACH). Previously, since 2008, Allis had been working as a Lecturer at the Federal University of São Carlos (UFSCAR). In 2012, he became a Visiting Lecturer at the National University Timor Lorosa'e (UNTL). His affiliation with the NMP authors is more recent (Allis 2016a, 2016b; Allis et al. 2017a, 2017b), and his first visit to CeMoRe took place in 2016, at which point he met Büscher – a meeting that was mediated by Camila Moraes, who studied under Freire-Medeiros during her doctoral research period in Lancaster. Allis went to Lancaster with other two opportunities: in 2019, when he was awarded the John Urry fellowship, and in 2017, during the International Association for the History of Transport, Traffic and Mobility (T2M), a conference hosted by CeMoRe. Other T2M conferences – in Florida in 2014, and in Mexico City in 2016 – had already enabled connections. In the first one, Allis met Sheller, and in the second one, he was able to establish a dialogue with some mobilities researchers not directly connected with Lancaster University: the U.S. geographer Tim Cresswell, the Argentinian sociologist Dhan Zunino Singh, and Jirón.[6]

With regard to the creation of new spaces for propagating the NMP and for a dialogue with Brazilians, the seminar Urban Mobilities: Foundations for Transnational Studies took place, which was organized by Freire-Medeiros and Urry. This 2011 academic event was hosted by FGV, in the city of Rio de Janeiro, and brought Urry together with researchers from Australia (Thomas Birtchnell), Brazil (Leo Name) and Spain (Javier Caletrío), for example (see: Freire-Medeiros 2018). More recently, Freire-Medeiros organized two thematic dossiers in important Brazilian journals (Freire-Medeiros et al. 2018; Freire-Medeiros & Pinho 2016), in which she interviewed Sheller and Elliott (Pinho & Freire-Medeiros 2016; Freire-Medeiros & Lages 2018) and wrote an *in memoriam* text to Urry (Freire-Medeiros 2016). In these editions, there are also two reviews: one by João Freitas (2016) – Freire-Medeiros's former master's student at FGV – and another by Moraes (2018), respectively about *Elite Mobilities* and *What Is the Future?* Portuguese-language reviews of *Mobile Methods*, *Mobile Lives*, and a talk by Urry at FGV, published in other journals, are also worth mentioning (Nogueira 2011, 2012; Freitas 2014), in addition to an interview with Büscher, also in Portuguese (Moraes 2016).

The two dossiers were announced in the First School of Advanced Mobilities Science (SPMobilities), an event organized by Freire-Medeiros and Allis in 2017, which congregated many of the main names of the NMP to USP. Its schedule included talks by Sheller (on Skype), Büscher, and Noel Salazar in English and by Jirón and Zunino Singh in Spanish. In Portuguese, there was a short course taught by Moraes and talks by Patrícia Pinho and myself. A second edition of SPMobilities in 2019 put on the same table some of the authors of this book, *Brazilian Mobilities*, edited by Moraes and Maria Alice de Faria Nogueira (who also studied under Freire-Medeiros at FGV). Each of us spoke (in Portuguese!) about the chapter that each of us had written (in English!).

As to the efforts toward making subjects from the Global South more sayable in the research on the new mobilities, Allis and Freire-Medeiros have been making headway. Since the beginning of his career, Allis has adopted a theoretical approach to tourism based on mobilities (Allis 2006), with special attention to means of transportation (Allis 2015, 2016b; Allis, Castro et al. 2017; Allis, Fraga et al. 2017) and to the comparison between Latin American countries (Allis 2006, 2015, 2016b; Allis et al. 2015). More recently, tourism as an economic alternative for postconflict countries and refugee immigrants has been his object of study (Allis & Pinto 2018; Allis & Santos 2016; Santos et al. 2014). Freire-Medeiros was likewise always interested in different mobilities (Freire-Medeiros 1997, 1999). In her PhD dissertation, she already defined Rio de Janeiro as a "traveling city", "whose identity is constantly constructed, and whose iconic images are reproduced around the world" (Freire Medeiros 2002, p. 7). Her articles on the mercantilization of the *favela* as a tourist destination, which is an unquestionable reference, analyze its ethical and aesthetic aspects and pay special attention to tourists, images, writings, souvenirs, and means of transportation put in motion by this market niche (Freire-Medeiros 2007, 2009a, 2009b, 2012; Freire-Medeiros & Menezes 2008, 2009, 2016; Freire-Medeiros & Name 2015).

These are highly original and complex subjects, unusual in Brazil, which have made it possible for Freire-Medeiros and Allis to publicize their ideas in international events, journals, and books, in addition to training new Brazilian researchers. Most importantly, they have presented the Global South not only as an object but as an epistemological location: capable of unveiling the Eurocentrism inherent to the NMP's conceptions of modernity and cosmopolitanism, which naturalizes the mobilities of the North and does not pay enough attention to the immobilities of the South.

These movements between so many demands, countries, and spaces for scientific dialogue have, however, demanded from Freire-Medeiros and Allis an effort to communicate beyond Portuguese. Taking their written (articles in scientific journals, books, chapters, or annals) and oral (presentations in scientific events, conferences, and talks) production since 2006 as an example, we have the following table:

Table 13.1 Amount and percentage of production, by type and total, according to author and language (2006–2018)

Author	*Type*	*Portuguese*	*English*	*Spanish*	*German*	*French*	*Total*
Bianca Freire-Medeiros	Written	42 (64%)	22 (33%)	-	1 (1.5%)	1 (1.5%)	66 (100%)
	Oral	29 (54%)	25 (46%)	-	-	-	54 (100%)
	Total	**71 (59%)**	**47 (39%)**	**-**	**1 (1%)**	**1 (1%)**	**120 (100%)**
Thiago Allis	Written	25 (61%)	12 (29%)	4 (10%)	-	-	41 (100%)
	Oral	16 (47%)	13 (38%)	5 (15%)	-	-	34 (100%)
	Total	**41 (55%)**	**25 (33%|)**	**9 (12%)**	**-**	**-**	**75 (100%)**

Source: based on data from the Lattes Platform (2019).

From each researcher's production – predominantly on the subject of mobilities, more than one third is in English. It is worth noting, on the one hand, that over the years, both have also communicated in other foreign languages, especially Allis, with significant production in Spanish (12%). On the other hand, in an effort to be read and heard by her peers in the North and South, Freire-Medeiros usually translates the same article or produces similar versions in Portuguese and English. That is the case of the articles on the installation of cable cars in the *favelas* (Freire-Medeiros and Name 2017; Name and Freire-Medeiros 2017), the tourist movements in these communities (Freire-Medeiros 2007, 2009a, 2009b), and the tourist market of their "pacification" (Freire-Medeiros et al. 2013, 2016). Her writing gave rise to challenges: how to translate and explain crucial research terms, such as *favela* and *laje* (Freire-Medeiros 2012).

And after all . . .

In fact, some scholars, writings, and ideas can also more easily move through space than others.

Discussions regarding the hegemony and the linguistic ideologies surrounding English and the analysis of the two most prominent Brazilian scholars of the NMP have helped us exemplify uneven mobilities led by the coloniality of academic communication. On the one hand, the scant number of translations of the works by key NMP figures into Portuguese is not a reflection of a small number of Portuguese speakers in the world. Most likely, it is a reflection of Brazilian scholars and the publishers' lack of interest in this analytical field – indicative of its lack of centrality in the global social sciences production, which exceedingly values certain universities and epistemological locations. On the other hand, efforts by Freire-Medeiros and Allis to move their ideas and to be more widely read and heard are in no way required of their peers in the North: it is truly impossible to imagine Urry, Sheller, Büscher, Elliott, Salazar, or Cresswell doing the work of translating their production into other languages in order to gain greater relevance.

It does not seem coherent that the NMP research, increasingly interested in unveiling uneven mobilities and claiming mobile justice, disconsiders or naturalizes inequities in the circulation of its scholars, writings, and ideas. Thus, though lacking pretensions of conclusion, it is important to end this text with preliminary notes toward a decolonization of academic communication and, consequently, toward greater solidarity in the dialogue between its Northern (predominantly English speakers) and Southern (not only Brazilian) scholars.

With regard to *language*, translation policies seem urgent. A Brazilian researcher's production should not be rendered irrelevant or invisible because it is written in their native language: if Brazilians are interested in translating NMP texts written by their English-speaking peers, why would the latter not translate into English the relevant production *already published* in Portuguese by the former? Leaving that task always to Brazilians is unfair.

Scene 1, which opens this text, shows that simultaneous translation is a crucial requirement. It is a well-known fact, however, that researchers and universities in the Global South, as in Brazil, often have scarce resources. Funding collaborations with CeMoRe and universities in the North connected with mobilities subjects are pressing, but in their absence, multilingual events with schedules having parallel sessions grouped by language seem promising to me. After all, one cannot presume to be heard by *all*: scientific universalism is laughable, and the universalism of the English language is a bad joke.

Scene 2 reveals the incongruences of the book the reader now holds. It is important that it be translated into Portuguese as soon as possible. More than that: it seems necessary to think of bilingual or multilingual NMP publications – why not? This facilitates the use of NMP in classrooms, choosing texts for each class-language-country. Moreover, if those who cannot read texts in English are numerous, would it not be fair for English speakers to be unable to read some texts written in Portuguese, Spanish, Aymara, or Guaraní? Publishers' unjust market interests should be confronted with the policy of open access.

Counterhegemonic geopolitics of knowledge must also bear in mind that fortunately, written texts and oral presentations are not the only forms of communication. There are other *registers* made possible through films, paintings, photographs, comics, music, engravings, sculptures, installations, performances, flash mobs, viewscapes, soundscapes, smellscapes and all sorts of media or artistic devices that are capable of – not necessarily in a verbal manner – communicating about new mobilities.

With regard to what is permitted to be *sayable*, it is worth noting that, up to this point, there has not been great interest in interviews with Brazilian scholars, or reviews of their work, in the widely circulated English-language journals or by key figures of the NMP. Is it not fair to reverse this situation? Co-authorship in any language and between researchers from the North and South, and especially between different intellectuals in the South, also seem highly welcome: it is in partnerships for the understanding of differences and similarities that epistemologies are renewed and advanced. The decolonial lens that leads this article also deems the Latin-American integration that may give the NMP a new face: a (also Latin-American) paradigm of the (old and) new (also Latin-American) mobilities, always permeated by the asymmetries of the coloniality of power.

Perhaps it is time for Brazilians to ask: why are we still writing and speaking in English? So that Europe and the United States will read us and listen to us? That is important, but would it not be far more important and urgent to write and talk together with and/or for *nuestros hermanos de América Latina?*

Notes

1 I thank Bruna Otani Ribeiro, Spanish and Portuguese language researcher from Brazil, with whom I had an informal discussion in 2018 regarding what she called "coloniality of academic register". My term derives from hers, with the change from "register" to "communication" meant to include aspects of the language and the sayable.

2 Portugal, Guinea-Bissau, Angola, Cape Verde, Brazil, Mozambique, São Tomé and Príncipe, Equatorial Guinea (co-official with Spanish and French), Macau (co-official with Cantonese), and Timor East (co-official with Tetum).

3 Contrary to the commonsense view that Portuguese is the only language in the country, more than 200 languages are spoken in Brazil: mainly indigenous languages, but also those of immigrant communities. See Oliveira (2000, 2003).

4 Part of the information presented in this section was gathered from Bianca Freire-Medeiros and Thiago Allis, who patiently answered questions in insistent electronic communications. I thank them for their affectionate availability.

5 In February 2019, having the beginning of 2006 (when *Mobilities* was launched) as the point of reference, I searched for English-language texts that had been published after that date and that had been translated into Portuguese. I used the Scielo, Redalyc, and CLACSO databases and additionally Google Scholar and Google Books. As to the production by Brazilian researchers, I identified it based on their CVs in the Lattes Platform, which is used by most universities in the country.

6 Zunino Singh and Jirón are part of an active Latin-American network of Spanish-speaking researchers on mobilities, in contact with Allis. See: Zunino Singh et al. 2017. eds.

References

Allis, T. 2006. *Turismo, patrimônio cultural e transporte ferroviário: um estudo sobre ferrovias turísticas no Brasil e na Argentina*. Ms. Thesis, São Paulo, Universidade de São Paulo.

Allis, T. 2015. Sobre cidades, bicicletas e turismo: evidências na propaganda imobiliária em São Paulo. *Caderno Virtual de Turismo*, 15(3), pp. 390–406.

Allis, T. 2016a. Em busca das mobilidades turísticas. *Plural*, 23(2), pp. 94–117.

Allis, T. 2016b. Transport e tourism mobility. In Netto, A. P. & Lohmann, D. G. eds. *Tourism theory: Concepts, models and systems*. Wallingford: Cabi, pp. 197–202.

Allis, T., Castro, R. T. & Fraga, C. 2017a. Airport concessions in Brazil and its influences on service quality: The cases of Brasília and São Paulo/Guarulhos airports. *Journal of Spatial and Organizational Dynamics*, 5(4), pp. 337–350.

Allis, T., Fraga, C. & Velazquez, M. 2017b. Railway for tourism in South America: An approach on its uses. *Journal of Traffic and Transportation Engineering*, 4, pp. 339–349.

Allis, T., Paula, A. T. & Raszl, V. 2015. Turismo de compras nas fronteiras brasileiras: panorama geral e perspectivas à luz das políticas vigentes. In Pieri, V. S. G. & Teles, R. M. S. eds. *Turismo e relações internacionais*. Rio de Janeiro: CENEGRI, pp. 83–110.

Allis, T. & Pinto, M. L. 2018. Turismo post-conflicto: desarrollo turístico local y estrategias para la integración social de refugiados. *Estudios y Perspectivas en Turismo*, 27, pp. 1003–1017.

Allis, T. & Santos, M. H. M. B. 2016. Tourism in east Timor: Post-conflict perspectives. In Pappas, N. & Bregoli, I. eds. *Global dynamics in travel, tourism, and hospitality*. Hershey: IGI Global, pp. 86–110.

Alperin, J. P. 2013. Ask not what altmetrics can do for you, but what altmetrics can do for developing countries. *Bulletin of the American Society for Information Science and Technology*, 39(4), pp. 18–21.

Ballestrin, L. 2013. América Latina e o giro decolonial. *Revista Brasileira de Ciência Política*, 11, pp. 89–117.

Büscher, M. & Veloso, L. 2018. Métodos móveis. *Tempo Social*, 30(2), pp. 133–151.

Cohen, E. & Cohen, S. A. 2015. Beyond Eurocentrism in tourism: A paradigm shift to mobilities. *Tourism Recreation Research*, 40(2), pp. 157–168.

Costa de Paula, M. F. 2002. USP e UFRJ: A influência das concepções alemã e francesa em suas fundações. *Tempo Social*, 14(2), pp. 147–161.

Elliott, A. 2015. A teoria do novo individualismo. *Revista Sociedade e Estado*, 33(2), pp. 465–486.

Freire-Medeiros, B. 1997. 'You don't have to know the language': Hollywood inventa o Rio de Janeiro. *Cadernos de Antropologia e Imagem*, 5, pp. 107–121.

Freire-Medeiros, B. 1999. Dos pântanos ao paraíso: Hugh Gibson e a (re)descoberta do Rio de Janeiro. *Lugar Comum*, pp. 51–67.

Freire-Medeiros, B. 2002. *The traveling city: Representations of Rio in U.S. films, travel accounts and scholarly writing*. PhD dissertation, Binghamton University.

Freire-Medeiros, B. 2007. A favela e seus trânsitos turísticos. *Revista Acadêmica Observatório de Inovação do Turismo*, 2, pp. 1–13.

Freire-Medeiros, B. 2009a. *Gringo na laje*. Rio de Janeiro: FGV Editora.

Freire-Medeiros, B. 2009b. The favela and its touristic transits. *Geoforum*, 40, pp. 580–588.

Freire-Medeiros, B. 2012. *Touring poverty*. London: Routledge.

Freire-Medeiros, B. 2016. In memoriam: John Urry (1946–2016). *Plural*, 23(2), pp. 138–141.

Freire-Medeiros, B. 2018. John Urry's adventures in Brazil. In Jensen, O. B., Kesselring, S. & Sheller, M. eds. *Mobilities and complexities*. London: Routledge, pp. 121–130.

Freire-Medeiros, B. & Lages, M. P. 2018. Mobilidades, espaços e identidades na economia eletrônica global. Entrevista com Anthony Elliott. *Tempo Social*, 30(2), pp. 301–316.

Freire-Medeiros, B. & Menezes, P. 2009. Fotografando a pobreza turística. *Revista Anthropológicas*, 20, pp. 11–21.

Freire-Medeiros, B. & Menezes, P. 2016. As viagens da favela e a vida social dos suvenires. *Sociedade e Estado*, 31, pp. 651–670.

Freire-Medeiros, B. & Name, L. 2013. Flying for the very first time: Mobilities, social class and environmental concerns in a Rio de Janeiro favela. *Mobilities*, 8(2), pp. 167–184.

Freire-Medeiros, B. & Name, L. 2017. Does the future of the favela fit in an aerial cable car? Examining tourism mobilities and urban inequalities through a decolonial lens. *Canadian Journal of Latin American and Caribbean Studies*, 42, pp. 1–16.

Freire-Medeiros, B. & Name, L. 'Peace, love & fun!': An aerial cable car and the traveling favela. In: J.Cidell & D. (Eds.). *Transport, Mobility, and the Production of Urban Space*. London: Routledge, pp. 98–111.

Freire-Medeiros, B. & Pinho, P. S. 2016. O turismo num mundo de mobilidades. *Plural*, 23(2), pp. 5–16.

Freire-Medeiros, B., Telles, V. S. & Allis, T. 2018. Por uma teoria social 'on the move'. *Tempo Social*, 30(2), pp. 1–16.

Freire-Medeiros, B., Vilarouca, M. G. & Menezes, P. 2013. International tourists in a 'pacified' favela: Profiles and attitudes: The case of Santa Marta, Rio de Janeiro. *Die Erde*, 144, pp. 147–159.

Freire-Medeiros, B., Vilarouca, M. G. & Menezes, P. 2016. A pobreza turística no mercado de pacificação: reflexões a partir da experiência da favela Santa Marta. *Cadernos do CRH*, 29, pp. 571–586.

Freitas, J. 2014. Vidas móveis. *Sociologias*, 16(35), pp. 340–352.

Freitas, J. 2016. Uma resenha de 'Mobilidades da Elite'. *Plural*, 23(2), pp. 126–133.

Goulart, S. & Carvalho, C. A. 2008. O caráter da internacionalização da produção científica e sua acessibilidade restrita. *RAC*, 12(3), pp. 835–853.

Gudynas, E. 2017. Sin nuestras propias revistas académicas latinoamericanas seríamos mudos. *Ecuador Debate*, 100, pp. 45–60.

Hannam, K., Sheller, M. & Urry, J. 2006. Mobilities, immobilities and moorings. *Mobilities*, 1(1), pp. 1–22.

Haraway, D. 1988. Saberes localizados: a questão da ciência para o feminismo e o privilégio da perspectiva parcial. *Cadernos Pagu*, 5, pp. 7–41.

Lander, E. ed. 2000. *A colonialidade do saber*. Buenos Aires: CLACSO.

Larsen, J. & Urry, J. 2011. Olhar e performance. In Pereira, A., Marques, I., Ribeiro, M., Botelho, M. L. & Nunes, P. eds. *O porto como destino turístico*. Lisbon: Media XXI.

Lohmann, G., Santos, G. & Allis, T. 2011. 'Los hermanos' visiting the South Region of Brazil: A comparison between drive tourists and coach tourists from Argentina, Paraguay and Uruguay. In Prideaux, B. & Carson, D. eds. *Drive tourism*. London: Routledge, pp. 49–70.

Mignolo, W. D. 1995. *El lado más oscuro del Renacimiento*. Popayán: Editorial Universidad del Cauca.

Mignolo, W. D. 1999. Espacios geográficos y localizaciones epistemológicas: la ratio entre la localización geográfica y la subalternización de conocimientos. In Caballo, F. & Herrera, L. A. R. eds. *Habitar la frontera*. Barcelona: CIDOB/UACJ, pp. 117–139.

Mignolo, W. D. 2000. *Historias locales/diseños globales*. Barcelona: Ediciones Akal.

Mignolo, W. D. & Escobar, A. 2010. eds. *Globalization and the decolonial option*. London: Routledge.

Moita Lopes, L. P. 2008. Inglês e globalização em uma epistemologia de fronteira: ideologia lingüística para tempos híbridos. *DELTA*, 24(2), pp. 309–340.

Moraes, C. M. S. 2016. Entrevista com Monika Büscher. *Trama*, 1(1), pp. 235–257.

Moraes, C. M. S. 2018. John Urry: What is the future? *Tempo Social*, 30(2), pp. 317–322.

Name, L. 2016. Geografias e imagens: notas decoloniais para uma agenda de pesquisa. *Espaço e cultura*, 37, pp. 59–80.

Name, L. & Freire-Medeiros, B. 2017. Teleféricos na paisagem da favela latino-americana: mobilidades e colonialidades. *GOT*, 11, pp. 263–282.

Nogueira, M. A. F. 2011. Mobile methods. *Interseções*, 13(2), pp. 396–400.

Nogueira, M. A. F. 2012. From land to landscape: o paradigma das mobilidades e a sociedade pós-carbono. *Ciberlegenda*. Available at: www.academia.edu/29854862/From_land_to_landscape_o_paradigma_das_mobilidades_e_a_sociedade_p%C3%B3s-carbono.

Oliveira, G. M. 2000. Brasileiro fala português: monolinguismo e preconceito linguístico. In Silva, F. L. D. & Moura, H. M. D. M. eds. *O direito à fala: a questão do preconceito lingüístico*. Florianópolis: Insular, pp. 40–50.

Oliveira, G. M. 2003. As línguas brasileiras e os direitos linguísticos. In Olveira, G. M. ed. *Declaração universal dos direitos linguísticos*. Florianópolis: IPOL.

Oliveira, G. M. 2013. Política linguística e internacionalização: a língua portuguesa no mundo globalizado do século XXI. *Trabalhos em Linguística Aplicada*, 52(2), pp. 409–433.

Pereira, M. V. 2013. A escrita acadêmica: do excessivo ao razoável. *Revista Brasileira de Educação*, 18(52), pp. 213–228.

Pinho, P. S. & Freire-Medeiros, B. 2016. Teorizações indisciplinadas: (i)mobilidade como metáfora, conceito e método. Entrevista com Mimi Sheller. *Plural*, 23(2), pp. 118–125.

Quijano, A. 2000. Colonialidade do poder, eurocentrismo e América Latina. In Lander, E. ed. *A colonialidade do saber*. Buenos Aires: CLACSO, pp. 227–278.

Santos, M. H. M. B., Allis, T., Ca, J. J. & Landim, C. C. 2014. Turismo na Guiné-Bissau: paradoxos e perspectivas para um país em conflito. *Revista Internacional em Língua Portuguesa*, 3, pp. 111–132.

Scheyerl, D. & Siqueira, S. 2008. Inglês for all: entre a prática excludente e a democratização viável. In Scheyerl, D. & Ramos, E. eds. *Vozes, olhares, silêncios*. Salvador: EDUFBA, pp. 17–30.

Sheller, M. 2016. Uneven mobility futures: A Foucauldian approach. *Mobilities*, 11(1), pp. 15–31.

Sheller, M. 2018. Theorising mobility justice. *Tempo Social*, 30(2), pp. 17–34.

Urry, J. 1990. *O olhar do turista*. São Paulo: Senac/Studio Nobel.

Urry, J. 2013. Sociologia móvel. In Lima, J. C. ed. *Outras sociologias do trabalho: flexibilidades, emoções e mobilidades*. São Carlos: Edufscar, pp. 43–72.

Woolard, K. A. 1998. Introduction: Language ideology as a field of inquiry. In Schieffelin, B. B., Woolard, K. A. & Kroskrity, P. V. eds. *Language ideologies*. New York and Oxford: Oxford University Press, pp. 3–20.

Zunino Singh, D., Giucci, G. & Jirón, P. eds. 2017. *Términos clave para los estudios de movilidad en América Latina*. Buenos Aires: Biblos.

Index

For Product Safety Concerns and Information please contact our EU representative GPSR@taylorandfrancis.com
Taylor & Francis Verlag GmbH, Kaufingerstraße 24, 80331 München, Germany

www.ingramcontent.com/pod-product-compliance
Lightning Source LLC
LaVergne TN
LVHW011131300926
849160LV00008B/609
9781032174242